A THOUSAND CAMPFIRES

A THOUSAND CAMPFIRES

A SCOUTER'S STORY

BY
JAMES T. HENDERSON

AMBUSH PUBLISHING
SAN ANGELO, TEXAS

International Standard Book Number:
Hardcover - ISBN 0-9631648-0-5
Softcover - ISBN 0-9631648-1-3
Library of Congress Catalog Card Number: 91-77729

A THOUSAND CAMPFIRES
Published by:
AMBUSH PUBLISHING
419 West Avenue C
San Angelo, Texas 76903
Printed in the United States of America

FOR DICK WYATT
My Best Senior Patrol Leader

Table of Contents

Table of Contents

Table of Contents

List of Illustrations

Original cover art, illustrations and cartoons by: J. T. Henderson

Foreword

When I first heard that J.T. had written a book called *A Thousand Camp-fires*, I knew it just had to be great. Everything J.T. did was great. If you don't believe this, just ask any one of his approximately twenty five hundred Scouts or their parents or their friends & relatives or anyone those Scouts might have talked to about J.T. or anyone of J.T.'s Girl Scouts or their parents or friends & relatives or some of J.T.'s Sunday school students or... well, I guess you get the picture.

Scouting is full of silent heroes & heroines. In my opinion, any Scout official, leader, volunteer or helper deserves the title. But J.T. was more than a hero, he was my Scoutmaster.

I first knew J.T., (we always call him by his first initials, never Mr. Henderson, that's the way he likes it) in our church where he was an usher and a Sunday school teacher. In fact, he and my father were two of the best teachers one could ever have. I have always been lucky, I had a wonderful family, I was born with a healthy body in a free country, and I had J.T. for my Scoutmaster.

J.T. is a bit of a "Maverick" and did not always see eye to eye with the official Scouting program. When he didn't, he would just "quietly" improve it and go on. I think, however, Lord Robert Baden-Powell, Ernest Thompson Seton, Daniel Carter Beard and the other "Fathers of Scouting" would look upon J.T. as I and the rest of his "Boys" do as the "Quintessential" Scoutmaster; Follow the lead, learn the ropes and think for yourself. J.T. could certainly think for himself and that's what he taught others. Some thought themselves into being: Doctors, physicists, merchants, clergy, clowns, writers, lawyers, soldiers, heroes, Scouters and more. Some even thought themselves into jail or out of this world. It was J.T. that kept us on the "Right Track" though some derailed on their own. But on or off track, J.T.'s faith in us was, and still is, always as solid as the Rock of Gibraltar.

Future Scouters could learn a lot from this book and others will find J.T.'s wit and charm captivating even if you know nothing of Scouting.

A tall, strong man with a powerful voice, he could sound like God Himself to a boy, or a grown man for that matter. Yet somehow, he was just a buddy, leading us through the dark thicket to the safety of our camp and the warmth of the campfire.

J.T. had many sayings that stay with you over the years. He could grab your attention and speak to you as man to man saying: "If you were to die tomorrow, could you look back and honestly say, that the world is a better place for your having lived in it?" Luckily for some of us, we haven't died yet!

Thanks to the J.T.'s of this world, it honestly is a better place, but we can always make it better. If you don't believe this, just ask J.T. Henderson.

If you are thinking of being a Scout leader, just do like J.T.; try it for about a dozen years, then take over another Troop in need, because you're asked, just temporarily, like twenty-seven years or so. It will be worth it, just ask J.T. For one campfire leads to thousands and one flicker of one flame can lead to eternal light.

J.T. always underplays his accomplishments, even in the title to this book. I think maybe it should have been *A Jillion Campfires*, but then, J.T. knew not to brag, he was a Boy Scout.

We who were his Scouts can't help but brag for J.T. Henderson was, and will always be, our Scoutmaster.

Eagle Scout 1967
Troop One
San Angelo, Texas
Concho Valley Council
Boy Scouts of America

This book represents fifty-seven years of Scouting. I couldn't begin to relate all of the events which happened during this period of time, but I did manage to assemble a few of the highlights of my Scouting life.

All of the people in this book are real people and only their names have been altered slightly to protect the guilty!

After serving thirty-nine years as Scoutmaster, I have come to one conclusion: Boys in Scouting are boys first and Scouts second.

To me Scouting was supposed to be fun. A boy sharpened his Scouting skills by learning to do these skills in a fun way. A Scout learned to be a better citizen in his community by doing civic good turns in a way that was fun.

Any Scoutmaster can look back and remember the many happy, funny things which happened in his troop. He may also remember a few sad, tragic ones which occurred, but I am sure that the humorous events far outnumber the sad.

So it is in this little book, the happy, humorous events far outnumber the sad, tragic ones. That is the way it should be because, you must remember, "Scouting is fun!"

Much work, apart from the actual writing, goes into any book and though many contributed, I want to thank certain individuals. I won't give their names but their initials are: Bubba Neligh, Louis Griffin, Milt Wyatt, La Ruth Jenkins, Bob Neligh, Rick Smith, Bill Kimrey, Diane Murray, Randy Marshall, Randy & Barry Rountree, Carla J. Jones, Ron Curry, and the offices of The Boy Scouts of America, The Concho Valley Council of the BSA, and *The San Angelo Standard Times*. Of course, my wife, Vivian, my family and the hundreds of Boy Scouts who made this book possible.

J. T.

Chapter 1
The Early Years

The little girl was drowning. Her small hands beat at the water and her cries were becoming weaker and weaker. People stood around, no one seemed concerned; no one was doing anything to help. Wearing my Boy Scout uniform, I pushed through the crowd of indifferent bystanders, jumped in the water, and rescued the little girl. I stayed around long enough to make certain that she was all right, then left before they could thank me.

This was a dream I had more than sixty years ago. It is still as vivid and clear as it was then. I was a young boy living in a small West Texas town in 1922. I had heard about the Boy Scouts, even though there was no Scout troop in our town. My mother had read to me articles from the *Fort Worth Star Telegram*, a well-known Texas newspaper. The articles told how the Scouts went on hikes, camped in tents, and learned all kinds of outdoor skills. But the thing which impressed me most was the idea of Scouts going about doing "Good Turns" and helping other people. About this time, to me, a Boy Scout was a combination of Sir Galahad, Babe Ruth and Tom Mix, three of my favorite people. And I know, after all these years that a Boy Scout is still a very real person.

But, to get back to the dream, it was quite a remarkable dream when you consider the fact that I was only seven years old, was not a member of the Boy Scouts, had no uniform and couldn't swim a lick.

After my mother's death, I lived with my grandmother in a larger West Texas town, San Angelo. There had been a Scout troop here, organized in 1910, supposedly with a charter from England. At one time, there had been more than 100 members in this troop. Through the years, the troop had gradually dwindled away, and at the time I moved here, there was no Scouting in San Angelo.

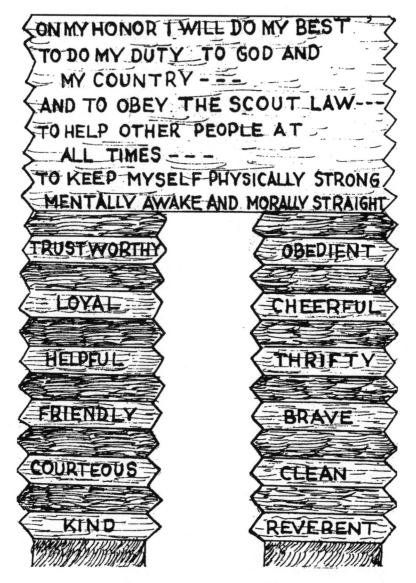

"On the Fire Station lawn a huge archway was erected. The Scout Oath and the 12 parts of the Scout Law were painted on this imposing structure. . . . "

In 1926 the present council was formed, chartered by the Boy Scouts of America. A bright young executive, Brice Draper, came to town and really started Scouting on its way. He had the ability to generate great enthusiasm among the boys and leaders, and frankly, I believed he might just be able to walk on water. If he gave you a job or duty to perform, he expected you to do it. He had an expression he used which has stayed with me all these years. If you were the one given the job, he would say to you, "do a good job or it's going to be you and me and me mostly." I used this gentle admonishment after I became a Scoutmaster, and several of my former Scouts used it in their troops after they became Scoutmasters. So Brice Draper, wherever you are, take heart in the knowledge that your words still live on in the minds of thousands of Scouts.

As you might expect, there was a lot of interest in Scouting in 1926. We had no Little League or organized baseball, no summer track, no tennis, swim program or soccer. Most of the boys in town were quite eager to get started in Scouting. I was so anxious to join, I persuaded my grandmother to check my birth certificate to be certain that I could become a Scout.

Before the actual organization of the troops, interested boys and their parents met next to the fire station on a huge lawn which covered about half a block. In later years, this same lawn was the scene of several field meets; we call them camporees now. The Scout Executive would stand up before the crowd and tell us some of the things we might expect to do as Scouts. He would wear his Scout uniform, with a colorful neckerchief around his neck and the broad-brimmed Scout hat. We always sang some songs such as "Old McDonald," "Clementine," "It Isn't Any Trouble Just To S - M - I - L - E," and "Gee, I'm Glad I'm A Boy Scout." A huge archway had been erected on the lawn. The twelve parts of the Scout Law were painted on the upright sides, and the Scout Oath was across the top. With my burning desire to be a Boy Scout, the words on the archway were almost as important as the tablets Moses brought down off the mountain.

At first, seven troops were formed. Four of these had churches as their sponsors. One was sponsored by the local newspaper, one by a service club and one by a church affiliated group. Four of these units are still going strong after more than fifty years. I was a charter member of one of these troops. At long last, I finally became a Boy Scout.

Our council now covers twenty three and a half counties and takes in quite a sizable chunk of West Texas.

Chapter 2
Our First Overnight Camps

Our troop had decided that camping was the big thing in Scouting and we were going to be a camping troop. Our Scoutmaster was the owner of a repair shop and didn't have much more camping experience than we had, which was none. Our first overnight camps were pitiful. We had no sleeping bags, which were unheard of in those days. I had two World War I blankets, which were worn so thin and slick, they looked more like khaki sheets than blankets. No one had ever told us about using a ground cloth. Our troop didn't enjoy the luxury of tents. When the weather got bad, we huddled under a blanket or quilt draped over some brush.

We had no practical instruction in fire building. It took us several camp-outs before it dawned on us that green wood produced smoke, while dry wood produced flame and heat. Each Scout felt obligated to carry a hatchet and a huge hunting knife dangling from his belt. Jim Bowie would have been green with envy if he could have seen some of the knives we carried. It was much, much later and after many, many camp-outs when we discovered "squaw wood." That was the wood you could gather from dead tree limbs without all that hacking, chopping and slashing.

Before we got our first Scout Handbooks, and before we read the information on campfire cooking, our first meals were disasters. Remember, this was before ice chests had been invented, and you were limited in the type of food you could carry on an overnight camp. Most of the dehydrated or freeze dried food available now were unheard of. Some dried fruit, such as apples, peaches and apricots, were in the grocery stores and some places handled dried beef, which tasted a little like beef flavored cardboard. We cooked the old standard stuff like eggs and bacon and stew. I'll never forget one campout when I took a bowl of stew for my Scoutmaster to try. He looked it over carefully and remarked, "I never tasted anything like this before, but I stepped in some once." I was crushed. I couldn't understand why he was so picky about a few ashes and sticks floating around on top of his stew.

Since there was nothing much to do in our town, we went camping sometimes two or three weekends a month. For a long time, it was Nature versus our camping skills, and Nature won most of the time. In fact, for many months I thought camping out was a combination of sleepless nights, eating half-charred, half-raw food, cooked over a fire of green, smoking wood, while the rain trickled down your back. But we gradually learned the basic outdoor skills, and found that camping could be fun instead of a survival test. We were tough—we survived—we were Boy Scouts.

On one campout, my Patrol Leader announced that he had brought a hammock and that he would sway gently in the breeze while the rest of us poor mortals would huddle on the ground amidst the dirt and weeds. The rest of our patrol decided that he should be taught a lesson in sharing. I, as Assistant Patrol Leader, was duly elected to do the teaching. After supper, our Patrol Leader slung his hammock between two trees, while the rest of us turned green with envy. After things quieted down, and we were sure our Patrol Leader was sound asleep, I went slinking through the brush, armed with a sharp hatchet. The hammock, with our illustrious leader in it, looked like a giant cocoon. The plan was for me to cut the rope on the end of the hammock where the feet were. Unknown to me, our P.L. had changed ends in the hammock. I cut through the rope in one slash and the hammock hit the ground with a thud. We listened for the cries of outrage, but there was only silence. We cautiously approached the crumpled wreckage of the hammock. We found that our leader's head had hit the ground, instead of his feet. The fall had about knocked him out. We brought him to and offered to go over and chastise the other patrols for doing something like this. He never found out that I did it or the Eagle Patrol would have been in the market for a new Assistant Patrol Leader.

Chapter 3
Our First Summer Camps

The first summer camps were very primitive. There were no permanent camps, so the camp facilities were very poor when you compare them with the modern camps with a permanent dining hall, a first aid lodge, a canteen or trading post, and a modern swimming pool. Cooking was done in tents using wood stoves or kerosene stoves. The mess hall was a structure, usually made of big cedar posts stuck in the ground with a sheet iron roof. This edifice was open on all four sides. If you happened to be sitting on the outside row during a blowing rain, your lower extremities were drenched. You might sit there, shoveling hot oatmeal in your mouth on one end, while the water was overflowing your shoe tops. We didn't mind—we were tough —we were Boy Scouts—cheerful to the end.

Since we had no swimming pool, we swam in the river. This was slightly dangerous because the swimming area was not roped off into sections for beginners, non-swimmers, and swimmers. The largest part of the river was for swimmers and was very deep. There was only a small section where the water was shallow enough for the other two groups. The whole area was watched by competent life guards and the "Buddy System" ruled supreme. This was the first experience for most of us with this system. We were warned to stay near our buddy. When the whistle was blown, you had to the count of five to reach your buddy and hold up his hand. If you failed to do this, both of you had to get out of the swimming area. This still works today.

Kitchen Police, or "K. P." is a snap today. In most camps, if you are on K. P., you go up about fifteen minutes before the meal is served in the dining hall. You make sure that your table has silverware, plates and glasses or cups on the table. Check the salt, pepper, mustard and maybe the peanut butter.

After the meal you stay long enough to clean off the table and clean the floor. On the early camps, K. P. was really a big job. One peeled potatoes, carried water for the cooks, kept the stoves burning and tried to shoo away the flies. But it was not all in vain. If you were lucky, occasionally, you might just be able to lick the bowl in which the icing for the sheet cakes was mixed.

The first camp in our council was Camp Geronimo I. This camp was at Christoval, a little town about seventeen miles from San Angelo. The camp was in a beautiful setting of big trees with the South Concho River on two sides of the camp.

Our patrol picked out a nice place to set up our tent. The site was a grassy area which sloped gently down toward the river. In fact, this area was almost like a shallow ditch with Bermuda grass growing in the bottom and on the sides. As we were preparing to set up our tent, a patrol from another troop came along and said this was their area. Since they were older and much larger, we graciously told them they could have our location while we beat a wise retreat. I believe we may have mentioned the fact that we hoped something terrible would happen to them, and it did. About three nights later it came a "gully washer" rain and our beautiful site, which they took from us, proved to be a drainage ditch for a large portion of the camp. When the water finally quit running through their campsite, most of their equipment, including their tent, cots, and most of their clothes was seen bobbing about in the river. After that, I always believed in poetic justice.

Our council was new and our knowledge of how to properly conduct Scouting ceremonies was scanty. One evening, quite a large number of people had come from home to visit the Scout camp. Everyone was standing stiffly at attention, the bugler was doing his thing, and all seemed to be going well. As the flag was being lowered our commissioner was standing at attention. He was wearing his "Smokey the Bear" hat and had a colorful neckerchief to top off his uniform. The only thing wrong was his salute. Instead of the conventional Scout Salute, he had his hand raised, the fingers were apart and the thumb was at about a forty-five degree angle to his fingers. As the flag was coming down, something caught his attention. He turned to look at the flag and it looked as if he might be thumbing his nose at the flag. A photographer from the local paper caught his picture, and he was kidded about his disrespect for the flag for years.

Homesickness is a terrible malady. During my years as a Scoutmaster, I saw all kinds of homesickness. There is the type where the boy gets really quiet. He doesn't want to eat. He is not interested in any of the camp activities. Then there is the type where the kid is hysterical. He is crying and screaming and about the only cure for this type is for his parents to come to camp and take him home. Then there is the type where a boy doesn't want the other boys to know he is homesick. He becomes defiant and very belligerent.

"Our Commissioner looked as if he might be thumbing his nose at the flag . . . "

But when his parents show up on visitors' night, we find that he is a changed Scout. His defiance is gone and we find that all of his troubles came from homesickness.

In my Scout troop, I used to tell my Scouts not to poke fun at any boy suffering from homesickness. I told them that I got homesick on my first council camp. I did something which, if one of my Scouts had ever done this to me, would have caused me to be tempted to wring his neck. On Thursday of the first camp, I was selected to pull K.P. duty for the noon meal. About 9:30 I was walking up to the cooking tents when the first wave of homesickness hit me. I decided I just had to get home somehow. Imagine my surprise and joy when I got to the cooking area. Joe, our milkman from home, was delivering milk to the Scout Camp. I asked him if he might be returning to San Angelo soon, and if I might ride back with him. He agreed and I got into the truck and came home. I told no one I was leaving, and never gave a thought to the trouble I was going to cause. My grandmother asked me about coming home but I told her I hadn't been feeling too well. I suppose I had been home about three hours when the phone rang; and when I answered it, our Scout Executive was on the other end. He asked me what in the "blankety blank blue blazes" I was doing home. He said they were getting ready to drag the river. I told him that my grandmother needed me and I felt it was my duty to help her even if it meant leaving the Scout Camp. I am pretty sure that he didn't buy it, but at least it kept the Scout Executive and my Scoutmaster from killing me.

Camp Geronimo II came along about a year later. This camp was in the same spot as Geronimo I. However, we Scouts were not the same. Most of us had fifteen or twenty overnight camps under our belts and many of us had attended the first council camp. We felt like old, seasoned campers and acted like it. We sent some of the younger campers looking for "tent stretchers," "sky hooks," and "strap oil." This last item was to be used on your tent ropes to keep them from drawing up in case of a rain.

Our Scout executive liked to invite Scouters from other councils, which had been in existence longer than ours. Some of these fellows would give us instruction in Scouting skills and several camped with us the whole camp session. We had a very well known Scouter from a Central Texas council, who was to make a talk to the Scouts and their parents on visitors night. I was quite awed by this man because of his long Scouting record. I would not have missed the Council Fire for any reason. We had the opening ceremony and then some members of the camp staff made a few announcements. We sang a few songs and then, it was time for our notable speaker to do his thing. Our Scout Executive made a flowery introduction, and said, "and now it is my pleasure to present Mr. Bill Woods." Our speaker had been sitting on a huge, dead log, which was used by our leaders as a seat in the council ring. Every one was clapping. Our speaker started across the ring, but just as he got to where our executive was standing, he went rushing across the ring, out into the darkness. Everyone sat there in stunned silence. Brice Draper, our Scout Executive, was lamely trying to make some sort of explanation, when our speaker appeared back in the light from the council fire. He had a very sheepish expression on his face, but we all understood when he explained his very hurried departure. It seems that, as he sat on the log, a couple of stinging scorpions had crawled into his Scout shorts. When he started walking, they started stinging and he had to retreat into the brush to remove the little critters by taking off his shorts and shaking them vigorously.

One day a man who lived on a ranch near our camp came into camp to ask the Scouts to help look for a lost man. The man was his father who had wandered away from the ranch and was lost. Our Executive called all the Scouts together and told us about the mission. In his talk he mentioned that the old man was not quite right in his mind, and they were afraid he might have fallen in the river. We were told that the man walked with a cane, and if we found any tracks, we were to follow them and send one of our group back for help. Trucks carried us to the search area, where we were divided into groups of three Scouts each. All three of us in my group were thirteen years old and we discussed this idea about the man not being quite "right in his mind." Before we had traveled 200 yards in our search, it had been decided that the man was stark, raving mad, and that he would probably jump out of the brush, hair standing on end, eyes glaring wildly, and maybe a small amount of foam trickling out of his mouth. We decided to take no chances. We cut a good stout set of clubs, and, armed with these, we set forth on our search. I guess that it was a good thing we didn't find the old man. We would probably have beaten him to death, in our terror, unless, of course, we could have found a place to run. I had already decided that, if we found him, I was going to be the one to take the news back to our leaders, and leave my two companions to the mercy of the "mad man."

The episode had a happy ending. The old man walked toward town, swam the river and was sitting in a filling station, drinking a soda pop, when they found him. They told us that he wasn't crazy, just senile—like I am today.

There was a Scout, a member of another troop, in camp that year who was obsessed with fishing. His Scoutmaster and Patrol Leader were constantly on his back for not working on any advancement or taking part in the many camp activities. He fished with a rod and reel during the daytime, and at night, he would set out a "throwline" from the river bank. He didn't catch many fish, but it wasn't because he didn't try. It got to be a joke in camp, and the Scout, Steve, took a lot of ribbing. One morning, several of us were doing a little laundry work in a shallow part of the river. A very large and very dead fish, a carp, came floating along in the river. We retrieved the fish and had a sudden burst of inspiration. We would put the fish on Steve's throwline. We did so and sent someone for our fisherman. When he arrived, he immediately went into battle landing his "catch." He put on a show which would have done credit to a man landing a 600 pound shark. When he finally got the fish on the bank, he realized the fish was dead and had been for some time. We all started laughing and snickering and we came up with a nickname which stayed with him the rest of his life. Ever after he was known as "Fish."

And that was Camp Geronimo II.

Camp Pioneer, one of our early camps, is best remembered for several events which happened during the session. One of these was "The Great Red Rooster Trial." The Red Rooster Patrol of one troop had a small bantam rooster as its mascot. During the day, the rooster was kept in a large cage. At night, the patrol had a long pole with a large birdhouse on top. The pole was slipped in a convenient hole in the ground. This lifted the rooster about twelve feet off the ground and provided a safe roosting place, out of the reach of predators. This was fine except the rooster crowed every morning about 5 o'clock and woke everyone in camp. Finally it was decided that there should be a rooster trial on charges of disturbing the peace.

The Scout Executive was to be the judge, two Senior Patrol Leaders from other troops were to be the prosecution attorneys and two members of the Red Rooster Patrol were to be defense attorneys. It was difficult to find twelve members for the jury. Everyone in camp, excluding the Red Rooster Patrol and the rooster himself, were all in favor of immediate execution. At last, a jury was selected and the great trial began.

The judge, the attorneys for the defense, and the prosecution all wore wigs made from unraveled rope. For want of better robes, all wore blankets draped over their shoulders. The trial lasted two nights. The jury was forbidden to discuss the case. It was rumored that the jurors had been approached by both the prosecution and the defense with the idea of a little bribery. The judge told the jurors that they were not to accept bribes, but if they did, he got half.

After moves and counter moves by each side, and after impassioned speeches which would have moved a stone idol to shed tears, the case was given to the jury. They retired to discuss the fate of the red rooster. After a short while they returned their verdict. "Not Guilty" on the grounds that the rooster was just "doing what comes naturally."

One of the bright moments of camp were the stewed prunes you were served for breakfast. I liked stewed prunes, but a lot of the boys didn't. The Scout Executive would explain that the prunes were to help you stay "regular." His little talks were ignored, so he decided that this called for more drastic measures. If you didn't eat your prunes, you had to report to the hospital tent. There you were given a small glass of a mixture of castor oil and Epsom salt. The prune consumption increased greatly.

One patrol of a troop in camp had a large wall tent. This was about a 14' X 20' tent. The patrol had taken all their cots outside and had the walls staked down. Some unsuspecting Scout would be sent to their tent for some "strap oil" to keep wet ropes from shrinking. When you knocked on the door, you were dragged inside and forced to run around the tent, while they belabored your hindside with doubled belts.

This had gone on for a couple of days until one morning at breakfast, Brice Draper, our Scout Executive, announced that he had something to award a certain patrol. After breakfast, the entire camp, except for the erring patrol, was to line up in two, long lines. The patrol was to run the gauntlet. I was near the end where they started and I figured that they would be running so fast that I probably wouldn't be able to swat but one or two. I came up with a brilliant thought. As the first runner came by, I would stick out my foot and trip him. This great idea had one defect. The lead runner was a big husky boy who weighed about 160 pounds. I weighed about 100 pounds, soaking wet. I tripped the runner, all right, but he was running so fast that I got knocked down in the pile of runners.

The erring patrol was squirming around on the ground, while the people from the gauntlet, proceeded to whack us good. I got quite a few good licks, some even from my own patrol. After it was over, they assured me that they couldn't tell it was me on the ground in all the bodies.

Needless to say, that was the last time anyone offered "strap oil" at camp.

Camp Kickapoo was one of our early summer camps, which was located a few miles from Menard, Texas, on the beautiful San Saba River. There were groves of huge pecan trees and live oak trees. There were some open areas, where we played games and had the archery range.

In the early days of summer camps in our council, there was a little chore called "guard duty." Each troop would patrol the area in the vicinity of their campsite. This duty would start after the nightly council fire and would last until five o'clock in the morning. Usually, two Scouts were on duty at a time for a two-hour watch. For illumination you carried a smoky kerosene lantern, with which, by straining your eyes, you might be able to see about six feet.

One night my Patrol Leader and I were on guard duty. Rumors had been circulating around camp that there was some strange animal prowling around. Several Scouts who had been on guard duty earlier in the week swore that they had seen "something." About 2:30 in the morning, we decided that we needed to use the latrine. We hung the lantern on a convenient nail and went about our business. When we had finished, we got the lantern and started out the door.

The moon was shining, but there were lots of clouds. Just as we stepped

Belt Honors

Awarded to each member of
patrol winning tent inspection.

Awarded for K. P. duty.

Awarded for taking part in
skit or stunt at Council Fire.

Awarded for each merit
badge earned in camp.

Awarded for running a mile
and going swimming each
morning before breakfast.

Awarded for serving
on guard duty.

out the door, the moon came out for an instant and we could see a tall white "Thing" about fifty feet away. The moon went behind the clouds and it got very dark again. We decided to retreat by going over the walls of the latrine. They were just too high; we couldn't make it. We went sneaking up to the door, which incidentally, was the only door. The "Thing" was still there. At one moment it would look like it was about five feet tall. Then it would seem to grow to about seven feet tall. To say we were terrified is putting it mildly. We were petrified, trapped with no way to run. Suddenly, the moon came out from the clouds and shone brightly. The mystery was solved. The "Thing" was a big white horse. When he had his head down grazing, facing us, he looked like he was five feet tall. When he raised his head to look around, he looked like he grew to over seven feet tall. Gordon, my Patrol Leader, and I decided that we wouldn't tell anyone in hopes that they would get the bejabbers scared out of them also.

I believe Camp Kickapoo was the first camp where a boy could earn Belt Honors. These were various symbols which were stamped on your web belt, and then colored with different colors of waterproof ink. There were quite a few a camper might earn, but the most prized one was a small white fish. To get this honor, you must rise at 5:30, put on a cold, wet bathing suit, assemble at the flagpole and then run a mile before breakfast. This had to be done each morning of camp.

Each morning, our troop, on the way to the flagpole, would pass through the campsite of another troop which was camped near us. Their Senior Patrol Leader, Mike, was the soundest sleeper I ever saw. When he went to sleep, he didn't just drop off to sleep—he died away. When he really started sawing the proverbial logs, it almost took an earthquake to wake him up. One morning we started through their camp and Mike was still asleep. We decided it would be fun to play a little joke on him. Four of us, gently, picked up the cot with Mike snoring away. We carried it a short distance to a shallow part of the river and placed Mike and the cot about thirty feet from the bank. We climbed back on shore and both troops combined to yell and scream that the river was on a flood. Mike finally raised up, looked around, saw all the water and then rolled off his cot. The water was only about six inches deep and Mike was feverishly trying to swim to shore. He skinned his chest and arms but finally made it to safety. He stood up in the shallow water and had this puzzled expression on his face. We all started laughing and giggling and finally Mike joined in. He told us that when he woke up and saw his cot surrounded by water, he was sure the river had flooded the entire camp.

So much for Camp Kickapoo.

Chapter 4
Field Meets

In the early days of our Scout Council, field meets—we call them cam-porees now—brought a lot of attention to Scouting and helped us to sharpen our Scout skills. We had many of the same events we have now: signaling, fire building, both flint and friction, first aid, knot tying and wall scaling. Every once in a while they would throw in a new event. One year this event was a "Tin Can Walker relay." There were eight members on a team. The "tin can walkers" were quart oil cans with a couple of holes punched in the top. A loop of wire went through the holes and reached up to between your knees and thighs. You held the wires with your hands. This was a relay. The first member started and ran on the walkers to a point about fifty feet away. He returned and touched the second member until all had run.

All the troops had made their walkers out of quart cans so it was evenly matched . . . except for one troop. They had used the very small size milk cans. When the starter gave the signal, their runner would jump straight up in the air, come down and mash the cans flat and then take off running. This worked so well that their entire team had finished before our number two man had finished. There was a great howl of outrage over using the collapsible cans, but this troop pointed out that the rules didn't specify any size of can. We had to admit that they were smarter than we were.

Another time, this same sneaky troop pulled off another good trick. "Wall Scaling" was one of the events which took a lot of team work. Eight men were on a team. Most troops would have four of their larger Scouts run to the wall, turn around and cup their hands about knee-high. Four smaller Scouts would run down and the four big boys would hoist them to the top of the wall. Then two boys would hoist two more and the last two would go over the wall. One would help his buddy to the top. He would stay on top and reach down to

*"A Scout had to have agility to keep his balance
in the Tin Can Walker Relay.'"*

help the last one over. Here again, most of the troops used this same procedure. But not our sneaky friends.

Their first four boys, wearing track shoes with steel spikes, ran to the wall. They helped the first four over. Then the four stepped back about three steps, and using the spiked shoes, went over the wall like a bunch of squirrels. There was a stunned silence, and then screams of outrage, "foul -foul." Once more this troop of Scouts pointed out that the rules didn't mention any ban on any type of shoes, so, they were legal. I often thought that most of those Scouts would grow up to be lawyers—and several did.

But one small footnote about the wall scaling event. In the years since the spiked shoes were worn, whenever there was a wall scaling, there was one stipulation: no shoes with metal spikes would be allowed.

One of the funniest events in the field meet one year was a signaling contest. Two receivers were about a hundred feet away from the signaler.

The only catch was, the signaler was perched atop a human pyramid composed of ten Scouts. Five boys stood on the ground with their arms around each other. Three Scouts sat on their shoulders and two sat on their shoulders with the boy sending semaphore signals on top. Since I was one of the smaller Scouts, I was one of the two Scouts directly under the signaler. The message was quite lengthy and I started slipping. By the time the message was finished, I had slipped all the way to the ground. The poor kid sending the message, was perched precariously on the one boy's shoulders. We won second place, but the sneaky troop won again. We accused them of reading lips, but once more they pointed out that the message was to be sent by semaphore, but nothing was said about a little added signaling, such as reading lips.

An event, in which we took a lot of pride, was the "Message Relay." There were sixteen members on a team. The first man was given a message and a few minutes to memorize it. At the start, he ran 100 yards, told the message to the next man, who in turn ran 100 yards and repeated the message. One of the Scouts running against me was one of the fastest boys in San Angelo. I made up my mind that I was going to run step for step with Benny. I felt that I was pretty fast myself and I had to prove to myself and to my team that I could run with anybody. The Scout on Benny's team and the Scout on my team reached us about the same time. They gasped out the message and we took off. I stayed right with Benny, but when I reached my teammate to tell him the message, I was so out of breath, I couldn't speak. My team mate, George, was a great big Scout. Later on, he played fullback on the high school football team. He was trying to get me to tell him the message and all I could do was gasp for air. He picked me up by the shoulders and shook me like a Great Dane dog shaking a little Poodle. By the time I finally got the message relayed to him, the rest of the runners were forty yards away. Needless to say, we certainly didn't win.

Chapter 5
The Exhibition Troop

The "Exhibition Troop"was one method used to create interest in Scouting in the smaller towns of our council. This troop was formed by Scouts from several different troops in our town. There was a try-out competition held to determine which boys would be selected to be in this group. There were four patrols; a Knot Tying patrol, a Signal patrol, a First Aid patrol and a Fire Building patrol. In the Fire Building patrol, the Scouts showed how to build a fire using flint and steel and also by the friction method.

We had two old Model T trucks, which should have been junked years before. One truck carried our gear and some of the Scouts while the rest of us rode in the other one. In these modern days when we put so much emphasis on safety and the dangers which come from riding in the back of an open truck or pickup, I shudder to think about our going all over this part of West Texas in those trucks. The motors in these two antiques were very bad. I'll never forget one of our trips to Junction,Texas, in the middle of the hill country. On the highway there were a number of steep hills and the trucks just couldn't make it up the hills going forward. The reverse gear worked pretty good, so when we came to a steep hill, we would all get out of the truck and the driver would back the truck up the hill. The tires were as bad as the motors. On one trip to Fort Stockton, Texas, about 170 miles from home, we had twenty-six flat tires.

When we reached the town where we were to put on the show, we would set up, usually in a high school gym or some public building. A lot of times, in the summer, we would put on a show in the town square. I was in the Knot Tying Patrol. Our Patrol Leader, Fred, was a big blond-headed Scout. He would tie knots with a piece of rope about one inch in diameter. This would help show our audience what the knot was supposed to look like.

The Signaling Patrol would demonstrate how to send messages using semaphore. This was the method used by Scouts then. Many of the people were very impressed with how you could make so many letters using the flags in so many positions.

The Fire Building patrol was usually the hit of the show. The boys who demonstrated fire building using flint and steel were very good. Most of the time they could build a fire in less than ten seconds, and one boy built a fire in one show in three seconds.

First Aid was also very popular in these smaller towns. Many of these people lived on ranches or on farms and some of these towns didn't even have a doctor. They were very interested in learning the proper methods to treat cuts and burns, and many were interested in learning Artificial Respiration. The Patrol Leader of the First Aid Patrol acted as a master of ceremonies for his event. He would have the other Scouts demonstrate bandaging and would also tell the symptoms of a victim in case of an accident. One first aid demonstration, which always drew a lot of comment was our treatment of snake bite. Many of our audience would say that our method was no good! They suggested pouring gunpowder on the bite and setting it on fire. Quite a few suggested the whiskey method—this was the treatment in which the victim was given liberal doses of whiskey to the point where he forgot all about the snake bite. Many of the old-timers leaned toward the whiskey treatment over our method of cutting the wound, applying a stricture bandage and suction. They insisted that this method was no fun at all and could hardly compare with the whiskey treatment.

Looking back, I firmly believe that the Exhibition Troop played a great part in bringing Scouting to boys in the smaller towns in our council. This was before the days of television, there were few radios, and even the newspapers did not cover the area like they do now. Most of the boys in our audiences got their first look at Scouting through the Exhibition Troop, and most of these small towns still have troops today, started long ago when we pulled into town and "did our thing."

Chapter 6
The Scout Village

The troops in our town had no permanent place to meet, no place to call their own. Since most of the troops were sponsored by churches, we met in the basements of the churches, in church school rooms, or any spot which was handy. After each meeting, all the Scout equipment had to be put away. Flags had to be stored, knot boards taken down, and any awards or ribbons had to be packed away. It was not a good situation and the troops sometimes felt like unwanted guests. Each patrol needed a room to call their own which they could decorate with patrol flags and all the stuff from hikes, summer camps and camporees. A room for a patrol helps to build patrol spirit and certainly makes a stronger patrol.

The adults in our community realized this and decided to do something about it. They planned to build a "Scout Village" where each troop would have their own cabin. There would be a cabin which the Scout Executive would use as an office and also a cabin for the Campfire Girls. The site was on the banks of one of the rivers which runs through our town. This location was about in the center of town which made it handy for the Scouts to attend their meetings.

We swam in the river. The drawback to this was there was no shallow place in the swimming area. A suspension bridge spanned the river and there were two dressing rooms across on the other side. We had tennis courts, volley ball courts, basketball courts and an archery range. Since there was not much in the way of any sort of summer recreation program in our town, the Scouts spent a lot of time at the Scout Village.

The cabins were started by volunteer help from the labor unions. Carpenters, plumbers, electricians and masonry men helped to start the build-

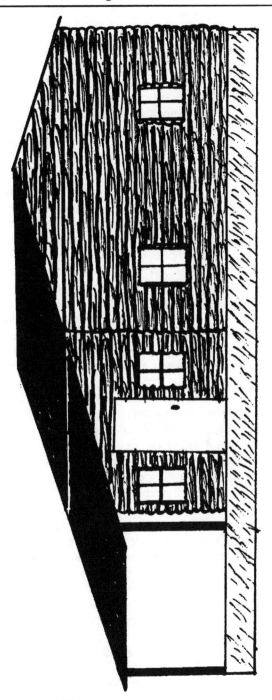

"Each troop had a cabin at the Log Cabin Scout Village."

ings. They put up the walls and roofed the cabins. The plumbers and electricians did their part in getting the cabins ready for the Scouts to finish. The boys put up sheetrock inside and painted the outside. The outside walls were made of wood siding. Slabs, cut from logs, were hauled in from a sawmill in New Mexico. These were nailed to the wood siding and made the cabins look as if they were really log cabins.

Each cabin had a large meeting room. There were four rooms for patrols and a room which doubled as the Scoutmaster's room and a place to keep our records and books. Each patrol was allowed to decorate their room, and it wasn't long before the walls were covered with snake skins, knot boards, pictures and all kinds of things to remind them of summer camps, hikes and weekend campouts. Two of the troops had totem poles, each about twenty feet tall, set in the earth outside their cabins. These had been carved by a local craftsman, Neal Sanders, and had been won by the troops in contests.

A suspension bridge was across one end of the swimming area, and we had a diving board and a tower which was used as a look-out platform for the life guards and also as a diving tower. The water was very deep in this area and the spot was called "dead man's hole." Stories were told about some people in a wagon who missed the shallow crossing about 100 yards downstream. They drove off in the deep part and all were drowned. One time, when we were swimming, we dived down and found parts of a wagon wheel. We just knew that this was part of the doomed wagon, which helped to make the stories seem all the more true.

All of the troops in town met on Friday night. In a way, this was good. We had inter-troop games and contests. We all kept up with what each troop was doing, and it helped to make you try a little harder on your advancement. Also, if you found out that some troop or patrol had a new idea for decorating their patrol room, you immediately tried harder to outdo them. Each troop and patrol developed a very competitive spirit, but, by all meeting on the same night, I think there was a good, warm feeling of brotherhood among all the troops in our Scouting community.

It was at the Scout Village where I had my first—and last—encounter with the use of chewing tobacco. One summer, most of the boys in town got on this kick of chewing Beech Nut tobacco. It was like this fad the kids had the last few years about dipping snuff. I, like a lot of my buddies, felt one had to chew tobacco to be with the in crowd. I didn't really enjoy it because I found there was a defect in my physical make-up. When it came to chewing tobacco, the glands in my mouth put out so much liquid that I had the sensation of being on the verge of drowning. To put it plainly, I just couldn't spit fast enough. I usually had a couple of small dribbles oozing from the corners of my mouth. I was constantly wiping these away with the back of my hand. The crowning blow, which brought an end to my tobacco-chewing career, came one summer afternoon, during a fast basketball game. I had a large chew in one jaw, and I jumped up to block a pass by my opponent. I blocked the pass, but I swallowed my chew. I turned several shades of green, up-chucked and finally staggered home, where my grandmother just knew I was "coming down" with some terrible ailment and went in to call the doctor. I stopped her and told her it was just something I ate. That was my last effort at chewing tobacco and I haven't touched any since that afternoon sixty-two years ago.

The Scout Village lasted for several years and helped Scouting to grow strong in our town. A flood in 1936 washed it away and the only thing left to remind you of the village is the concrete platform where the diving board and tower were and the large slab of concrete, which anchored the swinging bridge across the river.

Though there is not much left in the way of physical evidence of the Scout Village, I believe the wonderful memories of those happy times remain in the hearts of many boys who felt that the Scout Village was their second home.

Chapter 7
Moving Around

I stayed in Scouts in San Angelo for four years. During that time I served as Assistant Patrol Leader, Patrol Leader, Song Leader, Scribe, Assistant Senior Patrol Leader and Senior Patrol Leader. I learned some valuable lessons from Scouting. In looking back, I know that the happiest days of my youth were spent in Boy Scouts. I moved to Wink, Texas, where my Dad worked in the oil field. There was no Scouting program there but the Hi-Y had a good program and I spent many days camping in the sand dunes and in the Davis Mountains.

We moved to East Texas during the oil boom of 1931, and I served as Junior Assistant Scout master while I was still in high school. After graduation, we moved to New Mexico out in Gallup County. Actually, we lived about seventy-five miles from Gallup, which was the nearest town. There was no Scouting here but I learned some good ideas on desert survival from some boys about my age who were members of the Zuni and Navaho Indian tribes. They taught me how to recognize edible desert plants and where water might be found by digging a few feet below the surface.

I moved back to East Texas by myself and spent the next few years working in the "oil patch." I was away from Scouting for about four years. During this time I did one of the few smart things of my life. I met the young lady who was to become my wife, and after fifty-two years, I still count my blessings where she is concerned. She has been the soul of patience in my Scouting activities. She helped me to get ready for countless overnight camps, summer camps, jamborees, raft trips down the Rio Grande, canoe trips and Philmont. She sewed about a jillion neckerchiefs for the Scouts going to the jamborees. Vivian, my wife, also toiled over the sewing machine helping to make costumes for countless skits and expositions. I jokingly used to say that "I did my Scouting in spite of my wife." Actually, I couldn't have made it without her patience and understanding.

We moved to Seagraves, Texas, near Lubbock and I reorganized a Scout troop sponsored by the First Methodist Church. We had a good program and soon had about thirty-five boys in the unit. Camping was the main activity in our troop, even though there were very few good places to go in that part of the country. Cedar Lake was one of our camping sites. This was a rather large lake but it was very shallow. We had camped there at times when we could camp right next to the water. But if we had a hot, dry spell, the lake would evaporate and, when you went camping, you might have about 400 yards of red, sticky mud between you and the water. Also, the water in the lake had a bad odor, but the boys didn't seem to mind. After a hot summer weekend of camping, the boys said the lake didn't smell any worse than they did.

The father of one of our Scouts owned a ranch in New Mexico. The ranch house was located near a bunch of big sand dunes, where we always camped because there was a convenient windmill. We tried to plan our campouts when there would be a full moon. We would play "Capture the Flag" all night by the light of the moon shining on the white sand. Another game the Scouts liked was "King of the Mountain." One patrol was chosen as "kings" and they tried to prevent the other patrols from climbing to the top of the sand dune. There was a lot of scuffling and grunting, but the soft sand acted like a cushion when someone fell or was pushed. The only bad thing about this game was that I always ended up weighing about five pounds more from all the sand that I swallowed. My fondest memories of those days or nights was the moon shining over the sand dunes as we engaged in a life and death struggle of "Capture the Flag."

We met in the church basement and had to be careful about not tearing up the place. Our opening ceremonies were usually held inside, and if we were working on advancement, we would stay indoors. Our games were played outside on the church lawn. One night it was raining, so we had to have our game inside. The church held their church school classes in the basement, and were in the process of putting in a partition to make another room. The sheetrock was in place, but it hadn't been finished. Of course, the boys insisted on playing "Capture the Flag." The quarters were a little cramped but we were doing fine until one Scout grabbed the flag and was trying to get back across the line. He was running full speed and, as he passed by a boy from the opposing side, the boy gave him a tremendous shove and he went completely through the sheetrock.

The next morning the preacher called me and wanted to know what had happened. I explained and told him we would replace the damaged wall. He suggested, rather stiffly, that in the future, we should play our rowdy games outside.

We moved back to San Angelo, and have lived here since 1943. I have been in the Scouting program here since 1944. During that time I served as Scoutmaster for thirty-nine years, was on the Leadership Training Team for nine years, was Merit Badge Examiner for Swimming, Lifesaving, Pioneering, Camping, Cooking, Hiking, Canoeing, and Citizenship in the Community. I enjoyed working with Scouts on the various merit badges with one exception. The Lifesaving Merit Badge used to require the "hair carry" as one of the rescue carries. For several years, most of the boys wore their hair in the popular "crew cut." As I was the only one available with enough hair to grasp, I served as victim for about twenty lifesaving candidates in each of my classes. After a session of being towed ashore by my hair by several rescuers, my whole face felt as if it had been uplifted, by about two inches. This had one good result, though. It pulled all the wrinkles out of my face.

Chapter 8
Back in San Angelo

Back in San Angelo we became members of the First Methodist Church and joined the Friendship Class, a class for young adults, mostly couples. This class wanted to help the youth program in our community and decided to help form a Boy Scout troop and a Girl Scout troop to be sponsored by the Sam Houston Elementary School. All of the students of this school were of Hispanic origin. There had been a Boy Scout troop formed here several years before but had gradually fallen apart.

I was asked to take this troop as Scoutmaster, and decided to give it a try. Communication was one of my problems since I spoke very little Spanish. When the boys didn't want me to know what they were talking about, they would revert to Spanish. Also, there was a lot of distrust at first. The boys thought that this was some sort of scheme to exploit them, and they thought that I was getting paid to serve as Scoutmaster. Miss Ruth Rich was principal of the school and all of the boys thought she was the greatest. When I ran into some problems, I could count on her help to set things straight. We met in the school building and Miss Rich was very proud of the troop.

After a few weeks, more and more boys started coming to our meetings. We tried to plan some activity like knot tying or first aid and we played our games outside on the school lawn. Many boys would see the fun the Scouts were having and decide to join.

For a long time I couldn't get the troop to participate in any of the activities with the other troops in town. Our boys felt that they would not be welcome and would not join any of the district events. However, the district was having a Court of Honor on the steps of the courthouse. Our District Executive made a special point to come to our meeting to invite our Scouts to the

Court of Honor. Our boys attended, dressed in their uniforms and looking very sharp. The other troops made our Scouts feel so welcome that this was the turning point in our troop thinking about not being welcome.

Later on, during a big celebration for Boy Scout Week, our troop won first place for the best skit and won first for the best uniformed unit. After this there was no urging needed. The next event was a camporee, and Troop 36 won this, also.

One of the camporee events was knot tying. One of the mothers told me her son was so intent on winning that he carried his rope to bed and wore it to school like a belt. Another event was wood chopping. This was a cinch for our Scouts because most of them lived in homes where wood was used to cook and heat their homes. Chopping wood was something they did every day.

Our lack of communication with parents almost ended in disaster for the troop. We had played a game at the meetings called "Kelly Says." This was a takeoff of the old familiar "Simon Says" game. You know, you are given commands to perform some movement, but if Simon doesn't say for you to do it, you are out of the game. Our version worked the same way except we had taught the Scouts some simple drills like "right face," "left face," "about face," "parade rest" and a few others. If Kelly said for you to do "left face"and you did it that was OK. But if Kelly didn't precede the command, and you did it, you were out. We had a lot of fun with contests between the patrols to see which one could outsmart Kelly. The winning patrol usually got candy as a reward. The Scouts had gotten so sharp it was difficult to trick the boys.

One meeting night when I got to the school, there were only about five boys there. I asked them where everyone was, because we had been having about forty Scouts at the meetings. One boy shrugged and said something in Spanish to the others. I persisted and finally wormed it out of him as to the reason for all of the absentees. Two of my good friends, who were in the service, had been coming to the meetings to help me. Since it was wartime, the fellows had to wear their uniforms. The boy I was talking to told me that some of the parents had seen the men coming to the meetings in their uniforms. They would not let their boys come to the meeting because they were afraid we were trying to get them in the Army.

I got in touch with Miss Rich, and told her my problem. We had a good laugh over the idea of our trying to recruit those little elementary school kids for the military. She sent notes home to the parents of the boys and everything worked out all right. However, we didn't play "Kelly says" any more.

Our troop loved to camp out. We had very little equipment and no tents at all. In winter, if the weather turned bad, we would huddle under the truck or camp in a convenient shed used to shelter the sheep on a ranch. None of the Scouts had sleeping bags and used big heavy quilts for cover. I had a mummy type sleeping bag, which was made from the same material as an Army blanket. This bag was rather small and when I got in it, it was more like putting on a coat, rather than a sleeping bag. One cold night I just couldn't get comfortable. I turned and twisted a lot and finally dozed off. I awoke a little later and thought someone was choking me. I had turned and twisted until the zipper was on my back. I'm a good sized guy and the bag was so tight I couldn't reach the zipper. I struggled and finally decided that I would have to call the boys to get me out of this trap. I decided against this when I thought that they might just decide this was an opportune time to throw me and the bag in the creek. After a terrible struggle and a barrage of words unbecoming to a Scoutmaster, I finally managed to reach the zipper and free myself. I never used that bag again.

One weekend, my two Air Force buddies and I had promised the Scouts we would go camping. It was decided that we would hike to Ben Ficklin, a beautiful spot on the South Concho River about four miles from town. The wife of one of my buddies was going to spend the weekend with my wife. They questioned us about our plans and where we were going, but we told them it was a secret. They assured us that we would be sorry for not telling them. Later we were reminded how prophetic that statement was.

We hiked out with no problems and set up our camp right on the bank of the river. This "setting up" was not much of a chore. We still didn't have any tents, so, the main thing we did was to unroll our sleeping gear and gather wood for our cooking. We decided to go swimming and had a very nice time. We cooked supper and were planning a council fire after it got good and dark.

By this time there were some pretty ominous looking clouds building up in the northwest. One of the Scouts jokingly remarked, "Hey, man, those look like earthquake clouds." It got darker and the wind started to blow. And then the rains came. It was raining so hard that the drops were not coming down vertically or at an angle . . . "They were falling horizontally." There were no individual drops, the rain came down in sheets. The big pecan trees in the grove were swaying, and the ground seemed to tremble. Some of the Scouts were crying, some were praying, and a few of the braver or crazier souls were laughing. I was not one of the latter. You would huddle around on one side of the tree away from the wind and then the direction would change and you had the sensation of drowning, it was raining so hard.

It rained for about two hours and then stopped as suddenly as it had started. Everything was soaked—our bedding, our food, and our fire wood. I finally managed to get a fire started and we stood around shivering, with the water running out of our shoes. We took inventory and decided that our wisest move would be to return to town.

One of my military buddies had gone swimming in his underwear and had hung his shorts out to dry. When the storm hit, they were blown into the

"It wasn't raining straight down or even at
an angle . . . it was raining horizontally."

next county. I believe his wife never did accept his explanation as to why he came home without his underwear.

As I mentioned before, these Hispanic Scouts didn't have sleeping bags. A few of them had blankets, but most of them used a heavy quilt to sleep in. When these things got wet, they weighed a ton. We started walking back toward town. We were straggling along the road, at 1:30 in the morning. We three men were carrying what was left of our gear and most of the heavy quilts which belonged to the Scouts. Some of the boys just couldn't carry the quilts and wanted to just throw them away. We reassured them that we could make it if we just took our time and everyone helped to carry the wet mess.

We had one more small problem. The other two fellows were in the service and this was wartime. They had a curfew at one o'clock. If they were caught out after this time, they might be severely punished. After we reached town and delivered all the boys to their homes, we had the problem of trying to reach our homes without getting caught by the M.P. We went slinking down back alleys and side streets until one of the fellows was sure he could make it home. The other two of us still had about fifteen blocks to go. We tried to be quiet, but with all of the mud and water in our clothes and shoes, each step we took was like a cow pulling her foot out of a mud hole.

We finally made it home and knocked on our back door. My wife turned on the porch light and she and the other girl just cracked up into hysterical laughter when they saw their drowned heroes. They had talked about going to look for us when the rain started, but we had made such a secret about our destination, they had no idea where to look.

I was Scoutmaster of Troop 36 for six years. During this time the boys came to trust me. I believe that belonging to Scouts made them realize they were accepted and gave them a certain amount of dignity. Most of the boys I had in the early days of the troop are grandfathers now. I still keep up with most of them. Many come to see me on Christmas or summer vacations. This past spring, one of the Scouts, a grown man now, told me that I was the first Anglo who had ever seemed to care about the Hispanic boys. To me, they weren't Anglo or Hispanic, they were just boys—no, not just boys—they were Boy Scouts.

A young man, who had been a member of the old troop before I took it over, came home from the service. He wanted to get involved in Scouting again and expressed a desire to become Scoutmaster. I turned it over to him and they had a fine troop for years.

I have recounted here only some of the many happy, humorous, and a few sad episodes in my life as Scoutmaster of Troop 36. My Senior Patrol Leader, Alberto Hernandez, was killed in Korea. Two of my former Scouts got small acting parts in the movie "Giant." A couple of boys were elected to the City Commission, but most of my Troop 36 Scouts just grew up and became hard-working, good, family men—and I guess that is what life and Scouting is all about.

Chapter 9
Troop 1

Troop 1 was one of the original Scout troops organized in 1926 when our present council was formed. This troop was sponsored by the First Methodist Church and had a long record of outstanding Scouting. The Scoutmaster of Troop 1 was a member of another church. The members of his own church had been trying to persuade him to give up Troop 1 in order to start a Scout troop in his own church. He had agreed to do this if they could find someone to serve as Scoutmaster for Troop 1. They asked me to take the troop, and I decided to give it a try. This try lasted for more than twenty-seven years.

The first meeting night, when we met to reorganize the troop, there were only five boys present. Our unit grew very rapidly, and, in a short time, we had thirty-five to forty Scouts coming to meetings. We had the same old problem which plagues a lot of troops—we had no regular meeting place and had to use the basement of the church's educational building for a place to meet. After each meeting, we had to put all of our Scout equipment away, and there was no place to display things which help to build better patrols and better troop spirit.

The fathers of several Scouts in our troop got together and decided to build a troop cabin as a permanent meeting place. Our committee got permission to use some city property along the river on which to build our cabin. This location was just across the river from the site of the log cabin village which housed the original seven troops back in the late 1920's. This village had been washed away in the disastrous flood of 1936. The concrete foundation for the diving tower was about fifty yards from our cabin. The huge concrete block which was used to anchor the suspension bridge crossing the river, was about half a block away. To me, it seemed as if my Scouting had made a complete circle, and I was back in the same area, where I had spent so many happy hours as a Boy Scout.

Our cabin was built a lot like the old log cabins, except our new one was constructed of concrete tile blocks, instead of wood siding. The floor plan was about the same. We had a large meeting room, four patrol rooms, an equipment room, a bathroom and a room for a library and office. The building was heated by a huge fireplace and a central heating unit.

After our cabin was built, we really picked up in membership. We tried to provide a good year-round program of overnight camps, summer camps, and Philmont expeditions. We had about 60 Scouts in our troop and the cabin was getting a little crowded. There were three Scout troops in our city, whose Scoutmasters were members of the military stationed at Goodfellow Air Force Base. These three leaders were all transferred about the same time, and the troops sponsors couldn't seem to find anyone to take over the troops. The Scouts were without leaders and the units had folded.

About this time the phone started ringing. I would answer the phone and a little boy's voice would give me the sad story about his troop breaking up and how he had no place to enjoy Scouting. He would want to know if we would take him in Troop 1. I just didn't have the heart to refuse them, even though my wife would remind me about how crowded our cabin was. After a few dozen of these same heart-rending phone conversations, plus the news traveling via the grapevine, our troop had become huge.

At one time we had about 149 boys in our troop. I had no assistant Scoutmasters, but I had an excellent Troop Committee and the best boy leaders ever. But you can imagine the crowded conditions when you remember our cabin was designed to hold thirty-two Scouts. The patrols took over the equipment room and we moved the equipment into the bathroom. One patrol used the office as a meeting room and the rest of the patrols were good examples of true togetherness. The members sat in each other's laps, sat on the floor and spilled out into the main meeting room. It was crowded—but we still had a lot of fun and developed some great young leaders.

One of our Patrol Leaders, John Pipkin, was ready for his Eagle Scout interview. He had completed his requirements and his service project, and had to go before the District Advancement Committee. The Committee members didn't know John and were asking him a lot of questions about his leadership in our troop. He was asked in what position of leadership he served in our troop. He replied that he was Patrol Leader. The committee asked him how many Scouts were in his patrol. He answered that he had twenty-seven members. They said they didn't mean the number of members in his troop, but wanted to know how many boys he had in his patrol. When he assured them that there were twenty-seven Scouts in his patrol, they were flabbergasted. That was the end of their questions about leadership. The rest of the session

"Designed for 32 Scouts, our cabin was bursting at the seams when we had 149 boys in our Scout troop."

was spent in his telling them that our unit had between 140 and 150 Scouts, and that we had a great Scouting program in spite of overcrowding.

I could not have made it if it hadn't been for my great junior leaders and some of the best Senior Patrol Leaders ever in Scouting. About this time, my troop committee was something of an oddity. In most troop committees, the members have boys in the troop or have younger boys who may eventually join the troop. The only thing bad about this is, that when their boys leave Scouting, the committee members lose their interest and have to be replaced. For almost ten years, I had the same committee. There was not a man on the committee who had a boy, either in the unit or growing to Scout age. Several of the men had no children at all. The rest, like me, had girls. This same situation happens a lot when a Scoutmaster has a boy or boys in a troop. After his son leaves Scouting, in many cases, the Scoutmaster loses interest, also. But our committee really did a "bang up" job as Scouters.

I suppose I was too hard on some of the fathers of the Scouts in my troop. Some expressed a desire to come down and help at the meetings. I told them we would love to have them but we wanted them to be there each meeting night, and not just on the nights when there was nothing else more interesting to do. I told them I was too busy to be entertaining them, drinking coffee and sitting around "shooting the breeze." Why should we try to teach them to tie knots, do first aid, or use a compass? With my junior leaders, I could tell them to help a group in knot-tying and I didn't have to show them how to tie the knots. If the fathers wanted to come and learn the Scout skills, we would be glad to teach them. But if they were just going to attend the meetings, infrequently, I would rather have a knowledgeable junior leader to serve as Scout skill instructors.

On overnight camps, the fathers were welcome to attend, but I made it plain, that there were a few rules to follow. I didn't want the father setting up the tent, securing the wood and cooking all of the meals, while junior was skipping rocks in the river or off fishing. By the same token, I didn't want the father acting like a king and expecting his boy to wait on him hand and foot. We had many fathers attend our weekend camps. They were welcome to participate in our activities or do their own thing, such as fishing or hunting arrowheads and Indian relics. A few times we hornswoggled the dads into playing "Ambush" with the troop, but that is another story.

As more troops were organized in our city, the number of Scouts in Troop 1 was reduced. For more than ten years we had over 100 Scouts in our unit. For several more years we had between 75 and 100 boys in Troop 1. We added to our cabin and ended up with eight patrol rooms, two equipment rooms and finally got our office and library back from the patrol using it.

A good example of building troop and patrol spirit can be seen in the many plaques, trophies and ribbons in our cabin. These things cover the walls and about half the rafters in our meeting place. We have awards from summer camps, Philmont, canoe trips, Fifty Miler, Historical Trails awards, Rio Grande raft trips, jamborees, camporees, First Aid Meets, Swim Meets, expositions, and God and Country awards. Half of one wall has well over 160 Eagle Scout wall plaques, which represents many, many hours of outstanding Scouting. There are also pictures of twelve of our Scouts who made the "Report to the Governor" and two Scouts who made the "Report to the President." We have had Scouts from our unit attend national jamborees starting with the one in 1937 until the present time, and have had several Scouts attend international jamborees in various countries. In 1960, forty-eight members of our troop attended the Jamboree in Colorado Springs, Colorado. We had five natural patrols with regular leaders and each officer at the jamboree held the same position at home in the troop. This was one of the best jamborees I attended.

During my twenty-seven years as Scoutmaster of Troop 1, I enjoyed the friendship of a great many Scouts, who were very successful in later life. Among these are several lawyers, doctors, bankers, ranchers, college professors, some biochemists and some airline pilots. We also had several boys who ended up in the "slammer." The odd thing is, that when I recall the many boys I had in Scouting, sometimes the ones I remember most are the ones who got into trouble. I wonder if—maybe if I had spent a little more time with the boy or had given him the right advice at a bad time in his life—well, just maybe he might not have got off on the "wrong foot." I suppose that it is true; you remember your few failures more than your many successes.

Chapter 10
Hikes

When one thinks of Scouting, you just naturally remember the things most people associate with Boy Scouting. These are camping, cooking over a campfire and hiking. When I was a Scout in the early council days, hiking was a very simple matter. Our town was small and there were many places within a short distance of town. We had three rivers and Spring Creek, as large as the rivers, within a short distance from town. Troops could hike about five or six miles in any direction and find a good camping place on a river. All this has been changed. As the city grew, many of these spots are within the city limits and the others have been broken up into lots for people who want to build homes along the waterways. Many of the ranches have been leased by people who are raising thoroughbred horses, cattle and sheep and do not want Scout campers or hikers upsetting the animals.

Troops now are forced to travel to weekend camping spots in vehicles. Many of these sites are fifteen, twenty or even as far away as sixty miles. For a weekend camp, the distances are too great to hike out, spend the night, and hike back on Sunday afternoon. Many troops plan day hikes, in which the distance covered may be hiked in one day.

I suppose, since I first joined Scouting in 1926, I have participated in about a zillion hikes. Most of these hikes were very ordinary. We had our usual complement of blistered feet, the younger Scouts running out of water, falling into cactus patches, and all of us enduring the bites of various members of the insect family, such as ants, wasps, chiggers, mosquitoes and horse flies. The old hands knew just what to take to get by with the lightest load, while the younger Scouts carried everything but the kitchen sink.

One memorable hike I endured as a Boy Scout was something the Scout

Executive had dreamed up and called a "Bee-line Hike." The idea behind this hike was to travel in as straight a line as possible to reach your destination. Each troop was given a compass heading and told to follow this to a destination about fourteen miles away. To help keep you in a straight line, one of the Scouters, who owned an airplane, flew a straight line, from town to our destination. A helper went along with the pilot and threw five pound sacks of lime from the plane at intervals of about 500 yards.

To follow this "Bee-line" you were supposed to climb over hills or cross any body of water without going around it. It was suggested, however, that no one be foolish enough to wade through patches of cactus and "cat claw" bushes, but would be allowed to go around these natural hazards.

Several troops were hiking along together. The only equipment we carried were canteens and first aid kits. We were to be fed with a big barbecue when we reached our destination. We had a lot of fun climbing over hills, and fighting through dense underbrush, trying to keep a straight line to our goal. We finally came to the river and could spot the next sack of lime across the river. We had to cross the river to maintain our straight line. Since it was late summer, nearly everyone decided to just take off their clothes, roll them up in a bundle and swim across, holding their bundle out of the water. Two of my Scout buddies and I decided this method of crossing was "for the birds." We found two logs about fifteen feet long and decided to make a raft. We were supposed to use just natural items on our hike, so we decided to tie our raft together with ropes made from reeds growing in the water. We twisted them together and made a pretty good looking rope—so we thought—and lashed the two logs side by side.

We removed our shoes and socks and tied them around our necks, because we were going to sit astride the logs, with our feet dangling in the water. We launched our "ark" and were doing just fine. We were paddling with our hands and passed several swimmers in the water. We threatened them with dire consequences if they so much as touched our raft. We taunted them and, as I remember, mentioned the fact that they were suffering from a lack of intelligence not to have come up with a raft like ours. This sublime feeling of great accomplishment lasted about two-thirds of the way across the river. Our great dream came to a sudden stop. The ropes made from the reeds twisted together started to disintegrate, and as they broke up, our two logs started to separate. In a few seconds, we had to abandon ship and take to the water like the other swimmers. The great difference was they didn't have their clothes on like we did. We struggled to the shore and had to listen to the laughter and jibes from those poor "mortals," whom we accused of having an inferior brain and not being as smart as we were.

We finished the hike with no more problems. When the Scout Executive asked why we three were wet and the rest were dry, we just told him that we perspired more than the rest of the Scouts.

My longest hike in one day, took place when I was still a Boy Scout. Our troop decided to hike to Twin Mountains, which were about seven miles from where we met in town. We told our parents where we were going, and that we would probably be back in town by sundown. We hiked out with no problems and played around the hills for a short time. We decided to hike to where they were building a dam to make a new lake, Lake Nasworthy. This was about seven miles from Twin Mountains, so we started hiking. When we reached the dam site and rested a bit, my Patrol Leader discovered he had left his dad's binoculars at Twin Mountains. Our patrol decided to go back, and then the whole troop voted to go. When we got back to Twin Mountains, we had hiked twenty-one miles. After recovering the binoculars, we decided to go to Lake Nasworthy Dam, because we had been having such a good time throwing clods at one another and playing in the big ditches, gouged out to get dirt for the breakwater for the dam.

When we made it back to the dam, we had traveled about twenty-eight miles. We had a great time bouncing clods of dirt off one another's heads and playing "King of the Mountain" in the big ditches. It was getting near dark and we had been gone since seven that morning. We decided that we had better get started back to town. It was about nine o'clock at night and we were straggling along the road, a little leg-weary from all our hiking.

Suddenly, a car came down the road, and the driver stopped when he saw us shuffling along the way. He was a fireman from the local fire department, and he asked us if we were members of Troop 2. We assured him that we were and then he wanted to know what we were doing on the road to Lake Nasworthy when we had told all our parents we were going to Twin Mountains. We recounted our long hike and explained why we were in a completely different location from that in our original hike plans. He told us that the police department, the fire department and the sheriff's department all had men out looking for us in the Twin Mountain area. He said that he would go back to town and reassure our parents that we were all in the "land of the living." We tried to con him into giving us a ride. He said that there were too many of us to ride so we would all just have to walk.

A few days later, when we had recovered from our long hike and the tongue-lashings we received from our parents, we figured that we had hiked about thirty-five miles. That was my longest hike and the last one I ever took like that.

After serving as Scoutmaster of Troop 1 for several years, the boys in our unit came up with plans for a very ambitious hike. They wanted to hike to Camp Sol Mayer, about sixty miles away, to be there for the opening of the summer camp session. They planned to carry everything they needed for the five day trip and hoped to be able to obtain water from convenient windmills along the route. The boys were going to use freeze-dried food, which cut down the weight a lot. Each Scout carried a lightweight sleeping bag and a poncho.

We tried to cut down on the miles to be traveled by mapping the most direct route to camp. The father of one of our Scouts was a pilot with his own airplane. He flew a straight course from town and marked it on topographical maps. We checked with the ranchers over whose land we would travel, in order to get their permission. Some of them didn't much like the idea of a lot of people crawling over their fences, with the possibility of tearing down the strands. We came up with the idea of carrying a light weight aluminum step ladder to use to cross the fences. This seemed to pacify them, but one rancher pointed out something to which we hadn't given much thought. By using the direct route, there would be places where we planned to spend the night, which would be miles from any water. And in our area, where the mercury may climb to 110 degrees, water was a very essential commodity.

So we changed our thinking and decided to follow the road to camp. This route was a little farther, but at least, there were places where we could fill our canteens. We drove the route and got permission from the ranchers to camp by a convenient windmill.

Sixteen of the older, stronger boys were to make the hike. I could not get off from work to make the trip, but had an excellent Assistant Scoutmaster at this time. He offered to shepherd the little group and I accepted his offer.

We broke the group into two patrols which we named the "Holey Soles" and the "Flaming Feet." The Holey Sole flag showed a pair of worn out hiking boots and the Flaming Feet depicted a pair of bare feet with flames coming out the sides. We thought the names very appropriate.

Everything was in readiness, so, early one morning, Bill Kimrey, with his little group, started bravely on their long hike. Our troop had purchased some new aluminum pack frames for this group to use, and these frames would be used later by the other members of our unit. They started off very well with one of the youngest members of the hikers, Turk Pipkin, leading the way. Since we knew their route, it was possible for us to keep tabs on their progress. The first fifteen miles of their hike was along a well traveled road, and we got reports from drivers about their pace.

About one o'clock that afternoon I received a very disturbing report from one of the fathers of our hikers. It seems that he was worried about their welfare and he "just happened" to come back that way from a trip to San Antonio. He reported that the Scouts were having some difficulties. Some of the hikers had developed very painful blisters on their feet, and one of the windmills where they planned to refill their canteens, wasn't pumping. But the worst news was that the new aluminum pack frames were coming apart. It seems that the tubing, used in their construction, was too soft and the rivets were pulling out, allowing the frames to collapse.

When our troop hiked to summer camp one year, we felt that our two hiking patrols should have some appropriate patrol flags for their sixty mile hike. The boys thought that the "Holey Sole" flag would accurately depict the condition of their boots after walking over the rough West Texas terrain.

The name of this patrol was very appropriate for the boys on their hike to Camp Sol Mayer.

Since we were hiking in July when the temperature reaches well over 100 degrees, "Flaming Feet" became a reality for the boys making the hike.

This was one of our patrol flags carried by our Scouts on their sixty mile hike to Camp Sol Mayer.

I got in touch with two of my troop committeemen, whose boys were on the hike. We decided to go out late in the afternoon to where they were camped, to see if we could help out. We carried portable drills, pop rivets and extra canvas straps to patch the frames. We also carried about five gallons of ice cold milk and a bunch of fresh cookies.

On the way to their campsite, I worried that probably half of the hikers would want to come home, and forget about the hike. I had already catalogued in my mind a whole series of arguments concerning the reasons they should stay.

I guess that I didn't know my boys very well. When we got to their camp site, we found that they had come in, cooked supper, and were busy enjoying a cool swim in the rancher's stock tank. No one even mentioned not completing the hike. We repaired the packs, gave them their milk and cookies, returned home and quit worrying about them. They were tough—they were Boy Scouts.

The Fifty Miler Award was one of the goals the boys had in mind when they planned the hike. They had planned several good-turn projects to be completed along the way. One of the most notable took place one afternoon when they were camped near a little country store. They had made camp and gone to the store to enjoy a cold soda pop, the first they had had in several days. The little store was operated by an elderly man and his wife. The Scouts and the couple immediately became friends, and, in talking to the couple, noticed that their garden, which covered about two acres, had about a jillion rocks in it. The boys decided that this would be a good-turn project to clean out the rocks. The boys made a long line and started across the garden. They bent over and threw the rocks backward between their legs. The old couple watched in amazement and in a little while the Scouts had cleaned every rock out of the garden.

The last night of the hike, the hikers were camped about two miles from Camp Sol Mayer. It was the plan that we would carry fresh uniforms to them the last night out, so that they might make a triumphant entry into camp. We also brought along our troop flag, and we felt, that with the two patrol flags and an American flag the group would look very sharp. They planned to come marching into camp, flags flying, carrying their packs jauntily on their backs.

But Alas! Sometimes plans go awry and this happened to our courageous hikers. Early the next morning, they had cooked breakfast, packed their gear, unfurled their flags and changed into clean fresh uniforms. While they were waiting to make the last two miles, several of the boys wandered off to a little dry creek, which was located near camp. As boys always will, they found a humongus wasp nest in a tree and started pelting it with rocks. One Scout, Tom Bright, was standing directly under the big wasp nest. A rock knocked it loose from the tree, and it fell, striking Tom right in the face. About a dozen wasps stung him in the face and head, and in a very short time, his face was so swollen that he could not see out of his eyes. Bill had him lie down and put some medicine on the bites to kill the pain. After a short time, Tom seemed to recover from any ill effects except for the swelling of his face and head. Bill later told me that Tom looked like a cantaloupe which had grown hair.

The group decided to complete their plans to go marching into camp and make a grand entry. The only drawback was that they had to lead Tom, who could not see at all. So instead of a group marching smartly into the head-quarters area, they did come with flags waving, but had to lead their buddy, who came stumbling down the road.

The camp medic checked Tom, and found out that he was OK. Late that afternoon the swelling had gone down to where he could see fairly well, but for a couple of days, he looked like he was the loser in a good fight.

Since that summer, several troops have hiked to camp, but Troop 1 was the only troop to carry all their gear for a sixty mile hike. The others had trucks to carry their food and equipment, and about the only equipment carried by the individual Scouts was a canteen.

To me, hiking is still one of the Big Three in Scouting. We are lucky, in our area, to still have so many places for hikes. I know, that as long as we have Scouting, hiking will always be a big adventure for the boys.

Chapter 11
Summer Camps

Summer camps have always been one of the highlights of Scouting. After a week or two at camp, a Scout comes home with a feeling of great accomplishment. He has earned a merit badge or two, maybe even advanced a rank. He usually returns covered with glory, assorted mosquito and chigger bites, a little deeper tan or possibly a few more freckles. He has gained more confidence and may even joke about riding out a typhoon or braving the rigors of a tornado. In short, after a session of camp, you can be sure that he is a better Scout.

The first summer, after our troop was reorganized, we only had ten Scouts to attend summer camp. Through the years, our attendance increased to the point where we had sixty Scouts in camp one summer. Many times our Scouts could not attend camp with our troop because of Little League baseball, summer track or swimming, or maybe a conflict with the family vacation.

When we attended camp we tried to keep the natural patrols together as much as possible. Sometimes, when this was not possible and we had to combine Scouts from several patrols together in one patrol, we used special names for these patrols. Instead of our regular patrol names like Eagle, Panther, Tiger, or Roadrunner, we used special names for camp patrols. Some of these were a little on the "zany" side, but the boys thought such patrols as the "Knob Knockers", "Creepy Crawlers," "Skeeter Feeders," "Chow Hounds," "Things" and "Wyman's Heroes," named after our beloved Camp Ranger, were the greatest. I painted patrol flags with the appropriate pictures on them, and we were quite a sight as we marched to the Dining Hall with our flags flying.

At summer camp, we usually appointed one of the officers in our troop to be the "camp banker." The suggestion was made for the Scouts to turn their money into the banker for safe keeping. Many of the young boys would spend their week's allowance in one day and would be without any money until their parents came to camp on visitor's night, usually Thursday. The banker also had another function. He would try to persuade the boy not to spend any more of his money after he bought five cokes and seven candy bars in one day.

There was a lot of competition among the various troops in the camp inspection contest. After the Scouts had left camp in the morning to attend the various classes and instruction periods, the Camp Inspectors would come around and grade your camp. Neatness of tents, gear stored properly and cleanliness of the grounds were the things they checked.

A good friend of mine, Herbert Fields, who was Scoutmaster of another troop, had a very intense rivalry going with me about this inspection contest. After our Scouts had left camp, he and I would crawl around on our hands and knees, very carefully checking the ground. We would sift through the leaves and grass to be sure there were no bits of paper or any substance not of natural origin. One year his troop might win, and the next year our unit would win the inspection contest. One summer, his troop and my troop finished in a dead heat, so the Camp Director split the trophy right down the middle.

To generate a little competition among the patrols, and to help keep our troop campsite spotless, we had a patrol inspection in our troop. The winning patrol each day received $2 to divide among the patrol members. This doesn't sound very impressive, but along about the third day of camp, when the Scout's funds are depleted, twenty-five cents could seem like a bonanza.

We used a good method to help keep paper from being dropped or thrown down in our camp. Any member of our troop who saw another member drop or throw down a piece of paper just tapped the "thrower downer" on the shoulder and he had to pay the "tapper" five cents. If there was any static about not paying the nickel, the "tapper-on-the-shoulder" could appeal to our banker who would take it out of the "thrower-downer's" account. This worked fine, except, every once in while, the paper-dropper would accuse the other boy of planting a piece of paper in his pocket, so that it would fall out at the slightest movement. This method worked so well, it almost totally obliterated any bits of paper around our campsite.

For a long time, most of our Scouts would bring their clothes to camp in an Army-style duffle bag. This was the type which opened at one end, and had a strap on one end for carrying purposes. The mothers would spend a lot of time carefully pressing and packing junior's clothing. The first time the Scout needed to get something out of the duffle bag, it was invariably packed at the bottom. In his haste the boy would dump all the nicely packed clothes out on the ground. After retrieving the desired object, he would "cram" and "stuff" everything back in the bag. After a few sessions of "cramming" and "stuffing," his fresh clean clothes looked as if he might have slept in them several nights.

We eventually suggested that the Scouts use the duffle bag with a zipper along one side. The bag could be laid flat on the ground and then unzipped. The boy could remove the wanted object without causing the rest of his clothes to look like a disaster area. Footlockers or suitcases were also very good to keep clothing out of the dirt. These could also double as a place to sit in the tent.

After several years of summer camps, our troop came up with the idea of taking an extra tent to camp to keep our uniforms looking neat and clean. We would put a couple of extra tent poles in the tent and would hang our uniforms on hangers. This would help our Scouts look presentable, so that when we marched to the retreat ceremony and the evening meal, they didn't look like a bunch of refugees from behind the Iron Curtain.

For years, Scouts attending Camp Sol Mayer swam in the river. The swimming area was carefully roped off in various sections for non-swimmers, beginners and swimmers. A huge T-shaped pier was placed in the river in such a way that lifeguards using long poles could reach any part of any area if a swimmer needed help. This method must have worked very well. I can't recall any swimmer ever getting into trouble, in all the years we swam in the river.

The camp now has a beautiful swimming pool. The thinking of boys is hard to fathom, sometimes. At the last camporee held at Camp Sol Mayer, a troop asked for permission to swim in the river. They told us that several of their members had never been swimming in a river, and they had decided that it would be a change from swimming in a pool. Maybe a psychiatrist could come up with some solution for this kind of thinking.

One year at summer camp, our troop had a swimming period right before the noon meal. We would put on our bathing suits and go to the swimming area a short time before our session started. We would wait for the troop swimming before us to get out of the water and check out with the waterfront directors. This particular day, the waterfront director came to me and said they needed some help. It seems that one of the other troop members had not checked out of swimming and could not be found. A runner was sent to their campsite and some one checked out the canteen which was close by. No boy—so they asked our troop to get in the river to help search for him. He was a beginner in swimming, and the water in this section was about five feet deep. We were to hold hands and start walking across the area. One of my Scouts, a tall boy named Bill, was not too keen on looking for a drowned boy. He asked me what he was to do if we found him in the river. I told him, "Just yell, and we will try to get him out of the river." Bill was holding my hand on one side. He certainly wasn't enjoying this search. His face was white and I could feel his hand tremble in mine. We had gone about ten feet when Bill screamed, "I just stepped on his head." He literally walked across the top of the water to the pier where he sat, shaking like a leaf. He kept saying, "I stepped on his head! I stepped on his head!"

I moved over to where he had been walking, and felt around with my feet. I stepped on a round object and ducked under the surface to see what was there. The "head" proved to be a large round rock, which I removed from the swimming area. I couldn't talk Bill into coming back into the water. We started our search again, but it soon came to a halt. The "drowned swimmer" was observed coming down the path to the swimming area. He had gotten tired of swimming and decided to go watch the shooters at the rifle range. Between the waterfront director and the boy's Scoutmaster, it was a toss-up to see which one was to have the pleasure of committing mayhem on the Scout.

When a swimmer left the waterfront area, he was instructed to take his "buddy tag" and move it from the "swimming" side of the bulletin board to the "out of swimming" side of the board. If you forgot to do this little chore, the waterfront people had a nasty little reminder. When you entered the dining hall for your next meal, you were handed your "buddy tag" and told to go to the swimming area and place it in its proper position. This little punishment was very impressive, in as much as the swimming area was about 400 yards from the dining hall. By the time you had negotiated the 800 yards needed for the round trip, the rest of the "chow hounds" had gobbled up all the food. Most swimmers forgot their "buddy tag" only once.

We were enjoying a great summer camp one year and had gone to the council fire one evening. The Camp Director mentioned that we were in a "tornado watch." This is not as serious as it sounds. It simply means that the atmospheric conditions are such that it was possible for a tornado to form in our area. I didn't think much about the announcement until we started to get ready to return to our campsite. We lined up in patrol formation, and one Patrol Leader reported that one of his boys was missing. On questioning some of the other boys in his patrol, we learned that Pat, the missing Scout, had said something about "returning to the campsite to prepare for the tornado."

When we got back to camp, we found that Pat had prepared for the tornado in great fashion. He had taken nails, not little nails, but BIG nails, and nailed all of the tent flaps to the tent poles. We had a three gallon can of kerosene which we used for a lantern to burn at night in the latrine. Pat had gotten a shovel and buried the kerosene. When I asked why the burying process, he explained that, in case of a tornado, the kerosene can would not explode. He said that he had nailed the flaps shut on the tents to prevent the tornado from blowing through the tents. So much for tornado preventative

*"When we got back to our campsite, we found that Pat had used **BIG** nails to fasten all the tent flaps to the tent poles."*

maintenance. If you ever have a tornado watch, try this method—it sure worked for Pat.

One camp session, our troop and another troop of Scouts were working together on a camp good-turn project. We were building a couple of bridges along the river bank to make it easier for Scouts walking along the river trail. The drinking water for our camp is pumped from the river and filtered in a unit that is housed in a small building a short distance from the river bank. The chemicals used in the process are supplied in white plastic jugs which look like Chlorox bottles. There were several of these empty jugs setting on a shelf on the outside of the small building. Our Camp Ranger, Buddy Wyman, was working on the filtering unit. One little Scout asked Buddy what he did with all that Chlorox. Buddy replied that he used it to purify our drinking water. The little Scout thought a minute and then a grin came over his face. He said, "Mr. Buddy, you know, I bet I am bleached plumb white inside." This almost broke up our bridge building project as the guys in both troops were too busy laughing to work.

Many of our campsites were located very near the river. One year I let my troop talk me into camping near the river. I mean very near the river. Some of the boys were almost able to lie on their cots, and put their hands in the river. I warned them that they might wake up with snakes in the tent and that the mosquitoes would be very blood thirsty. Also, I reminded them, that if the river came down in a rise we would have to move our camp up to the next level above the water. All to no avail. The Scouts said that I had promised that we would camp near the river, and that this was as near as you could camp, unless you were members of the Sea Scouts.

In the hot daytime it was cool under the big trees, but the insides of our tents were covered with mosquitoes. However, the pesky critters hardly ever bothered us in the daytime. They waited until it got dark and then descended on us for the feast. As far as mosquito lotion was concerned, it was like putting syrup on pancakes. The lotion just whetted their appetites. After about three days and nights of this, I had made up my mind that we were going to move our campsite. I didn't have to make up my mind—Mother Nature took care of that. It started to rain—and then it started to pour. This rain didn't last as long as Noah's, but it must have equaled it in intensity. The river started inching up into our tents and we had to move up higher to the next level of the river bank. I exercised great self-control. I didn't remind them, much, that the old man had warned against camping so near the river. The river was still rising, and we had to pick up our tents like the Arabs, except maybe not so silently, and move up to the next level.

We were very smug in our belief that we had finally outsmarted the river. We felt sure that the river would not get up this high. I woke up the next morning and the water was running through my tent. It was about four inches deep, but it might get deeper. I hastily jumped up and started waking up the boys to inform them that the river had won again. Three boys were sleeping in a big Army tent. I hammered on the tent and roused them. One Scout, Jim, rolled off his cot and I heard him yell. When I got to him he was in a hole up to his shoulders. I pulled him out and then checked out the hole. Several years before this campsite was used for camping, a large, deep hole on the site was used as a garbage dump. It had not been filled in, and over the years, grass and weeds had grown over the top. A thin layer of dirt had covered this over and made it appear to be solid ground. When the water came into camp, this was all that was needed to soften the top of the hole. When Jim came off his cot, he just went through the opening. I reminded the boys that if they had listened to me, The Great Wise One, all this moving and falling into garbage pits would never have happened. To this day, I am sure that my "I told you so's" never did make much of an impression on the troop.

Have you ever had a dream when you dreamed you had lost all your clothes, and you rushed about frantically trying to cover your nakedness? Well, this happened one summer to one of our troop members and it wasn't a dream —nightmare, maybe—but not a dream. Dick, our Junior Assistant Scoutmaster, and another young man were in charge of the waterfront. It had rained for several days, and all waterfront activities had come to a halt. This was before our camp had a swimming pool and these two waterfront directors had time on their hands.

There was a long, deep hole of water in the river, then you came to a shallow crossing, almost like a causeway. This led down a narrow chute to another deep hole of water. The deep holes were normally flowing very gently, but the rains had caused them to have quite a strong current and a few rapids, and it made the river quite dangerous. Our two young men from the waterfront decided to run the rapids in two of the boats, called "river runts," which were used at camp. These craft were not very stable. They were made of one by twelves covered with canvas. The sides were only twelve inches high and their flat bows and sterns were not the best shape for running rapids.

The two heroes, one in each boat, put in the river above the shallow crossing. Their plan was to run the chute and be in the calmer water of the lower deep hole. Alas! So much for plans. When they hit the chute, the high waves and their inability to steer the clumsy boats caused their boats to capsize. They were not wearing life jackets, but, luckily, the very force of the current helped them to reach shore. One boy was swept to the camp side of the river, where he managed to get out. Unluckily, Dick was swept to the other side where he hung onto some willow trees hanging over the water. The force of the current was so strong that it was difficult for him to get out. He finally was able to pull himself into the branches and get to shore. He had escaped, but the river exacted a terrible toll. The current was so great, that, as he hung there the water stripped off his shoes, Scout shorts, and even his underwear. The only piece of clothing left was a Camp Sol Mayer T-shirt.

He yelled across to the Scout on the camp side that he was OK, and that he was going to a neighboring ranch house close by. He started trudging up the road to the house. Dick later told me that as he walked along, he was trying to figure out how would be the best way to hide his nakedness with one wet T-shirt. He finally decided that the best way was to wear the T-shirt like an apron. He finally got it secured in front, and knocked on the ranch house door.

Mrs A., the ranch woman, told me, that when she opened the door, and saw Dick standing there so wet and miserable, she wanted to cry, but she just broke up into hysterical laughter. She knew Dick and invited him in to see about finding him some clothes. She said he was very careful to walk around her, keeping the covered part of his body always turned toward her. When her husband came in from the pasture, he got on the phone and called camp to let them know our wanderer was fine. By the next afternoon, the river had gone down enough that they could get Dick back to camp. And this became known in camp history as "The Great River Runt Caper."

When Scouts go to summer camps they sometimes get a little irregular in their going to the bathroom, pardon me—I meant latrine. Some boys just seem to not have the time to stop and go to the latrine. There are too many things to capture their attention at camp. Another thing is that sometimes habits are changed a little from home life and many kids don't like to use the facilities in a latrine where togetherness is the theme.

So, many Scouts get a little "irregular" and the camp staff is always trying to alleviate this condition. I told you earlier how this was handled when I was a Boy Scout. You were fed stewed prunes at breakfast. If you didn't eat your prunes you were sent to the hospital tent where you were given a glass containing a mixture of Epsom salts and castor oil. After one dose of this, stewed prunes looked pretty good.

Each Scoutmaster was supposed to keep a check on his Scouts to see that they didn't get too "irregular." One morning, at breakfast, the camp director made quite a pitch about the importance of each leader making sure that his boys had a B.M. (bowel movement) each day. The leaders listened, but the Scouts could have cared less. About 98% of the kids absorbed absolutely zilch about the importance of B.M.s.

Later that morning I was coming back from the swimming area when I caught up with one of my charges walking back from the trading post. He was carrying a large coke in one hand and two candy bars in the other. I thought that this might be the opportune time to begin my B.M. check. I asked him, "Jody, have you had a B.M. today?" He studied his handful of loot care-

fully and replied, "Well no, I haven't had a B.M., but I had two Snickers bars and a Hershey's." Needless to say, I didn't pursue the questioning on the B.M. caper any longer.

Many things in Scouting haven't changed much since my first summer camp in 1926. When you attend a council fire, you see and hear the same ancient, moth-eaten skits which I enjoyed as a boy. The hazing still goes on with the older Scouts sending the new campers looking for the "key to the flagpole," "rope oil"—to keep your tent ropes from drawing up in a rain storm, "sky hooks," and a new one: "snollygoster traps." These last are used to catch snollygosters—little animals which live on the banks of the San Saba River and eat old Montgomery-Ward catalogues.

Poison ivy is always bad business at summer camps. The camp staff tries to clear out this pesky stuff, but leaving a little for identification for the boys walking the Nature Trail. It seems that Scouts still manage to get in the ivy, and for some, it turns out to be a disaster. Some of the kids get such a bad case that they are not allowed to go swimming, and the discomfort is very extreme.

We had a young District Scout Executive, Jerry, who had about the worst poison ivy allergy I have ever seen. When he got infected, he broke out all over his body and sometimes had to go to the hospital. He jokingly said that, "All I have to do to break out in poison ivy is to just read the name in a book or paper." Another one of our camp staff was a junior counselor named Bill, who for several years was in charge of the Nature Trail at camp.

Bill had a cute trick which he would perform. As he led his class down the Nature Trail, he would stop by the poison ivy and call attention to "leaflets three—let them be," and would tell the Scouts to be sure to remember this. After the "Nature Trailers" had completed the circle and were coming back to their starting point, Bill would stop along the trail and ask them questions about the trees and flowers they had seen. When he reached the poison ivy, he would stop and casually break off a twig and start chewing on it. His class would be horrified and would start yelling that he was chewing poison ivy. He would take the twig from his mouth, look at it carefully, tell the Scouts that they were absolutely correct, and remind them not to try this little stunt. For some reason, Bill would not react to poison ivy. I guess that there must have been something in his chemical makeup which made him immune to poison ivy.

I kidded him about the fact that someday his cute little trick might backfire. One year at summer camp, poison ivy got back at him with a vengeance. The Scout office called me to ask if I might be able to take over the summer camp. When I asked what had happened to Jerry, who was camp director, I was told that he was in the hospital with a severe case of poison ivy. When I asked about Bill, I was really shocked to hear that he was also in the hospital with poison ivy.

When I visited the two sufferers in the hospital, I was prepared for the way Jerry would look. He was completely covered with the rash from the top of his head to the soles of his feet. He was coated with some sort of "yellowish-green" ointment, and he looked like a victim in the last stages of jungle rot. But, as bad as he looked and felt, he was still able to get a belly-laugh out of the way Bill looked.

Bill was not covered with the rash like Jerry was, but the poison ivy was really concentrated in just one area of his body. His face and lips were swollen so much that he couldn't see out of his eyes, and his lips looked like those of the African natives who put big pieces of wood in their lips. This was done until their lips were as big as saucers. Bill looked like a West Texas Ubangi. Jerry pointed to Bill, who couldn't see us and then cracked up into hysterical laughter. I tried to suppress a few giggles, and Bill promised us all sorts of terrible consequences if we didn't quit laughing at him. I don't believe that Bill ever pulled the poison ivy trick again.

One summer when my troop went to camp, I was not able to go with them. We had planned a Rio Grande raft trip later in the summer, and I just couldn't get off for both events. One of the Scout Executives who was going to camp the first session, was just going with no official council duties. He volunteered to go as our troop leader and everything had worked out fine. I went to camp and helped them get "set up" for the camp.

Early one morning I got a telephone call which scared me badly. The camp director called to say that there had been a tornado in camp. One of my Scouts had been taken into town to the hospital. There had been no word on his condition. I asked about the troop equipment I needed to bring. He told me that quite a few of the tents in our camp site had been torn to pieces. I asked if there were any other injuries, but he told me that the rest of my Scouts were OK. I went to our Scout cabin, grabbed several tents and some extra poles. I got out on the highway and started driving. I was running between 65 and 70 miles an hour. The more I thought about those poor kids having been in the tornado, the faster I drove. The last 25 miles I was driving between 95 and 100 miles an hour. I had visions of the Scouts in hysterics and I was very worried about the boy who had been injured. I turned into the camp gateway and the first thing I saw surely didn't help my peace of mind. Two huge revolving ventilators, about four feet wide were laying just inside the gate. They had been blown from the top of the dining hall about 4 blocks away. I turned up the road leading to our campsite, and was really shocked. The tents had been erected again, the gateway was in place, and except for several tents, which had been literally shredded, the place looked normal.

I just knew that when I drove up, the hysterical kids would run out and grab me. They would be crying and in a "state of shock." I looked around and couldn't find a soul. I decided I would walk to the dining hall, where, I figured they would have our troop, giving them liberal doses of traquilizers.

I was walking along the trail to the dining hall when I saw our troop walking to camp. When we got near, I could not detect any tears, shock or hysterics. In fact, they seemed surprised to see me and asked what was I doing in camp so early.

I told them I had come to camp as soon as I had heard about the tornado. When I asked them where they had been, they told me they had decided to go swimming. I asked about Roger, the boy who had been injured, and they reported that he just had a bruise on his back.

The tornado touched down in the area where the camp staff were housed in tents. Most of them were at the dining hall at the time. The funnel rose up once more and ripped the ventilators from the roof of the dining hall as it picked up in the air. It touched down between the hall and our campsite and made splinters out of a huge oak tree.

The tornado rose once more and was rising when it went over our campsite. Tents were shredded and a large dining fly in the center of our camp was never seen again. We had carried some of the heavy benches from our scout cabin to be used by the boys as they did some of their paperwork on merit badges. These benches were constructed from 2x12 lumber and were very heavy. Roger was hit in the back when he decided to go out of his tent and put in a few more stakes. The wind sent the bench hurtling through the air and it hit him in the back. After the doctor examined him, he found only a bruise on his back. The boys kidded Roger and told him the bench suffered a more severe injury than he did with his bruised back. We had a large folding banquet style table setting under the dining fly. I found it in small pieces all the way to the highway, about fifty yards away. Yet, a rickety clothesline, which had been set up next to the dining fly, didn't even blow down.

I never cease to wonder how boys can bounce back from the experience of going through a tornado or some other shattering experience. I was so sure that the Scouts would have been in shock, and I must admit, I maybe was just a little disappointed that they had snapped out of it without my guiding hand. When I was risking my neck driving at a very unsafe rate of speed, I consoled myself with the thought that I was doing something noble—I would arrive in camp like the conquering hero to rescue my laddies from the "old tornado trauma." Then it was quite a let down, when, in their hysterics and shock, they decided to go swimming—so much for the conquering hero bit.

I did gain back a little satisfaction in the thought that there was one thing which really shook the kids. They were very upset about their latrine. This beautiful structure had been finished right before the first camp session and was not only beautiful in design, but also, was very functional. When the tornado struck, it ripped all of the redwood siding off the wall next to the highway, a short distance away. The boys were asking, "How can we use the latrine? People driving along the highway can see us as we are going to the bathroom." I pointed out that most of the drivers had better things to watch than little kids using the bathroom. But to relieve their fears, we strung up a canvas tarp to give them their desired privacy.

Many of the Scouts in our camp that summer brought home pieces of the tents destroyed in the tornado, and hung them on their patrol walls to remind them of "The Great Tornado Disaster."

Throughout the years I have seen many cases of homesickness, but the case of Dicky was a classic. Dicky came to camp on Sunday afternoon, helped his patrol set up their tents, took a physical, and had a swim check. He was assigned a table in the dining hall and attended the retreat ceremony. The first night he appeared to be all right, but by breakfast the next morning, he was beginning to show symptoms of homesickness. He helped his patrol to police the area around their tents, and rolled up his sleeping bag. As the other Scouts left camp for their activities, I took Dicky aside and told him to report to Mrs. Wyman, our camp ranger's wife. He looked sort of startled but didn't ask any questions. For years, Mrs. Wyman had been "mothering" homesick Scouts and the boys all loved her. Dicky reported to her and she put him to work helping her in her home. Dicky must have really liked this arrangement. Each morning he would eat breakfast with our troop. He would help his patrol get ready for inspection and then he would light out for Mrs. Wyman, D. H. (Doctor of Homesickness).

He spent the entire week at camp and didn't seem to suffer the pangs of homesickness any more. Later I was asked what was accomplished by his staying the whole camp session, if he didn't work on any advancement or enjoy any of the many activities of camp. I reminded my questioners that if he had not stayed in this fashion, he would surely have gone home the first day of camp. Who knows—maybe he got as much out of camp as some of the boys who run their legs off trying to do everything.

Chapter 12
Overnight or Weekend Camps

To my way of thinking, overnight camps were always the backbone of Scouting. Many Scouts were unable to attend summer camps because of Little League Baseball, family vacations and church camps. On the other hand, our troop went on overnight camps once a month, winter and summer, rain, snow or shine.

These camps gave a boy a great opportunity to sharpen his Scout skills and to work on advancement. Instruction was usually available to the Scouts in most of the outdoor related merit badges such as camping, cooking, swimming, lifesaving, pioneering, nature, bird study, and soil and water conservation.

Our troop had equipment such as buck saws, hatchets and axes. We offered the Scouts instruction in their proper use and even suggested that the individual Scout should not buy his own hatchet. We suggested that a good pocket knife was much more useful than the sheath knife and was safer to use. However, you could always spot the new Scout. He came to his first overnight camp sporting a brand new sheath knife, which hung almost to his knees.

For seventeen years, our troop camped in the same campsite at Camp Louis Farr. There was the trunk of a huge old oak tree which had fallen in a storm many years before, which lay alongside our campsite. Through the years, the new campers with their new shiny hatchets had chopped on this old log. Their choppings had looked like a giant rat had been gnawing on the log, but in seventeen years, they had been unable to cut through the log.

After a campout or two, the new campers learned to use "squaw wood"— that wood which may be broken from dead limbs of trees and requires very little preparation to use in a fire. Even with instruction in the use of a hatchet or ax, I always tried to tell my Scouts that they were not in the same league with Paul Bunyan in tree felling. I suppose our instructions must have paid off. Through the years, we have never had a wood chopping accident—no Scout ever cut off the toe of an onlooker—and more importantly—never cut off any of his own toes.

On one weekend camp, our troop was camped near a troop from our own town. As we were setting up our tents, one of my Scouts came to me and seemed very excited. He reported that the other troop had some experts in tent pitching, cooking, and use of ax and hatchet. He couldn't understand why our unit could not get some experts to put on some demonstrations for us. I replied that I felt that we had some very good instructors, among the members of our junior leaders who would stack up very well against most experts.

My words were very prophetic. The first evening, the axe expert cut his foot and had to be taken into town to have a few stitches. The tent-pitching expert was not quite as good as his reputation. When we checked their campsite the next morning, we found about half of their tents were sagging badly or were flat on the ground. The crowning blow to the experts came when the cooking expert turned a boiling pot of coffee over on his leg, and I was asked to take him into town to the hospital. He was treated for second degree burns over most of his lower leg and foot.

When I got back to camp, I reported to their troop about the fate of their last expert. My kids came up to me and said, "Boy, if those guys were experts, we will just stick with our own Junior Leaders."

So much for the so-called experts .

We went camping, winter and summer, and in all kinds of weather. Our troop prided itself on the fact that we hardly ever called off a campout because of bad weather. In our latitude, we seldom get a whole lot of snow in the winter. However, when we get what is called a "blue norther," the weather can get very disagreeable. The winds blow from the north at a high rate of speed and are accompanied by freezing rain, sleet, and some snow to add to our discomfort.

One of our coldest campouts started with all the bad ingredients. It rained first and got the tents thoroughly soaked. Then the rain started freezing, and it turned to sleet. It snowed on top of this frozen rain and sleet, which had built up to a thickness of about two inches. The wind was blowing right off the North Pole, and the cold was bitter. We got everything ready for a very cold night. I checked to be sure all the boys had plenty of cover and made sure everyone had plenty of bedding, including a waterproof ground cloth placed under their sleeping bags.

It takes a few cold campouts before a Scout learns the importance of having plenty of bedding under him. I have seen boys come on an overnight with six blankets. They put one blanket under themselves and five on top and wonder why they freeze to death. The same thing happens with cots. We had an unwritten law in our unit that no one used a cot except at summer camps. Anyone using a cot on a weekend camp was liable to be tossed in the river. A cot is like a highway bridge in bad weather. The first thing to freeze was the bridge, because the air could circulate under the bridge. The same thing happens with a cot. The cold air flows under the cot, and you sleep a lot colder than you would on the ground.

On this particular cold campout, the wind-chill factor must have been about thirty-five degrees below zero. The next day when we were getting ready to come home, there was so much ice on the tents, you could pull the poles out from under the tents and the tents still would stand up. There was no way the tents could be folded properly, so we rolled them up loosely, being careful not to break the tents. We took them to our troop cabin and hung them from the rafters. It took about a week for the ice to thaw and the tents to get dry.

On our campouts, we usually were camped near a river or creek in a grove of big trees. We warned our boys of the danger of camping under a big limb which might fall or be blown down in a storm. On one campout, we had two new campers, who were camping in a three-man trail tent. This tent is almost like a large pup tent, inasmuch as it has no ridge pole. These two boys had pitched their tent under a big limb, a likely looking "widow maker." I suggested they move their tent because of the hazard. They replied that it looked okay to them, and, as for a storm—there wasn't a cloud in the sky.

We ate supper, had our council fire, and turned in. Well, so much for our weather forecasting. The rain and wind storm sort of "snuck"up on us. The rain started coming down in buckets—or maybe it was tubs. The wind was moving the big trees around pretty good, and my first thought was for the two boys under the big limb. I got up, put on my slicker, and decided to check to see that everyone was doing OK—that no one was drowning in their sleeping bags. I found everyone seemed to be weathering the storm in great fashion. The two "under the limb" boys were sound asleep, so I returned to my sleeping bag and listened to the sound of the rain on my tent.

It was barely getting light the next morning, when one of my Scouts came rushing into my tent. He yelled, "Come quick! I think Doug and Bill have been killed!" Doug and Bill were my two Scouts who had camped under the "widow maker." I jumped up, ran to their tent, and my worst fears were realized. The big limb had broken off the tree and had fallen squarely across their tent. We picked up the limb and threw it aside. We burrowed into the wreckage of the tent, expecting to find two crushed Boy Scouts. Imagine our relief when we found that they were not even scratched—in fact, they hadn't even awakened when the limb fell on their tent. After that, I never had any trouble persuading Scouts not to camp under big dead limbs.

One weekend camp found us camping on the council property near Lake Nasworthy. There is a large concrete dam, and then the earthfill dam, or levee, runs for about a mile. Right opposite the campsite, the levee is about thirty to forty feet high. A road runs along the top of the levee, and trees have been allowed to grow on the side away from the lake. We camped near this earthen dam, which gave us a lot of protection in case of high winds coming from the southwest, west, or northwest.

When we got to camp that afternoon, we found out that we were under a tornado alert. This meant that a tornado had been spotted somewhere in the area covered by our weather station at Mathis Field, our local airport. The boys asked what they should do to get ready for any eventual bad weather. I had the boys move some of their tents nearer the levee in order to get a little more protection from the expected high winds. We put in extra stakes and—in Navy terms—we decided to "batten down the hatches." We got everything ready and sat back and waited for the storm.

It started off like a scene from a Hollywood movie. The lightning was constant and lit up the whole sky. You could see the huge black clouds moving in from the southwest, and the rain looked like a gray wall coming across the lake. It was really a classical storm—if there is such a thing. The wind didn't blow—it howled. Your ears took quite a pounding from the terrific noise from the rain, the howling wind and constant crash of the lightning and thunder. After about an hour, the storm moved away and we went outside to assess the damage.

We were very proud that not one of our tents had blown down. We were prouder yet when we turned on the radio in one of the pickup trucks and heard that Mathis Field had clocked the winds at ninety-two miles an hour.

A huge oak tree grew near our campsite. Many of the dads going on campouts with us had parked their vehicles near this mighty oak. When we checked, we found that the two main trunks of this tree had been torn apart by the terrific wind. One of these trunks, about three feet in diameter, had fallen right across the favorite parking places of the dads. Luckily, none of the fathers had accompanied us on this camp, so we did not have to explain to any irate mother why her husband had ended up with the family limousine smashed under a tree limb.

Many of the younger campers on their first campout would assure you that they knew all about cooking, fire building, and tent pitching. We tried to tell them about pitching their tents so that the front faced away from the wind. We also tried to show them that camping in a low spot was a very good way to go swimming in your own tent in case of a good rain.

On this particular campout, we had three young Scouts, Steve, Buddy,

The water was about 8 inches deep in their tent. They had piled all their equipment on the only high spot in the tent. Someone suggested that they had better watch for sharks!

and Benny, who were on their first "overnighter." As usual, instead of camping with the older, more experienced Scouts, the "greenhorns" insisted on camping by themselves. They were amazed to find a nice open spot almost in the very center of our camping area. The reason this spot was open was that it was the lowest portion of our camping area. All the water drained down to this area when it rained. I suggested that they might move their tent, but their argument was, "We've got it set up and we have tarps under our sleeping bags." I pointed out to them the very reason the spot was open was because, in the past, other new campers had camped in this same spot and had found the water trickling into their sleeping bags following a hard rain.

All my arguments went for naught. We went to bed and then it started to rain. It wasn't just your gentle summer shower—it was pouring, coming down in bucketfuls. In East Texas, a rain like this is called a "frog strangler." In West Texas, we fondly refer to a deluge like this as a "cow chip floater." As the rain was coming down, I wondered how our three new Scouts were faring. As soon as it let up a little, I went slogging over to their tent to check on them.

In their tent, there was one high spot, about a yard square, which was not covered by about eight inches of water. They had piled most of their gear on this island and were sitting on top of the heap. They reminded me of three turtles trying to rest on one lily pad. Some of the other Scouts came over and jokingly reminded them to be sure to check for sharks swimming around the tent. The three boys had a sickly grin on their faces and promised to be more careful about their choice of campsites in the future.

Two of these three boys stayed in Scouting and earned their Eagle award. They went on many other camps, summer camps, survival camps, and hiking camps, but I believe their very first "overnighter" made more of an impression than any of the other camps. After all, how many other camps do you attend where you wake up and find the river flowing through your sleeping bag?

A Scout is thrifty—the ninth part of the twelve parts of the Scout Law. I used to get a little vexed at the boys because they would not take care of their personal equipment. The troop equipment, we could control. If a Scout didn't take care of the troop equipment, we could penalize him by forbidding his use of the equipment for a certain period of time. His own gear was a different matter. We could only plead with him and suggest that he think about all the money his parents had spent for his equipment.

One year a little boy joined our troop on Tuesday night. We were planning a campout for the weekend. The boy went home, got a Boy Scout catalogue, and marked about ninety percent of the items in the book. He told his mother that he absolutely had to have these things before he could go on the camp. She called me and told me her problem. She said that she figured the cost of these "must have" items at about $300. I told her that all he needed for his first camp was something to sleep in—quilts and blankets were fine if he didn't have a sleeping bag. He needed something to cook in to prepare a simple meal. I suggested a small skillet and a can opener. He could take a plastic cup and a few paper plates. Also, have him bring something to wash his dishes with.

I suggested that he attend a camp or two before he decided on a lot of equipment which he might never use. I didn't think he needed a beadwork loom, a bugle, or a red patch vest. I told her he might bring a small pocket knife, but to leave the bucksaws, the axes, and the hatchets off his list. Our troop had all that equipment, and we would rather that he not use these deadly weapons without a little instruction in their proper use.

One situation we saw over and over was where the boys would place their sleeping bags too near the fire. We never had anyone burned when their sleeping bag caught on fire, but we had quite a few bags which were turned to ashes. On a campout, a Scout had borrowed his father's $200 down-filled sleeping bag. The camp was in the late fall of the year, and the nights were getting a mite nippy. His dad had bought the expensive sleeping bag for a trip to Alaska. The Scout told us that his dad had told him to check out the bag before his dad's hunting trip in about three weeks. Joe and two other boys were sleeping in one tent. I told the Scouts to be sure that their bags were a safe distance from the fire in case a spark popped out of the fire and landed on their sleeping bags.

That night was uneventful, and then came the dawn. After breakfast, we would have inspection to be sure the sleeping bags were rolled up, the dishes washed, and the area around the tents were checked for anything like paper or foil. We broke up into some groups for advancement, and the classes went in several different directions. After about an hour, the boys returned and went to their tents. I heard a cry of dismay from Joe's tent, and he came running to me. His face was about the color of ashes, and he was so shaken he couldn't talk. He just grabbed me by the arm and pulled me over to his tent. The expensive sleeping bag was a charred pile of rubble. When he rolled up the bag, he left it too near the fire. A spark must have blown or popped out of the coals. The down bag burned just like the cheaper ones.

Joe's father was very understanding, as well he might be. He was an antique car buff, and just two weeks before the tragedy of the down bag, he had been cleaning the motor of a 1929 Chevrolet auto. The cleaning mixture was inflammable. It caught on fire, burned up the antique car and half of a two-car garage. When he came to pick up Joe at the campout, he just patted his son on the head and said, "Son, I think you and I need a course in fire prevention."

Two Scouts came on one of our camps with each sporting a brand new sleeping bag. They had just bought them the afternoon of the camp. The two were going to share a tent—in this case a pup tent. This was right after World War II, and tents were hard to find. There were plenty of surplus pup tents available, and we used them for several years, even though the National Boy Scout Office didn't approve of the little tents. As you know, pup tents have no ridge pole. There is a guy line in the back and one in the front, which holds the tent erect.

Our two campers put up their tent, spread out their new sleeping bags, and got ready to prepare supper. For some unknown reason, they built their fire under the front guyline. After eating, everyone was engaged in a life and death struggle called "Capture the Flag."

One Scout had grabbed the flag and run past the opening of our camp-site. He yelled that there was a tent on fire. When we ran over to the tent, it was plain to see what had happened. The guy line had caught on fire and, as it burned in two, the tent collapsed. The burning guy line swung into the tent and caught the two new sleeping bags on fire.

We put out the fire and scrounged up enough blankets for the two to sleep comfortably. The boys' egos were a little scorched to think that they had pulled such a dumb stunt. It was quite an expensive lesson, but never again did they build their fire under their tent guy line.

One year, our Scout troop had planned an overnight camp for late January. The weather had been miserable, but we decided to go anyway. The local newspaper was planning a whole section on Boy Scouting to be published during Boy Scout Week. They had called and asked to send a photographer and reporter out to our camp to take some pictures to be used in the paper. We told them to come out the next day and that we would be ready.

We had planned to camp at Camp Louis Farr, a former council camp. There were a few buildings left there, including a huge two-story dining hall. The camp was not used by our council any longer because we had two more camps in our area.

When we arrived in camp, we found that our plans were all wet. I mean literally all wet. The entire camp was covered in water about four inches deep, and the sleet and snow were still coming down. We had brought bales of hay and tarps to put under the tents, but the depth of the water in the camping area made it seem very foolhardy to try to camp there. We decided to camp out in the big dining hall. There was also a big cabin which had been used by the Order of the Arrow for some of their meetings. About six of the Scouts decided to sleep there. Both buildings had nice fireplaces, and there was plenty of wood stacked outside on the porches.

We rolled out our sleeping bags and cooked supper. After the boys ate, they decided on a game of Capture the Flag, inside the dining hall. We took several of the bales of hay and made two big piles of hay, one at each end of the game area and surrounding the two flags.

It was one of the wildest Capture the Flag games that I have ever seen. The kids would come barreling down across the hall and literally dive into the hay. To catch a player, one had to grab the rope hanging out of their belt. Some of the smart players tied their rope to the belt loops in their pants. When someone grabbed one of the "tied" ropes, the "tier" suddenly found himself without about half of his pants. We finally changed the rules so that no one could tie the ropes.

After an epic struggle in which each side won great honors and covered themselves with glory and hay, we decided to call the game a draw. I had brought along the "fixings" for hot chocolate and popcorn. After gorging themselves, the kids settled down and asked if I would tell them some ghost stories. I had several in my repertoire of far-out tales which were guaranteed to curdle your blood and make your hair stand at attention. One of these eerie tales had to do with a well-known outlaw, "Black Jack Ketchum," who roamed these parts at times. He was caught and hanged, and the rope snapped off his head. The legend told that he still roamed these parts looking for his lost head. At night, if you listened carefully, you could still hear the sound of hoofbeats as he rode around looking for his head. The camp was covered with huge trees, and, with the wind blowing, your imagination could almost make you believe you could hear this sound.

We spread out the hay and put tarps over that. We put our sleeping bags on the tarps and built up a big fire in the fireplace. The floor of the dining hall was stone, and I warned the Scouts that the night was going to be a mite nippy. The six Scouts who were staying by themselves seemed to be a little reluctant to go to their cabin, about fifty yards away. I told them to build a good fire in the fireplace and to keep it going all night. There was plenty of wood on the porch of the cabin. After a cold night in that cavernous dining hall, we got up and started cooking breakfast. In a little while, here came our group from the O.A. cabin. They were so cold, some of them were shaking. I couldn't understand why they didn't keep the fire burning in their fireplace. After some "hemming" and "hawing," they sheepishly admitted that the ghost stories scared them so badly that they were afraid to step out on the porch and replenish their firewood. That was the last time I told any ghost stories before going to bed.

When we went on overnight camps, we had a schedule which we used most of the time. We would:
Set up camp
Free time for fishing or arrowhead searching
Cook supper
Wide game
Council fire:
Songs and "moth-eaten" skits

Closing

Curfew: All in tents by 11:00 PM, asleep by 12:00 midnight

We explained to the newer Scouts that we had a very hectic day planned for the next day. They needed all their sleep. After 12:00, I would warn the "talkers" and "gigglers" once. The second warning carried a terrible penalty. I would get the "non-sleepers" out of their tents, and we would go to the council fire, now just a bed of coals. I would give each boy a large rock to carry in each hand. He had to trot around the fire twenty-five times and then reverse this direction. The first few circuits of the fire seemed like a lot of fun. But, as the rocks got heavier, the breathing was a little more labored. After about five minutes of jogging, I would stop the participants and ask if they thought that sleep might come to them. One hundred percent of the runners always agreed that the night was made for sleeping.

Breakfast

Devotional

Advancement

Inspection of individual tents

Wide games:

A compass course covering two or three miles,

Capture the Flag,

Hare and Hounds,

Pioneers and Indians,

Ambush—our favorite, we shall devote a chapter to this game.

We tried to impress upon the boys the importance of keeping our campsites neat. We tried to leave them in better shape than they were when we first arrived. To help arouse a lot of interest in "better housekeeping," we had an inspection during camp, and I would have an inspection after the boys had gone into town.

The competition was very keen. The boys in one tent were competing against all of the other tents in camp. On our first meeting night, after a weekend camp, I would present each Scout in the winning tent with a nice pocket knife. In some cases, it was difficult to find anything wrong while inspecting. I was forced to declare that two, sometimes three tents, had all tied for the honor. This appeased the Scouts, but it sure was expensive for me.

This inspection bit helped the boys to realize the importance of leaving the campsites in excellent condition. As in most parts of America, in our area it is becoming more difficult to find places to camp. We tried to impress the landowners with the idea that we really appreciated the use of their land. We have been camping on some of the ranches for more than twenty years.

Mike was Senior Patrol Leader for our unit. He had very large feet. In fact, they were so large that the other Scouts nicknamed him "Snow Shoe." Usually on campouts, Mike and I shared the same tent. There was something very peculiar about this boy's feet. No matter how large the tent, whether it was winter or summer, when he woke in the morning, his feet were always sticking out from under the tent. The kids all agreed that his feet had a separate set of lungs, because of their size, and, for this reason, had to crawl out from under the tent flaps to get more air. Even in the winter time, when the weather was very cold, the feet could be seen protruding from the tent. Mike took a lot of kidding about this odd habit, and I always wondered what his wife thought about this after they were married in later years.

Milt Wyatt, our council executive, had three boys in our Scout troop. He went on a lot of campouts with us. His boys dearly loved to con him into coming on an overnight in order to get him to participate in one of our Ambush games. In this way, the boys could bounce a sack of dirt off their father's head without fear of retaliation. On Monday, after one of our camps, Milt would complain of having "thrown his arm away" after having thrown several dozen sacks in mortal combat.

One thing we all enjoyed when he came camping with us was his ability to spin a yarn at our council fires. You have heard of an audience hanging on every word of the speaker—well, that's an understatement in the case of Milt and our Scouts. The boys didn't "hang" on every word, they were "glued" to every word. In fact, it would be so quiet that you felt that each boy was holding his breath. When Milt would finish one of his yarns, you could hear a sound from all around the council fire which sounded as if every Scout had been holding his breath, and then let the air out of his lungs in one great "whoosh."

One yarn which Milt told several times was a story about this "mysterious blue mist." This was a natural phenomenon which occurred at certain times of the year around some of the canyons of West Texas. This mist would rise from the bottom and sides of the canyon, and was a bright blue color. Many scientists had checked this mystery but could come up with no plausible explanation. If you stood very near the edge of the canyon and happened to breathe this mist, you started floating like a balloon filled with helium. Milt would have the kids close their eyes and his voice would weave such a spell, you really got the sensation you were floating in the air. I would open one eye and sneak a glance to be sure I was still firmly seated around the campfire.

For as long as I live, I'll never forget one story Milt told. This had to do with his being up in the north woods where he had some trouble with a nasty, arrogant lumberjack. Now, this character wasn't quite as large as Paul Bunyan, but he would rank a pretty close second in size. After a series of run-ins with this lumberjack, Milt and this first cousin of "Big Foot" got into a terrible fight. They fought all day and fought all night. The adversaries used clubs, rocks, knives and very sharp axes. Just about the time in the yarn, where you believed Milt would come up with some new weapon or some sneaky trick, he would pause for a second or two and then say, "and then he killed me."

The kids would sit in stunned silence and then crack up into laughter. As one Scout told Milt, "This is probably the way some stories should end—the good guy doesn't always win."

Chapter 13
Ambush

I felt the need to devote one complete chapter to this game we called "Ambush." Over the years, I know that we moved hundreds of tons of dirt, as our troop engaged in the life and death struggle of Ambush.

The rules of the game are quite simple. Two teams are chosen, usually by Scouts who are to be the "Captains" of their respective team. One team will be given a certain amount of time to hide, then the other team goes looking for them. The game got its name from the theory that the team, which is hiding, is supposed to ambush their adversary. This is theory only, as the "ambushers" sometimes became the "ambushees."

The ammunition used is made from small paper bags. The sack is about half filled with dirt and then the top is folded over and taped with brown paper tape. Each player can carry as much ammunition as he can "tote." Army survival vests with lots of pockets and ammo belts were the favorite items of dress among the warriors. Some boys would carry extra ammunition in back packs, but this had two bad "drawbacks." The pack was heavy and this made it extremely difficult for one to beat a hasty retreat, running through the brush, with ten of the bloodthirsty enemy, breathing down your neck, trying to banish you from the game with a well-aimed sack of dirt. The other bad thing about a pack was: under the rules of the game, if you, or any part of your equipment were hit, you were "dead." So, a back pack presented too much of a target.

When we first started playing this game, we felt that we had to use flour, to better mark a "hit" made on the enemy. We used to go to one of the wholesale grocery firms in our town and buy flour, which contained weevils. This was great for a while. But as our troop grew, it got to be too expensive. The last time we used flour, our intrepid warriors threw about 600 pounds away in paper bags. Even at two cents a pound, this was too much to spend on "sackfiller," when we had about a "zillion" tons of good old dirt for free.

Our troop usually bought the sacks and tape from a wholesale paper company. On a good weekend of Ambush, we would often use about 6000 paper bags. We got the tape in long rolls. This tape had to be moistened to stick. You could always tell an old ambush player, because he suffered from a dread malady called "Mucilage Tongue." This was caused by licking several thousand feet of brown tape. Aside from the dirt, which seemed to adhere to your mouth and tongue, there was another bad side effect from "mucilage tongue." Everything you ate for days after a campout, seemed to have the distinct flavor of glue. One thing which helped a lot was to drink large amounts of liquids such as Cokes, root beer, and Mountain Dew. This helped relieve the discomfort caused by the "mucilage pucker," but it had its own deadly side effect. After consuming several gallons of liquid, you "sloshed" as you ran through the brush, and the noise revealed your hiding place to the enemy.

There were several rules which had to be observed. When one was hit, you put your hands on top of your head and went back to camp. You could not tell your team members where the other team was or warn them of an ambush. For all purposes, you were dead. You might give any ammunition you had to your teammates; you didn't have to turn it over to the enemy. Most "dead" warriors would return to camp and start making ammunition for the next game.

The game was played sometimes until all the members of one team had been vanquished. At times, there was a time limit on a game and the team with the most live heroes at the end of the time period won.

We used to play this game at night, but decided that it was too dangerous. "Ambushers" and "ambushees" stumbled around, running into trees and occasionally falling into a patch of cactus. No one was foolish enough to turn on a flashlight because the beam attracted great numbers of flying sacks from the enemy, as well as from your own team. It was very difficult to be able to see who was behind the light at night.

Also, one night our troop was playing another troop. The Scoutmaster of our enemy troop was wearing a khaki shirt and pants. I had chased him near the house where the Camp Ranger stayed. The Ranger heard the commotion outside and turned on the porch light. He had come outside, but I didn't know that. I saw a figure dressed in khakis, standing in the light with his back to me. I drew a bead and nearly knocked him down with a sack of dirt in the back. When he turned around, I saw I had "killed" the Camp Ranger instead of the enemy Scoutmaster. I beat a hasty retreat into the darkness and hoped he hadn't seen who clobbered him with a sack of dirt.

We had a lot of funny incidents happen when engaged in Ambush. One of our Scouts, who is a local attorney now, was on his first campout. We were playing Ambush and he had run out of ammunition and had gotten separated from his team. Several of the enemy were in hot pursuit and Tom was running down the trail, dodging sacks with every step. In the wild chase, Tom lost his shoe. We looked, but could never find it. I guess that it is somewhere out there on the battleground, an example of the utter terror caused from being chased by a bunch of yelling "Ambushers."

For several years, our troop had gone camping on a ranch near a place called "Red Creek." The bed of this creek was, for the most part, dry, but there were several holes of water along the area where we camped. In this area, the creek made a very sharp curve and the banks on one side of the creek had been cut away to where they were 100 feet high. In one part of these high banks, there was a very peculiar formation. About half way up the wall was a thing which looked like a gigantic cinnamon roll. One of the Scouts father was a geologist and he told us this formation was called a "mud slide.". Although rare in the United States, they were common in many parts of the world. Many of the local geologists have been to this ranch to look at this formation.

One year, there was a national convention of geologists, which met in our city. A geologist of international renown, was the principal speaker, and during his speech, suggested that anyone having any questions, might check with him after the speech. Our Scout's father had gone up to congratulate the speaker on his talk and was standing behind another man who seemed to have a question. This fellow had a picture of the mud slide and was asking the famous geologist about it. The man replied that this formation was rare in the U. S., but rather common in some parts of the world. The man with the picture said there must have been a lot of geologists out viewing this formation recently. He told of finding countless numbers of sacks, filled with samples of dirt. The thing he couldn't understand was why the geologists would go to the trouble to collect the samples and then throw them down. Our geologist father had to turn away to keep from bursting out laughing. Our troop had camped there very recently, and of course, we had to have our regular game of Ambush. The "samples" were the remains of the ammunition used in our epic struggle. The visiting speaker could not explain the reason behind the geologists collecting the dirt samples and then throwing them down. And we never told them.

In our part of the country, several years ago, the federal government had a project to eradicate the screw worm. This is the larva of a fly which lays its eggs in a cut or scratch on any animal like a cow, deer, horse or sheep. If left untreated, the screw worm can cause the death of the animal.

The federal government developed a project to wipe out the screw worm

*Dodging sacks at every step, Tom tries to evade
the ambushers, but, alas! he loses a shoe.*

plague. Sterile male flies were dropped from airplanes in the areas where the screw worms had been found. These sterile flies would mate with the females, but there would be no new flies born.

These treated flies were dropped in cardboard boxes, which came apart in the air, and let the flies cover a large area.

We had been camping one weekend on a ranch where this screw worm eradication program had been started. On Monday, after our campout, some of the sheepherders found these little brown paper sacks, neatly taped, and filled with some unknown substance. They took them to the ranch owner who contacted the county agricultural agent. He didn't have any information about any sacks and suggested that the rancher contact the U. S. Department of Agriculture. The federal agency could not shed any light on the mysterious sacks, and the rancher was getting ready to send some of the sacks to Texas A&M University, to have the contents of the sacks analyzed. He happened to run into the father of one of our Scouts, and mentioned the mysterious sacks. The father knew of our love for Ambush, and told the rancher the sacks were the ammunition the Scouts used in some kind of war game.

I still have a clipping cut from the paper about the strange sacks. The headline reads: "Mystery of the Sacks Solved."

We played many a game of Ambush in the twenty-seven years I was Scout-master of Troop 1. This game was the great equalizer. Strength and size were no assets in Ambush. An adult had no advantage in this game. The adults' greater size just presented a larger target for some seventy-five pound runt of a Boy Scout to bounce a sack of dirt off your rib cage.

A boy's chemical make-up is such that he has to throw something. This can be rocks, balls, clods of dirt or Ambush sacks. Ambush provides a natural outlet for this youthful disease called "throwing." After Ambush, even the most avid throwers would decide that they had enough throwing to last for some time.

After the geology incident, and all the uproar caused by the "mysterious sacks" in the screw worm project, our Scouts used to wonder what would happen in the future, if by chance, one or two of our sacks were preserved. Maybe a sack or two rolled down a prairie dog den, or was sheltered from the weather in a niche in some rocks. They could picture the poor, puzzled geologist, a hundred years from now, as he turned the neatly taped sack over in his hands, and before he opened the sack, it would probably be X-rayed to be sure it contained no explosive or items used in germ warfare. After opening, the contents would present more of a puzzle. It just made no sense that anyone would go to all the trouble to sack up a bunch of dirt.

Of course, it's just possible, that all the geologist would have to do is get in touch with a Boy Scout. Because, a hundred years from now, I'll bet Troop 1 is still playing Ambush.

Chapter 14
Food and Cooking

There are not just twelve parts of the Scout Law. There are thirteen. The thirteenth part is: A Scout is hungry. He eats what he can, when he can, out of a can.

When anyone mentions Scouting, you immediately think of cooking gourmet meals over a campfire, with the sound of crickets in the background and the murmur of a brook close by. Well, "it ain't necessarily so." Since primitive man first learned to use fire to cook a little mastodon meat, there have been good campfire cooks and there have been bad. This has been the way it was in Boy Scout cooking. I have eaten some very good meals, cooked by a Boy Scout, and I have eaten some horrible messes.

Nearly every new Scout on his first overnight camp, would assure me that he could cook like a chef. We suggested that the new Scouts stick pretty much to canned food for their first campout or two. Even this wasn't fool-proof—about fifty percent forgot to bring a can opener, and of those who did bring an opener, many could not understand how to use the tool.

For years, many of our tents had beautiful murals adorning the sides and flaps. These murals were the results of exploding cans of soup, pork and beans, stew, and chili, which the boys forgot to open before placing them in the fire to heat. Luckily, no one was ever injured by these "gourmet grenades," but our tents were adorned with paintings which looked like they might have been done by Salvadore Dali or Picasso.

I used to tell the mothers that if they could see what their sons cooked, and then ate, they would spend a little time instructing their children in the mysteries of cooking.

Many of our Scouts on "overnights" were always eating a meal ahead of

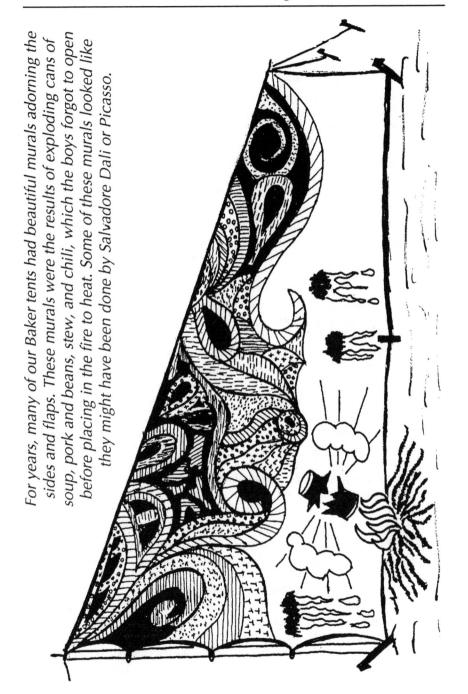

For years, many of our Baker tents had beautiful murals adorning the sides and flaps. These murals were the results of exploding cans of soup, pork and beans, stew, and chili, which the boys forgot to open before placing in the fire to heat. Some of these murals looked like they might have been done by Salvadore Dali or Picasso.

what they should be doing. Let me explain this statement. When we left to travel to the ranch or campsite about 1 P. M., many of the boys, who hadn't eaten in at least thirty minutes, would start eating their food planned for the evening meal. When it came time to cook the evening meal, it had been devoured, so the kid cooked the breakfast food for the evening meal. The next morning, the breakfast was all eaten, so the boys had to cook the food planned for the noon meal for breakfast. By then, there wasn't very much food left for the noon meal, so the Scouts scrounged all kinds of food from one another in order to keep from "starving," as one kid said. No one ever starved to death on one of our campouts in thirty-nine years of camping —there was enough food, but some of the mixtures were utterly horrible.

I'll never forget one very cold ,wet, miserable campout. The wind was blowing, and it was sleeting a little. One boy was squatting by his fire, holding a big, black, cast-iron skillet over the flame. In the skillet was a big hunk of brick chili. (See, he was eating his noon meal for breakfast.) Brick chili is usually very greasy, and this piece was no exception. The bottom of the skillet was covered by a thin film of red grease as the hunk slowly melted. The kid sat there shaking the skillet every once in a while as he took a few swallows of Dr Pepper from a bottle in the other hand.

Another Scout came by and said, "Hey, Bob, are you going to put some of the Dr Pepper in the chili?" Bob looked at the bottle thoughtfully, and said, "Yeah, you know, that might taste pretty good." With these words, he poured about half the drink in the chili, and started stirring it up together. I had to turn away to keep from "up-chucking" at the thought of eating a mixture of greasy chili and Dr Pepper for breakfast.

The kid ate the mess and seemed to enjoy it. In fact, several of the other boys came by to try the conglomeration. They all agreed that it was very tasty and planned to try the same "mess" on their next campout.

While planning a hike one time, one of our troop committeemen had told the Scouts that he would demonstrate the technique of cooking on a flat rock with no utensils. As we hiked along the road and through the fields, Elmo Curry, our committeeman would pick up a flat rock, carry it awhile, and then discard it in favor of a better one. Just before we got to the river where we were to cook our meal, our "flat rock cooking instructor" found a large white rock like you find in the beds of rivers. He announced that this was "the" one. Elmo started his fire and put the flat rock on to heat. He put a nice piece of steak on the rock and covered the rest of the top of the rock with sliced potatoes. This was frying very nicely, and the boys were quite impressed. Many expressed the desire to try this on our next hike or campout.

I was cooking my food over my fire about thirty feet away from Elmo. All of a sudden, there was a great explosion. I jumped around to see what had happened and found that Elmo's fire had been completely blown out. The first thing that popped into my mind was that one of the boys had slipped a firecracker into the fire. All pleaded innocent, so I went over to where the fire had been to see if Elmo had been hurt. I was amazed to find he wasn't even scratched. He had been leaning down over the rock, stirring the potatoes, when the rock blew up. Instead of the force coming up into his face, the rock blew sideways and scattered his steak and potatoes into the bushes. I can still remember how silly we must have looked as we got down on our hands and knees and peered into the grass and weeds and brush, searching for the elusive steak and potatoes. Needless to say, this was our "first"— and "last" endeavor to cook on a flat rock.

Our troop, through the years, had gone on several "survival camps." Now, when you think of survival training, you immediately picture a survivor eating bugs, grubworms, lizards, snakes, and grasshoppers. The only trouble with a survival hike covering only one weekend is that you don't get hungry enough to eat all those things which most of us feel a little squeamish about eating. However, we learned the skills necessary to survive, and a few of the hardier souls would try a little grasshopper or bug flesh.

On the survival camps, no one was permitted to carry any cooking utensils, matches, fishing supplies, or bedding. You had to build a fire with flint and steel, and cooking had to be done on a stick or buried in the coals.

On this particular survival camp, one of our Scouts had managed to catch a fish, a bass, which weighed about three pounds. He had heard about planking a fish—cooking a fish on a slab of wood. He decided to try this method. The scales are scraped off the fish, the fish is cleaned, and then spread out on the slab of wood. This fish is fastened to the wood by means of sharp splinters, and the slab is put in an upright position close to the fire. The idea is that the wood acts like a reflector oven and cooks the fish with the heat from the fire. So much for the theory—Tom didn't know that you were supposed to use green wood, and the chunk he was using was very dead and dry.

The cooking of the planked fish progressed very well for a while. Then the dry chunk of wood started to turn black and smoulder, and the fish did the same thing. After a short time, some of the other Scouts, who had been green with envy when Tom caught the fish, came by and suggested that Tom throw away the fish and eat the chunk of wood. I didn't say anything, but I was inclined to agree with them.

Back in the days when "foil cooking" was first getting a lot of publicity, our Senior Patrol Leader, Mike, announced that he was going to demonstrate this type of cooking on our next campout. We had never seen any foil cooking and were anxious to get some instructions and then try this type of cooking.

When we arrived at our campsite, Mike dug a hole in the ground and built a good fire in it. He kept building up the fire until he had the hole filled with coals. He raked the coals away and put the whole chicken, wrapped in foil, in the hole. He pulled the coals back into the hole and put a layer of dirt on top of the fire. He left part of the foil, which had been folded around the chicken like a bag, sticking above the ground.

We all stood around watching this new type of cooking. In a few minutes, the steam started coming out of the open end of the foil. A short time later, Mike announced that the chicken was done. It was "done" all right, for, when the coals were raked away and the foil was opened, we noticed that Mike had forgotten one small detail. He hadn't cleaned the chicken. The meat was cooked and very tender—but the odor was just a little rank. In fact, after this cooking disaster, it was some time before I could choke down a piece of chicken.

My wife could never understand why, when I went on a weekend camp, I brought home most of the food I had carried. I tried to explain that on most weekend camps, we usually had from fifteen to twenty Scouts working on their Second class or First class cooking requirement. Each one felt that I had to taste his culinary triumph, and, after about twenty of these "mess tasting" ordeals, I could not choke down much food. Many of the Scouts eventually became good cooks, but quite a few, to this day, cannot boil water successfully.

Through the years, I witnessed many examples of cooking disasters. Some of these were so terrible that they have been indelibly etched on my brain. The only good thing about these disasters was, as bad as they were, the humor of them kept you from "blowing your mind."

We were camping one bitterly cold winter day and had stretched some tarps between the trees to give us a little shelter from the sleet. I was sharing a campfire with Tom, a newcomer to our troop. Tom was one of those kids who never seemed to pay attention to what he was doing. As he cooked, he seemed to be watching everything except his cooking. He was using a big cast-iron skillet and had opened a can of green pea soup and dumped it in the skillet. It was so cold the soup stood up just like a pale green cylinder. Tom would shake the skillet a little, but the soup wasn't melting much. As he shook the skillet and moved it around over the fire, he managed to collect a few ashes in his soup and a twig or two.

I looked up from my own cooking in a few minutes and saw Tom eating his soup. The soup hadn't melted much, and he looked like he was eating green ice cream which had been molded into a cylinder, the shape of the soup can. He gobbled it up like it was good—but to this day, I have never been able to swallow green pea soup.

I used one example of cooking for years to teach my Scouts how not to cook over a campfire. I would tell my boys how one Tenderfoot Scout came on a campout and was going to endeavor to cook a steak. Not just an ordinary, run-of-the-mill steak—no, sir! This kid had a steak that would have easily fed a family of six and was about two inches thick, in addition to its great size.

Our cook built a huge roaring fire which resembled a council fire more than a cooking fire. Then he took this huge steak and draped it over the skillet, part of a Boy Scout cook kit. The steak was so large that the only part of the skillet visible was the handle. The steak hung over all sides of the skillet and was hanging down about six inches from the lip of the skillet.

I suggested to Hamp that he cut the steak up into smaller pieces so that they would fit in the skillet. He assured me that his way would work and went about his "cooking." The fire was so hot he had to shield his face with one hand while he held the skillet in the other. The part of the steak hanging over the sides of the skillet was slowly turning a dark black color as it became burned and charred. He had punched the center of the steak down into the skillet, and a sort of bloody froth was bubbling in the middle of the meat.

I looked over in a few minutes, and Hamp was eating the steak. A bloody trickle oozed from each corner of his mouth and ran down his chin. I said, "Hamp, isn't that meat a little raw?"

He replied, "No, that's the way I like my steak cooked—rare."

For years I used his cooking as a horrible example of how "not" to cook. I told my Scouts about the huge fire and Hamp"s inability to get close enough without scorching his face. Also, I told my Scouts it was impossible to cook a fifteen-inch steak in an eight-inch skillet without cutting the steak up into smaller pieces.

On my last campout as Scoutmaster, I really got a laugh when I saw what an impression my words must have made on some of the boys. One of my Eagle Scouts, a high school junior, came to me and told me he wanted some help on cooking a steak. When I got to his fire, I just cracked up. Brian had a fifteen-inch steak, trying to cook it in an eight-inch skillet. He pretended to be very serious about needing some help, but finally he couldn't hold back his laughter any longer. He told me that he had heard me tell the story so many times that he felt obligated to try to see if one could cook a big steak in a little skillet.

Take it from me—it just won't work.

Many of the Scouts became very good campfire cooks. On campouts, several of the patrols used to see which one could serve the tastiest meal. There was a lot of good-natured competition and each patrol tried to keep the others from knowing what fancy dishes had been planned. I encouraged these cooking contests because I was usually called upon to determine the winner. I would tell the chefs that I needed a few more bites or a more generous helping of this or that to be sure theirs was the best.

This cooking skill helped them on Jamborees, Philmont treks, canoe trips,

Through the years, I used Hamp as a horrible example of how <u>not</u> to cook a steak.

and float trips down the Rio Grande, but, as I said once before, some of them never learned to cook properly and had difficulty boiling water.

The reason why some of these lousy cooks managed to get by was—I have become convinced—a Boy Scout will eat anything, no matter if it is charred on one side and raw on the other.

The hungry ones survived—they were tough—they were Boy Scouts.

Chapter 15
Snakes

If you were to make a list of things which fascinate boys, in the order of their importance, I am sure that food would be at the top of the list. But running a close second would be snakes. I don't know what it is about these slithery reptiles that makes boys want to touch them, hold them, and occasionally carry them tucked away inside their shirt. Some kids don't like snakes, but I think they are a minority.

At summer camp one year, we were lined up to march into the dining hall. One of the Junior Staff Members spotted a suspicious bulge in the shirt of one of the Scouts. Upon checking, they found he was carrying a snake in his shirt. Not just the common house variety of snakes—oh no! He was carrying a coral snake. These are beautiful snakes, and the boy said he thought it was just a garter snake. Lucky for him, a coral snake, although very deadly, is not very belligerent or aggressive and must bite something like a toe or finger. The coral snake does not strike like a rattlesnake, but bites and chews. The Junior Staff Member removed the reptile and placed it on display in a cage in our reptile section. The camp director warned all the boys about the extreme danger of being bitten by a coral snake. At the time, the nearest antivenom serum for this snake was kept in New Orleans.

For the remainder of that session, I don't believe anyone was guilty of carrying snakes around in his shirt. For several days after that, each Scoutmaster checked for suspicious bulges in shirts. Outside of a few candy bars stashed away to prevent starvation, the "snake-in-the-shirt caper" became just one more episode concerning a boy and his snake.

When I was in Boy Scouts, our troop was attending summer camp at Camp

Kickapoo on the San Saba River near Menard, Texas. My Patrol Leader was Gordon. He was one of the smartest Scouts I ever knew, but he had some odd habits. Gordon was probably the only Scout in camp who wore pajamas at night. We kidded him a lot, but he insisted on wearing them. One afternoon, some member of our Lion Patrol found a harmless, little green grass snake about eighteen inches long. We decided immediately it would be great fun to put the snake in Gordon's cot that night. We kept the snake out of sight and could hardly wait until he went to bed. We had slipped the snake under his blanket, and all seven of us were lying there in great anticipation. Nothing happened for so long, I became convinced the snake must have crawled off the cot.

I was just about asleep when the uproar started. Gordon came out of his bed ripping the buttons off the top of his pajamas. He was yelling, "Snake! Snake!" Seven cots were gently shaking as we tried to suppress our giggles. Our victim grabbed a hatchet and threatened to behead the snake and the guy who put him in his cot. We all pleaded innocent and assured him it must have been the members of the Eagle Patrol. He finally calmed down, and we asked him what had happened. He said that he went to bed and was almost asleep. I guess that the snake stayed quiet until Gordon was falling asleep. When things got still, the snake started crawling up under the Scout's pajama top. This was when Gordon realized that he was not alone in his cot, and the button ripping started. I was never real sure that Gordon bought the story about the Eagle Patrol being the culprits, and for days I made sure that there were no slithery guests in my cot.

When I was still a boy in Scouts, our camp had an instructor from the University of Texas who was an expert on reptiles. He taught us how to recognize the poisonous varieties of snakes and how to catch them. This was before the days of the fancy snake catchers used now. He showed us how to use a forked stick to pin the snake to the ground and then pick up the reptile by holding it behind the head. In our estimation, we ranked favorably with Frank "Bring 'em Back Alive" Buck and all of the great snake catchers of history. We could hardly wait to get home to try out our new skills.

My patrol decided to take a hike before school started to discover and catch a bunch of snakes. Early one morning, we hiked out west of town to Twin Mountains. We searched diligently all day with very little success. We found one rattlesnake—so far back in a crack in a huge rock we could hardly see him. We were terribly disappointed because we had wanted to try out our newfound skills of catching snakes alive.

It was late in the afternoon when we started back to town. We were walking along through the brush and cactus patches when we got a glimpse of a big snake crawling into a patch of cactus and yucca plants. One of our Scouts, Joel, a big, redheaded, freckle-faced kid, yelled out, "I'll get him!"

"*Joel fell back with the snake hanging on his nose.*"

Now, Joel was very clumsy and uncoordinated. In fact, he had difficulty walking and whistling at the same time. He ran up to the patch of cactus, grabbed his Scout hatchet, and started swinging it at the cactus. We heard him scream and saw him stagger backwards—with the snake hanging on to his nose. He fell to the ground, and the snake crawled back in the brush.

We could not tell for sure what kind of snake it was as we were about thirty feet away when it bit Joel. When we got to the victim, he was lying on the ground propped up on one elbow. His face was white as a sheet, and those big freckles stood out like drops of blood. You could see where the snake had bitten him—there was a trickle of blood running down the side of his nose. Joel was moaning and crying and saying in a pitiful tone of voice, "Tell my mother I love her and tell my dad I'm sorry for all the trouble I got into. I'm going to die and tell my sister I'm sorry I was so mean to her."

I had a snake bite kit, but I wasn't sure about tying the stricture band around Joel's neck. I was getting it out to start cutting when one of the Scouts nudged me and pointed. A big bull snake, a non-poisonous variety, came crawling out of the cactus. These snakes are very belligerent and will strike at you when cornered or when you hit them. I guess that when Joel was swinging his hatchet, he must have hit the snake or come mighty close. The snake struck at the first thing he could see, which was Joel's face, as he leaned over the cactus.

We started mocking our snake bite victim—"Tell my mother this, and tell my dad that, and I promise never to be mean to my sister again." Joel hadn't seen the snake crawl out of the brush, so he didn't know that he was not in immediate danger of dying. He started crying and accusing us of making fun of him as he lay dying out on the cold prairie.

When we finally told him about the bull snake, he grabbed up his hatchet and chased us around through the brush, vowing that he would kill the whole patrol for laughing at his misfortune. He finally calmed down enough that we could continue our hike back to town with a minimum of danger of having our heads sliced off.

For years after this, if you walked up to Joel and said in a pitiful voice, "Tell my mother this or tell my dad that," his face would turn red, and you were in imminent danger of being clobbered.

This was our first—and last—"great snake hunt."

One year, when our troop was setting up the tents at Eagle campsite at Camp Sol Mayer, we were very near a nice latrine. The kids remarked that this was a welcome change from having to traipse a hundred yards at night to a latrine. Most of the boys, if they had to walk that far, forgot what they had come for in the first place and would only make the trip in dire need.

As we erected the tents and got everything ready for a week of camp, one of the Scouts yelled at me to come to the latrine quickly. When we got

"He caught a little movement out of the corner of his eye, and found himself staring eyeball to eyeball with a snake which was in the commode tank."

there, we found the cause for his alarm. It seems that he was sitting on the pot, and the top of the commode tank was pushed a little to one side. As he sat there, he caught a little movement out of the corner of his eye. He turned to see what it was and found himself staring eyeball to eyeball with a snake, which was in the water in the commode tank. To say he beat a hasty retreat is putting it mildly—he rushed from the latrine with his trousers at half mast, yelling at every breath.

We got rid of the snake, which happened to be a non-poisonous water variety, and checked the rest of the commode tanks. I assured the boys that there was only a thousand-in-one chance that a snake would ever crawl back in a commode tank. I don't think I reassured them, and I must admit I never felt comfortable using that latrine again. Our new, nice, handy latrine was not used much—at least not by our troop. The kids said that they had rather walk the hundred yards to the old one. At least, no one had ever found any reptiles in the commode tanks there.

On our first night of summer camp, we found that we were going to need some more stakes. I went to the home of the camp ranger, Buddy, and we walked over to the quartermaster building. It was dark outside, and as he opened the door, he flipped on the light, a single bulb suspended from the center of the ceiling. The room was full of boxes, crates, and tent poles stacked at one end. The single bulb didn't give a great amount of illumination, and there were lots of shadows in the room. Buddy started across the floor to a box filled with tent stakes, and I was walking about four feet behind him. We had taken a few steps when we heard a rattlesnake rattle. We froze and stood there trying to locate the snake. It could have been anywhere in among all of the stuff stacked around on the floor. We couldn't spot the snake and decided to take another step or two to see if the snake would rattle again.

There was a large burlap bag hanging from the rafters, and the bottom of the bag came to about our shoulders. As Buddy took another step and brushed against the bag, we heard the rattle again. This time we pinpointed the place from where the noise was coming. It was coming from the burlap bag. If the snake had struck at him as he brushed against the bag, he would have been in great danger of being bitten in the shoulder or arm. Luckily, the snake didn't strike.

We left the bag there, I got my stakes, and Buddy did a little detective work to find the culprit who had left the snake in the bag. It was one of the Junior Staff Members, who was in charge of Reptile Study merit badge. He had caught the snake late in the afternoon before all of the cages were ready in the reptile display area. He decided to put the snake in the burlap bag where it could get air. Buddy, in a nice, chewing-out manner, told him how dangerous it could have been. Someone could have brushed against the sack and been bitten in the face or neck. Every time I went to the quartermaster's building during that session of camp, I always looked around to be sure that no "unwanted varmints" were lurking in the shadows and there were no sacks of surprises hanging from the rafters.

Many people have a terrible fear of snakes just like some have a fear of heights or a fear of close places. At one summer camp, we had a young medic from the local Air Force base serving as camp medic. As boys will, they found out that he was afraid of snakes. I told my Scouts not to try to scare him because a person with that fear of snakes, when frightened by a snake, may hurt someone because they are not totally responsible for their actions.

One afternoon after retreat, we were lined up, getting ready to march into the dining hall. I was standing on the porch just outside the front windows. Jack, the medic, was standing inside the dining hall looking at the troops lined up in formation. I saw a Scout walking across the dining hall, behind Jack, carrying a paper sack. He walked up to the medic, pulled a snake out of the bag and tapped Jack on the shoulder. The medic jumped completely backwards over one of the dining hall tables. He pointed his finger at the boy and told him that he was afraid of snakes and that he better not try a stunt like that again.

A few nights later, one of the staff members stepped out from behind a tent holding a snake and shoved it into Jack's face. The medic knocked him about twenty feet and brought to an end the cute stunt of scaring people with snakes.

Most people who have a fear of snakes suffer from this phobia all their lives. I had one Scout who was able to overcome his fear and who demonstrated his victory in a convincing manner. When Randy first joined our troop, his fear of snakes was such that the mere sight of one made him physically ill. If some other boy happened to come around Randy and he was carrying a snake, the boy and the snake were both in imminent danger of being clubbed to death. The other Scouts found out about Randy's fear and respected it. They didn't try to scare him with a snake, because he made it very plain that— first—he would dispatch the reptile—and then—they would be next in line.

But one summer before summer camp, I was amazed to find out that Randy had applied for camp staff and had specifically asked to be in charge of Reptile Study. I couldn't believe it until I called him on the phone. He told me that he had made up his mind to get over his fear of snakes and that a family friend, who was an expert on snakes and lizards, had been working with him. This friend had let him handle some snakes, and Randy had gradually overcome his fear.

He decided that the ultimate test would be to teach Reptile Study at summer camp sessions. The first morning of camp when the merit badge sessions had started, I just had to go down to see Randy handling the snakes. He showed several varieties of snakes, both poisonous and non-poisonous, and showed the Scouts the do's and don'ts of handling snakes. When he let a large bull snake hang around his neck, I knew that he had whipped his fear. But Randy was one of the few people who are able to really overcome their fear of snakes.

We live in a part of the country where four varieties of poisonous snakes are to be found. There are ten different types of rattlesnakes, two different types of copperheads, one cottonmouth water moccasin, and one type of coral snake. Through the years, I have tried to teach my Scouts the latest recommended treatment for snake bite, but sometimes you find that your words just don't make an impression.

Each year at camp on Saturday, there were a number of inter-troop contests and games such as marksmanship, volleyball, archery, swimming, rowing, canoeing, and the turtle race. Awards were given and there were epic struggles as the troops tried to win an award to take home to their Scout cabin.

The turtle race was always a lot of fun. Sometime during the week, each troop would catch a turtle and keep it around their camp to be entered in the great race. The idea was to find a speed demon turtle, a real barn burner. This was quite a search because most turtles are built more for comfort than for speed. One session, the camp staff tried to run in a ringer. They tied a turtle shell to the back of a big lizard and tried to convince us that they had found a new type of turtle.

Our troop had a big turtle staked out down by the river, which was very near our campsite. We had tied a string around one of the turtle's back legs and placed him near a log which stuck out into the water. The reptile could get in the river or crawl up under the log to get out of the sun.

At camp one evening, our troop was getting ready to go to the retreat ceremony and eat supper. The kids were dressed in their uniforms and looked very sharp. One of my Scouts, Craig, said that he was going to go check on the turtle. I told him to hurry because it was just about time to go to the retreat ceremony. He had been gone just a minute or two when I heard him yell. He came running through camp, holding one finger up in the air, yelling that a snake had bit him. He took off in a cloud of dust toward the hospital building. I was trying to catch him, calling for him to stop. I had tried to teach the kids that, if you're bitten by a snake, violent movement can help spread the poison, and you are supposed to remain as quiet as possible. Craig had forgotten all this, and his only thought was to break all existing world records for the 400 meter dash to the hospital.

In my younger days, I used to pride myself in the fact that I could hold my own in a running race with any of the boys in my troop. Not this day. The last I saw of Craig, he was still running, holding one finger aloft and equalling the speed of a world class sprinter.

He had already reached the hospital building, and the medic had him

"Craig came running through camp, holding his injured finger in the air. He yelled that a snake had bitten him, and took off in a cloud of dust for the hospital."

sitting down when I finally arrived, puffing and out of breath. The medic calmly checked the bite on his index finger. He said that he didn't think it was a bite of the pit viper family, which includes rattlesnakes, cottonmouth moccasins, and copperheads, because the bite hadn't started to swell. He said that it might be a coral snake bite, but he didn't think it was.

I asked Craig where he was when the snake bit him, and he told me that when he went to check the turtle, the snake bit him, but he didn't wait around to check the identity of the reptile. I told them I would go back to the log to see if the snake might still be there. When I got to the log, I rolled it over and a harmless water snake came crawling out from under the log. I reported to the medic, and he cleaned the bite and put a band-aid on it.

As Craig and I were going to retreat, I reminded him that he did everything that we had taught him not to do in case of snake bite. He grinned and said that all he could think about was getting to the hospital building as quickly as possible—and, I have to admit—he certainly did just that.

Chapter 16
Jamborees

Jamborees are a camping get together with Scouts from all of the United States, plus a sprinkling of Scouts from many foreign countries. When you see 50,000 Scouts marching to one of the big arena shows, one gets the feeling that Scouting is a Mighty Big Movement. Members of our unit have attended each of the jamborees since the first one in 1937. Also, several Scouts have attended World Jamborees in various countries.

My first jamboree was in 1953 at the Irvine Ranch near Santa Anna, California. We traveled by train in two special cars to Fort Worth, Texas, where we hooked on to a special train carrying 600 Boy Scouts.

One member of my troop was an expert on railroad trains. At first the other boys thought that he was pulling their leg, but after checking with several members of the train crew, we found that he really knew his trains. Allan and his dad and brother were train buffs. If you were invited to their house to hear a new long-playing album, you did not hear the Boston Pops Orchestra or even Montovani. You sat and listened to 45 minutes of train sounds. Allan was our train expert and gave us a lot of interesting information.

On our ride to the West Coast, we stopped several times to stretch our legs. We leaders had to make certain that none of our little charges had strayed from the vicinity of the train station. As a result of our vigilance, we hadn't lost a single boy when we arrived at the Grand Canyon.

Our train was to be here for several hours, so we were able to get in a little sight-seeing. We hiked to an observation point where a park ranger told us about the canyon. We went back to the area where there was a concession building with a cafe, snack bar and a lot of souvenirs. This was where I first found out that Scouts, at this age, are not very interested in the scenery.

They would walk to the retaining wall, look down to the bottom, wonder if they could throw a rock that far, and then go back inside. They spent most of the time at the Grand Canyon drinking malts and cokes, buying postcards and playing the pinball machines.

We bought quite a bit of fresh fruit here and the Scouts were upset about a rumor that we could not take fruit into California. They gorged themselves and then decided to hide all the rest of the fruit on the train. They hid the sacks under the seats, in the restroom and all along the luggage racks. The kids found that there were very few good hiding places on a train.

We went to sleep and must have crossed the state line about midnight. We woke up to find that all our fears were for naught—I don't think the inspectors even checked us. I think the boys were a little disappointed because they felt that their skillful hiding of the fruit would have fooled even a veteran inspector.

We arrived at the jamboree site and marched to our own section. The grass covering the hills was very dry and dead and about knee high. Even as we hiked in we saw one hillside smoking where seventeen tents had burned down. We leaders made a mental note to warn our campers about the dangers of fire getting started.

Native Californians were complaining about the dry grass and told us that they hadn't received any rain in three months. We countered by saying that we hadn't received any rain in five years. We told them that it was so dry back home, even "the jackrabbits had started carrying canteens." That dry grass was a real fire hazard, and a number of tents caught fire. Luckily, we didn't have any such misfortunes.

We set up our tents and got the lister bags ready for water. We got our combination table and benches and nailed them together. The design for these things was pretty good, but the guy who picked out the nails for them, made a slight error. The nails were too short and this caused the benches to collapse without any warning. We finally found some slightly longer nails, but even this didn't stop the benches from collapsing. We finally solved the problem by piling dirt under the benches. This was not as nice looking but was safer.

The first day there we had just set up our camps in a temporary manner, in order to sleep the first night. The next morning we got up early to straighten up our tents, gateways and displays. It was cloudy and cool and several of the Scouts worked without their shirts. This was a sad mistake, as the sun burned right through the haze and cooked you good. This was the first hard lesson we learned about the West Coast.

The second lesson we learned was that charcoal was almost impossible to start anywhere within 200 miles of the ocean. There was enough moisture in the air to be soaked up by the briquets and make fire starting a curse.

All of our Scouts were used to cooking on wood fires and charcoal cooking was a mystery to them at first. Where wood fires get hot at first and then gradually cool off as the fires burn down, charcoal fires get hotter the longer they burn. The cooks learned to hoard the milk cartons and any other flammable material to start the fires. One Scout lost a highly prized grass skirt from Catalina Island, when he had put it in the chuck box for safe-keeping. The fire builder could not get the fire going and used the skirt as a last resort. This worked fine but made fire starting a little expensive.

Another discovery we made at the jamboree was that most Scouts just didn't have the know-how to prepare a meal for eight or ten people. Usually a couple of the leaders ate with patrols at different meals. This would bring the number of diners up to ten, and sometimes more, if we had a guest from the section staff. We leaders quickly learned which patrols had the best cooks and tried to get invited to dine with them.

Since we were so near Hollywood, we had scads of movie stars. They appeared in the arena shows and even showed up in your own camp area. One morning I was coming back from the trading post and saw this big open-top limo. There was quite a crowd of Scouts around the car, and, as I got nearer, I saw that Vice President Nixon was in the car. He was busy signing autographs and talking to the boys. We were told not to ask the V.I.P.'s for their autographs because signing your name 50,000 times might get to be quite a chore. However, he didn't seem to mind. I heard later that some Scout had absconded with the vice president's pen. As this was near the trading area, I'm sure the Scout traded Mr. Nixon something for the pen, but the V.P. was never really sure just what it was.

Swimming in the ocean was a new experience for most of us old West Texas boys. In the first place, the warm Pacific was anything but warm. Before our Scouts learned how to gauge the waves, large quantities of salt water were swallowed .

The safety measures were excellent. Usually 5,000 Scouts swam at one time, and I never heard of anyone getting into trouble. Lifeguards were stationed at short intervals all along the beach, and we leaders waded out a short distance and faced the shore. All swimmers stayed between us and the beach. Amphibious vehicles patrolled about 100 yards offshore and helicopters constantly flew overhead.

One very cool morning it was our turn to go swimming about 8:30 A. M. We boarded the bus and rode to the beach area. We leaders waded out in the cold surf, teeth chattering, with our skins turning a beautiful shade of blue. Some of the kids ventured out in the water but beat a hasty retreat back to the shore. They covered each other with sand to stay warm while we gradually froze to death in the ocean. After a short stay, we all decided that we had had enough morning swimming and went back to the bus. This episode forever ruined my idea of the warm Pacific Ocean. As one little Scout so aptly put it, "Man, this water is colder than the river back home in the winter time." I kind of had to agree with him.

One of our side trips was a voyage to Catalina Island. Our Scouts were very excited about this because most of them had never been out on the ocean before. We saw a lot of flying fish and the deck hands pointed out several sharks to the kids. The Scouts had another new experience, which was not so pleasant. Sea sickness sneaked up and grabbed about half of our troop. At first, a sick Scout would go off by himself, when he felt the queasiness coming on, but after a short while they were lined up on the rail, elbow to elbow. Many were certain that they were going to die before we reached shore. Any mention of food brought cries of protest and some even vowed that they would never eat again.

As I have mentioned before, kids have that ability to shed misfortune like a duck's back sheds water. We had hardly docked when the boys disappeared in all directions to find something to eat. Later in the day, we ate lunch at the football field, and their appetites had miraculously returned. I warned them that we had to return, by boat, to the mainland, but they assured me that they had the sea-sickness thing whipped. And they did—on the way back, not a single Scout got sick. I told the captain that they must have acquired their sea-legs and considered themselves old salts.

To me, one of the most impressive things at jamboree is the sight of thousands of Scouts marching to the arena. Since the Scouts come from different parts of the jamboree grounds and have to travel different distances, the timing of the whole maneuver is a thing of beauty. Sections start out marching; they are joined by other sections; then the different regions all come together at the big arena. I don't believe the military could have done a more precise job of getting thousands of Scouts together at the same time to meet at the same place. At the first big arena show we saw a great pageant showing the scenes which make us proud of our heritage. We saw Columbus, the Pilgrims, Washington at Valley Forge, wagon trains crossing America, the Alamo, the gold rush and many others depicting great moments in our history.

After all this pageantry, each Scout was given a candle. After lighting it, 50,000 Scouts and Scouters rededicated themselves to the high ideals of the Scout Oath and the Scout Law. The entire arena was covered with a soft glow from the lighted candles, and you realized that Scouting was a mighty big and important movement in the world.

For those of you who enjoy movie stars and hero worship, the Hollywood arena show had everything—and everybody. Bob Hope was the Master of Ceremonies and there were literally dozens of movie stars. Most of them arrived in convertibles, and were greeted by loud cheers and shrill whistles.

Danny Kaye was the hit of the show, though he arrived in an old Model T with a smoking chimney on the back of the ancient car. The doors on this antique didn't swing open in the usual fashion—oh, no! They let down like loading ramps on a cargo plane. The crowd was estimated at 100,000 people, who had come to see the Scouts and all of the movie stars. The fireworks display was tremendous, as the ground actually shook from the exploding aerial bombs. And the huge crowd would "oooh! and aaah!" in unison as a particularly beautiful burst of fireworks would light up the whole countryside.

Caveat emptor is a Latin phrase meaning "let the buyer beware." This should be changed to "caveat trader" or "let the trader beware." Although the first part of the Scout Law, "A Scout is Trustworthy," possibly was not broken, I believe it was dangerously bent in some instances of jamboree trading. Scouts, who brought items native to their part of America, sometimes pawned them off on poor unsuspecting souls as something other than what they really were.

I saw cockle burrs traded as porcupine eggs. One troop, whose home state was bordered by the Mississippi River, seemed to have a never ending supply of small, neatly labeled bottles of Mississippi River water. I wondered how they managed to carry so much water across half of America. My wondering came to an end one day when I happened to go by their campsite. The boys had a regular assembly line going—one group was putting a small amount of dirt in the bottles; another was filling the bottles with water; while the last bunch busily stuck the labels on the bottles. All this activity was taking place around the water faucet, which supplied them, and the rest of us, with good old California water.

One night at the trading tent I noticed two Scouts carrying around a large ice chest. My curiosity got the best of me and I had to find out what they had to trade. They opened the chest and displayed a shark, about three feet long. The shark was packed in ice to preserve it long enough for the two Scouts to trade it to some poor trader before the shark started to smell. I always wondered who finally ended up with that piece of trading material.

Rattlesnake rattles were not too good for trading. It seems that most of the states have rattlesnakes. Oddly enough, the skins of these snakes were very much in demand, and some of our own Scouts did quite well in trading rattlesnake skins.

One troop from Oklahoma had beautiful arrowheads to trade. They told us the arrowheads were authentic Indian points and were made by Indians. Later on, we found out that the boys made the arrowheads, and that there wasn't a single Indian in the whole troop.

Various patches make good trading material. Camp, camporee, Philmont, Order of the Arrow, and regional patches are very sought after. Our regions, Region 9 and Region 2, had patches which were very hard to obtain. These regions issued patches only to leaders who were attending a national Scouting event, and this rule made it difficult for Scouts to get these patches. The boys did manage to get their hands on these patches somehow, and were able to trade them for a large assortment of patches in return. Some of these patches, Regions 2 and 9, brought as much as $25 from some traders who needed these to complete their collection.

The jamboree came to an end, and we dismantled the tables, benches, lister bags, and all of the equipment furnished by the national jamboree organization. We packed our personal gear, including all of the trading goodies we had scrounged from some poor unsuspecting souls. We boarded the buses to take us to Santa Anna to begin our long trip home via Salt Lake City and Royal Gorge.

The majority of the Scouters on the section and regional staffs were very helpful, considerate, and willing to listen to our troubles. A few were "puffed up in their own conceit and wise in their eyes." One such gentleman, who I will call Scouter "X," was the last contact we had with the jamboree, and he left a nasty taste in my mouth.

We rode for about an hour and came into the train station. When we checked about our railroad cars, we received the distressing news that the railroad had lost one of the cars. This meant that our entire contingent would have to crowd together in one car. We growled, but the railroad company said there was nothing they could do about it. When we went to the buses to tell the kids what had transpired, they didn't seem to be upset nearly as much as the leaders. However, they said they needed to go to the bathroom, and I assured them that little chore would be accomplished.

Before we left home for the jamboree, Truett McClung was appointed to be the tour group leader. We were told that if we had any problems we were to go through the tour group leader, instead of several of us bothering someone with the same problems. This had worked fine until this last day.

The leaders from our contingent and Scouter "X" were standing around in the train station yard. We were in a small circle, and I told the Scouter the boys needed to use the restroom, either the one outside or the one inside the station. Scouter "X" said that he didn't want anyone running around in the yard and the boys were to stay on the buses until the train was ready. I reminded him that the kids had been on the buses, then, for almost two hours and that they needed to go to the restroom.

The fine gentleman said that the Scouts were to stay on the buses, regardless, and he didn't care if they "wet their pants." After finding that we had lost a car and the inconsiderate statement made by this Scouter—well, that was the last straw. As I said, we were standing in a tight circle. I told Truett that it was my understanding that we were to go through him if we had a beef. So, I said to Truett, "Would you please tell this gentleman that I am going to let the boys off the buses to use the restroom, and if he makes one move to stop me, I am going to mop up the ground with him." The man looked sort of startled, but he didn't make any move to stop the kids.

After we finally got on the train, we found that being a car short brought about a feeling of true togetherness. We were so crowded that eleven of us had to sleep in the aisle on the floor. I volunteered to be one of these aisle sleepers and put my sleeping bag at the very end of the car. Our one car was the last car on the train, and I decided that any sleepwalking Scout would have to crawl over me in order to fall off the train.

The first night, we left Santa Anna and went north to Salt Lake City. Every hour or so, the train would stop and an employee of the railroad would get on the train carrying a small chunk of ice. The water cooler was in the opposite end of the car, so the guy would have to pick his way over the eleven aisle sleepers to get to the cooler. As he tiptoed over and around the sleepers, the chunk of ice would drip and some of us wound up getting a dash of ice water in the ear or face.

About 2:30 in the morning, another ice toter came up the steps by my head and said, "Hey! What have we got here?" After the lost car and the inconsiderate Scouter episode, this was the last straw! I raised up and told him, the cooler was in the other end of the car and for him to go to the cooler end to get on the train. He looked a little startled and hesitated like he might come on down the aisle. I said, "Fella, if you come down this aisle and step over me with that dripping ice, I'll bite you on the leg." He backed up and got off the train, and then went to the other end of the car.

To me, the jamboree had been a huge success, but these three little things —Scouter "X," the lost car, and the dripping ice—left a bad taste in my mouth, and I think I stayed mad the entire trip home. After sleeping on the hard aisle for three nights, someone offered to trade with me. I had to go back to the aisle, though, because I had become used to the hard floor and couldn't stand the softness of the seats.

I was tour group leader for the 1957 Jamboree at Valley Forge, Pennsylvania. Once more we traveled by special train to the jamboree. We left home and went to Fort Worth, Texas, where we hooked up with a train carrying about 600 Scouts. When we got on the train, we carried only our personal gear because the rest of our equipment was locked in the baggage car. This car would not be opened until we reached Philadelphia, where trucks would carry our equipment to the jamboree ground.

This meant that anything alive for trading purposes had to be carried in the cars with us. The first night out from home, we took an inventory of the live trading material in our car. There were over 600 horned frogs, 23 snakes (non-poisonous), 31 terrapins, 11 coons, 5 possums and 11 cigar boxes filled with doodlebugs—ant lions to you—and 4 descented skunks. One Scout had brought about 60 small pin cushion cacti, mesquite beans, and screw beans. All this—along with a zillion patches, countless neckerchief slides, neckerchiefs, rattlesnake rattles and skins, and several dozen cow horns and bull whips—made a very impressive display of trading materials. In fact, before we had hardly cleared the station and with the parents' tearful farewells ringing in our ears, the Scouts had already started trading among themselves.

Each morning, the porter would bring mops, brooms, buckets, and trash cans for us to police the car. About the second morning out, a couple of the snakes got loose and were crawling around in the car. The Scouts didn't pay much attention to the snakes, but the porter sure did. He opened the door, saw a loose snake, and threw the cleaning material about twenty feet. He said if we wanted to get equipment to clean up the car, we would have to check with the conductor, as he wasn't coming back to our car anymore unless we got rid of the snakes. The kids tried to convince him the snakes were not poisonous, but he said, "A snake is a snake, and I'm afraid of all of them."

Scouts that age are certainly not interested in scenery. I would try to interest them in something along the tracks, but they kept their noses buried in funny books. The only time anything outside seemed to get their undivided attention was when there was a three-car pile-up on the freeway which ran near the tracks.

To give our troop a West Texas flair, I had decided to paint animals, birds, reptiles, and insects, native to our part of the southwest, on the front flaps of the Baker tents. The Texas Parks and Wildlife Department had printed a series of pictures, suitable for framing, of these representatives of Texas wildlife. These pictures were in natural color and had information on the back about this particular specimen. We got several hundred of these pictures for the boys to give visitors at our jamboree campsite. For instance, the boys in the tent with a skunk painted on the flap had pictures just like the tent flap to be given away. We had a great many visitors who had heard about our tents and wanted to see them.

Many of the Scouts from other states who attended the jamboree, looked on Texas Scouts as a bunch of braggarts. We bragged about the size of our state and felt that everything in Texas was bigger and better. At this particular jamboree, I decided to try to convince all of the Scouts from other states that our troop didn't fall in the bragging group. For our gateway, I took pieces of 4' X 8' plywood and cut out prickly pear cactus. For the thorns, I drilled over 1800 holes in the wood and glued double-ended toothpicks to represent the thorns.

My little daughter came home from school one day with a verse, which I felt expressed exactly what was needed to dispel the idea of bragging Texans. It went like this:

Two six foot cowboy boots, holding up a star, on which were painted the six flags of Texas, gave a West Texas flavor to our 1953 jamboree gateway.

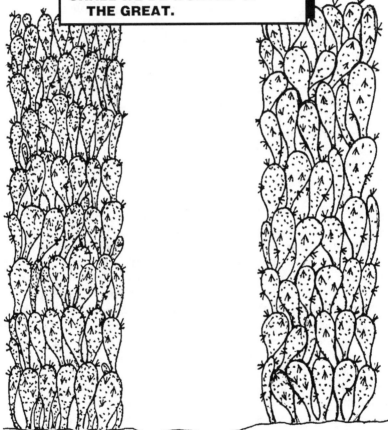

WE TEXANS KNOW
THAT <u>NOT</u> WHEN WE BOAST OF
WHAT OUR FATHERS DID,
NOR OF THE MANY MILES
WITHIN OUR STATE,
BUT WHEN OUR DAILY LIVES
ARE TRUE AND FINE,
SHALL WE BE WORTHY OF
THE GREAT.

Our 1957 jamboree gateway was made of plywood cut out to resemble cactus. Double-ended toothpicks were glued into the cactus to look like thorns. The little verse at the top caused many people to remark "that we were the only <u>modest</u> Texans at the jamboree."

"We Texans know:
That not when we boast of what our fathers did
Nor of the many miles within our state,
But when our daily lives are true and fine,
Shall we be worthy of the great."
This little verse on our gateway brought a lot of comment from Scouts of other states. They would read the verse and then say, "Well, what do you know? A bunch of modest Texans."

We were camped very near the big memorial arch. We had lots of visitors, and our painted tents made quite an impression on the people. One day a Den Mother from Phoenixville, Pennsylvania, which was very near the jamboree site, brought her Cubs to visit our camp. Each of the little Cubs really wanted a horned frog but didn't have anything to trade. Our Scouts got together and gave each Cub one of the little reptiles. The kids couldn't have been happier if you had given each one the Hope Diamond. At first, some of the Cubs were a little hesitant to hold the horned frogs because of their ugly appearance. Some of the kids dropped their prizes, and then there would be a mad scramble to catch the little critters.

The next day I had been to the section headquarters to check on some information I needed. When I returned to camp, about half of our troop was standing around my tent. They all had a sly grin on their faces, and I immediately suspected the worst. I figured that they must have released a King Cobra inside my tent or had dug a pit for me to fall into. I hesitated and they all urged me to go on in—the boys assured me that I had a pleasant surprise for a change. Still expecting "no telling what," I gingerly ducked under the tent flap, and there it was. Reposing on my cot was a great, beautiful cake—it must have been two feet wide by three feet long. There was a note attached to the cake, and, after reading it, I realized it was from the Den Mother of the Cub pack which had visited with us. She said that the Cubs were so thrilled with the horned frogs that they decided to do something for our troop. She was elected to bake us a cake, and she thought that a nice big one was necessary to give each of our boys a very generous slice.

As I had said earlier, our campsite had a great many visitors. Two of our Scouts got together to provide a little entertainment for the people. John probably might have weighed a hundred pounds soaking wet, a skinny kid. Bill was a very muscular Scout who weighed about 165 pounds. These two great entertainers had worked up a routine which went like this: When there was a large group of people visiting our campsite, these two would get into a violent argument. Their voices would get louder and louder, and finally, Bill would threaten John with terrible bodily injury. By this time, all of the people would be looking at these two combatants, and probably wondering why I hadn't stopped the brawl. Bill would rush at John like a runaway train bear ing down on a Model T stalled on the tracks. Just as Bill reached John, the smaller kid would throw the larger boy over his shoulder with a wrestling hold. Bill would hit the ground with a very loud grunt, then get up to rush John again. Our visitors would be herding their children away from the gladiators, and men would protect their wives from the terrible carnage. After about three of these bull-like rushes, I would stop the kids and explain to the people that it was all a gag. As the jamboree progressed, so did the great fight episode improve. Each time, all of the people were pulling for John to wallop the big bully who was picking on him. In one of my scrapbooks, I have a great picture of Bill in the process of hurtling through the air.

When word got around that we had a lot of horned frogs, many visitors came to our camp wanting to buy these little reptiles for their children. One day a man and wife and three kids came into our campsite. He told the Scouts that they wanted to buy some horned frogs for the kids. One Scout had about thirty frogs left and went to get the box he kept them in. This crate was a shallow box with screen wire on top. It had sand in the bottom and was about four inches in height. The horned frogs were in the sand, and, when the kid removed the top, some of them started to scurry about. The children were excited and crowded around the box. In one corner of the crate was a very large, very dead horned frog. The man studied the reptiles for a few minutes and then said to the Scout, "That sure is a big horned frog there in the corner. However, he doesn't seem to move around like the others."

The Scout, never cracking a smile, assured the man that the reason the big frog didn't move around much was because he was hibernating. I had to walk away to keep from bursting into hysterical laughter. The man finally decided to buy three horned frogs but decided to shy away from the "hibernating frog."

While I was attending the jamboree, my wife and daughters had planned to visit my wife's brother who lived in Boston, Massachusetts. They were driving, and I worried about their driving in New York and on the turnpikes. They came by the jamboree one morning, and I got to visit with them for a short while. I told my wife to be very careful about her driving because she wasn't used to driving in traffic like she would encounter in New York and New Jersey. They left, but all that day, in the back of my mind, I had a nagging fear for their safety.

We were to leave the jamboree the next morning to start home. Our troop was busy packing all of our gear, when a messenger came to our camp and said that I had a telegram at section headquarters. I went in a high lope to headquarters, and as I ran, I just knew that my family had been involved in a traffic accident. When I arrived, I was told that there was a telegram for me, but it had been taken to regional headquarters. I muttered a few choice un-Scout-like words and started out the door of the tent. Our section chief, seeing how agitated I was, offered to drive me to the regional headquarters. When we arrived there, I was told that the telegram had been sent back to our section headquarters, by a Scouter driving a jeep. This was beginning to look like a version of "Keystone Cops," except it certainly wasn't funny to me. On the way back, we stopped every Jeep but couldn't find the right one.

It was getting very close to the time that we had to board the buses to ride into Philadelphia to catch our train. I knew that I was going to have to leave very soon and was half sick with fear for my family and frustrated that something like this foul-up could happen. When we got back to our section headquarters, we were told that the guy with the telegram had been there, but, when told I had gone to regional headquarters, he decided to try to catch me there.

By this time, I had to leave with our contingent to board the buses. I told the headquarters people to make sure the telegram was put on the train. By this time, I was so mad and frustrated that I wasn't a fit companion for man or beast.

We had been on the train for about thirty minutes when they brought me the telegram. Frankly, I was afraid to open it. I just knew that it contained bad news concerning my family. When I opened it, all my fears went floating out the window. The telegram didn't contain any tragic news about my family but was, instead, a telegram from Lyndon B. Johnson, congratulating me on being a leader at the jamboree. At the time this took place, I believe I told someone, "if I could get my hands on LBJ right now . . ."

I still have the telegram in one of my scrap books. Once in a while, I happen to run across it and can laugh—now—that this little paper caused so much trouble and anxiety for me.

After we had settled down on our train, the Scouts started showing all of the items they had traded for at the jamboree. One Scout had traded his Texas snakes for some from other states. They were the non-poisonous variety and were allowed to roam freely around the car. The first night out from the jamboree, the air conditioning in the car had been turned down very low. It was cold, and our sleeping bags felt good. About 1:30 in the morning, I woke up and felt something heavy on my chest. I reached up and found a snake coiled up in a tight ball. I guess the cold was affecting him, too. I suppose, as a good Scout, I should have shared my sleeping bag with him but decided against it. I picked up the cold reptile and pitched it across the aisle to my sleeping neighbor.

We saw this snake several times on our way home and tried to get its owner to corral it. He promised he would, but the last night on the train, the varmint was still enjoying the run of the car. When we got ready to leave the train the next morning, we couldn't find the snake anywhere. We decided he had crawled up into the upholstery on some of the seats and couldn't be found.

We never did find the snake and I always wondered what would happen if the snake came crawling out of the upholstery on one of the regular passenger runs. I watched the paper for days but never heard of a railroad car being mysteriously overturned as the passengers had panicked.

A few times in one's lifetime, you may have the good fortune to meet a man who is dedicated to his job and who puts the needs of others as his first priority. Such a man was Mr. Daryl Bones, the liaison officer for the Santa Fe Railroad. He accompanied us on the train from Ft. Worth to Chicago and then was on the train as we returned home. There were sixteen passenger cars in this train, and ours was the last car on the train. Mr. Bones went out of his way to make the Scouts' journey pleasant, and any problem we had —he would come up with an answer.

After we left Chicago on our way home, we noticed that one of our boys was ill. James seemed to have symptoms of the flu, and we were worried that, if it were contagious, we might have a flu epidemic on the train. We tried to isolate James as much as possible, but it was a pretty hopeless task. We called Mr. Bones, as usual, and he suggested that we move the sick boy into his quarters. In this way James would be more comfortable, and he would be more isolated from the rest of the Scouts.

The sick kid said he didn't want to move. He knew that he was going to die, and he wanted to die among his friends. Mr. Bones said that he would call ahead and have a doctor meet the train about eight o'clock that night at the next town of any size. The doctor met the train and examined James. He said he thought that the sick boy had pneumonia or a case of the Asiatic flu, which was just coming into the United States. He said that he had never seen a case of this new flu, but a colleague of his was a doctor in a town further along on our trip home. Mr. Bones said that they would radio ahead and have the doctor meet the train when we arrived in this town, about midnight. Mr. Bones said that he would come back to our car in plenty of time, so that we would not have to hold up the doctor too long. After making James as comfortable as possible, we went to sleep. The first doctor had given him a couple of shots and they seemed to relieve his pain and congestion.

The next thing I knew, Mr. Bones was shaking me to tell me we would be in the town in about five minutes. To really appreciate what Mr. Bones had done, you have to know a little about the conditions on a train carrying about 600 Scouts. When the Scouts go to sleep at night, they assume odd positions in the car. Some sleep with an arm or leg sticking out in the aisle. Some sleep with their feet across the aisle. Some packs and containers filled with scout equipment and trading items invariably seem to find their way out into the aisle. To walk through sixteen cars of wall-to-wall humanity, finding your way with the aid of a flashlight, is above and beyond the call of duty. This fine liaison officer did just that. Not just once, but several times to check on the sick Scout.

When the doctor examined James, he told us that he definitely had Asiatic flu. He gave him some shots and told us to keep him as cool as possible. Mr. Bones again suggested that we move the boy to his quarters, but the Scout didn't want to go. The doctor said that it would probably be better to let him stay where he was if he were more content there.

When we arrived in Fort Worth, it was a little before noon. Our car was put on a siding because we would not leave Fort Worth until late that night. It was hot and I wondered how we were going to keep James cool. Good old Mr. Bones, in his usual manner, solved that problem. He had the railroad employees hook up a big portable air conditioning unit to the car and the sick boy was kept cool. Most of the Scouts and leaders had gone into town to do some sight-seeing and eating. I stayed with James and had them bring me something to eat. We always kidded James about being the one who brought Asiatic flu to Texas.

I never knew whether or not Mr. Bones was a Scouter. I only knew that man about seven days, but to me, he personified everything good and noble which you find in the Scout Oath and Scout Law.

Mr. Bones, where ever you are—I salute you!

I was the tour group leader for the 1960 Jamboree. We had three troops from the Concho Valley Council, and we had 46 boys from our own Troop 1 to attend. This was great, as we had five natural patrols, using the same Patrol Leaders and assistants, and we used the regular officers in our troop for Senior Patrol Leader, Quartermaster, Junior Assistant Scoutmaster and Scoutmaster and Assistant Scoutmaster.

We tried something new for this jamboree. We decided to have permanent cooks whose only job would be cooking. We obtained menus for all the jamboree meals, and the cooks got some prejamboree experience in preparing just what we would have during the jamboree. Someone complained that the rest of the patrol would not get any cooking experience at the jamboree. In polling the Scouts, most of them said they didn't want to cook for eight to ten people and would just as soon leave the cooking chore to the permanent cooks.

I suppose I had another motive for the permanent cook caper. In two prior jamborees, the food and cooking left a lot to be desired. The food was fine, but most Scouts hadn't had enough experience cooking for about ten people. Also, the charcoal cooking was a new thing with most of the chefs, and they seemed to have problems with their heat. After eating some of the "food" at the 1953 and 1957 jamborees, I was about ready to see about arranging to have our meals catered in by Howard Johnson.

When we had selected the permanent cooks from each patrol, we would give them some practical experience in cooking on charcoal. This really worked out fine. I never had better food at any jamboree, with the exception of the 1964 jamboree, where I served on the section staff.

Since our Jamboree Troop was to be composed of just Troop 1 Scouts, we talked it over and decided that the Baker tents would be painted with Indians on the front flaps. I let the two boys who were to occupy a certain tent pick the Indian or Indian scene they wanted painted on the tent. One Scout had found a picture of or Indian scene they wanted painted on the tent. One Scout had found a picture of Placido, the famous Tonkawa Indian chief and wanted me to put it on the tent. One of the two Scouts sharing the Placido tent had a special interest in Chief Placido, Chief of the Tonkawa Indians. It seems that Jim's great-great-great-grandfather owed his life to Placido. The Tonkawa Indians were friendly toward the white people and were serving as scouts for a group of Texas Rangers who were trailing a large group of hostile Indians. At the Battle of Plum Creek, Jim's distant relative had his horse shot from under him. He was about to be clobbered by a group of hostiles when Placido dashed in and rescued him. So, you see, our Boy Scout had a lot of family history depicted by the picture of Placido painted on the flap of the baker tent. Another boy had a picture of a famous Sioux warrior, who was a distant relative, and asked me to paint this warrior's picture on the tent flap.

I did a lot of research on Indians and wanted the paintings to be as authentic as possible. I tried to get pictures of Indians from all parts of the United States to use to get a cross section of Indian dress and ornaments.

I painted twenty-four tents, beginning in October. I finished in July right before the jamboree. I used textile paints which are very waterproof. Quite a number of these tents are still in use, and the colors are as bright and vivid as they were in 1960.I didn't have any good place to paint, so I painted them in my house. I would usually have a tent drying in the living room, one over the dining room table, and possibly one or two on the back porch.

My poor wife suffered through all this tent painting. I would paint a lot at night on the living room floor. The rest of my family would go to bed to try to get a little sleep. This didn't work out that way. I loved to listen to records as I painted and sometimes would get carried away with the volume. One of my favorite recordings was Bing Crosby singing a bunch of Irish songs. My wife would stumble into the living room about 2:30 a.m. and ask me to please cut down the volume on "Who Threw the Overalls in Mrs. Murphy's Chowder?"

It's a wonder my wife hadn't slipped some arsenic into my coffee. She had put up with tents drying all over the house for several months and been blasted out of a sound sleep by the strains of such recordings as "Ghost Riders in the Sky" or "Rancho Grande." The only thing which saved me was her understanding—especially when I had to tell her one night that I had spilled about a quart of bright yellow paint on the carpet in the living room. She had

Since "Indians" were the theme for our troop at the 1960 jamboree, we spent a lot of time searching for pictures of authentic Indians to be painted on our Baker tent flaps.

Chief "Stand-In-The-Mud-And-Bawl-For-Buttermilk" looking for the proper Indian pictures!

*We painted Indians on our tent flaps and even
had a few adorning our gateway.*

We found lots of Indian pictures but never found one which looked like the above character.

the answer to that problem—I just had to buy her a new living room carpet. The only good thing to come out of using this textile paint was our sink trap in the kitchen. After I had mixed up several colors, I usually had a small portion left. It was too difficult to try to keep this until the next painting session, so I would empty it into the sink trap. For years we had the most beautiful sink trap in all of Texas. However, this wasn't much of a conversation piece as it was sort of difficult to get guests to go traipsing into the kitchen to look at our designer sink trap.

We traveled by bus to Colorado Springs, with a stopover at Amarillo Air Base. Once again, I was impressed by the lack of appreciation for scenery the Scouts showed. We got off the bus at the jamboree site, and I was eagerly showing the kids Pike's Peak and other scenery. They would glance at the famous peak and grunt unenthusiastically and poke their heads back into funny books.

It was late in the evening and we hurried to set up our camp so that we might spend the night out of the cold. We were busy getting everything ready in our campsites when one of my Scouts came up to me and said, "Hey, look! See what I bought!" He opened his hand and showed me a Region 9 patch. I asked him what he paid for it and he told me $5. I chewed him out and told him he was going to run out of money before the jamboree was over. About three nights later after we had been to the trading tent, the same boy came up to me and said, "You know that Region 9 patch you got on me for buying for $5? Well, I sold it tonight for $20." Once more, the learned Scoutmaster had to take his lumps and eat a generous helping of crow.

Most of our Scouts had a good sun tan, but we found that the rare mountain air of Colorado didn't cut out much of the sun's rays, and some of us ended up with some very painful cases of sunburn. I was among those with this problem. In fact, I had clear blisters in several spots on my legs and had to quit wearing my scout shorts until they healed. Luckily, I had brought along a couple of pairs of long scout pants, and I managed to get by.

The water from the showers was about as cold as any I have ever tried to use to bathe. Rumor had it that the water came from the snow run-off in the mountains and that the water stayed at about thirty-eight degrees. I don't know about the temperature reading, but it would take your breath away when you stepped in the shower and turned on the shower head.

I used to use the cold shower as a little disciplinary method for those Scouts who were a little late getting back to our campsite at night. If we went to a night show at the big arena or the Scouts just wanted to go to the Trading Post or trading tent, we set a time for a curfew. If one was late, one must pay the consequences. The penalty was to take a cold shower when you got back to camp. If the water seemed cold during the heat of the day, you should try it about 10:30 at night. This method of curbing the curfew breakers proved to be very effective.

There was a contingent of Scouts from the Corpus Christi, Texas area camped right next to our campsite. There was a little Scout in this group who refused to take a shower. His philosophy was: If you were careful, you didn't get dirty, hence, you didn't need a shower. We had heard the other Scouts in his group threaten him several times with all sorts of dire troubles if he didn't take a bath.

One afternoon, I was taking a shower and happened to look out the door of the shower building. Down along the jamboree street came this group of Scouts with the non-shower taker being half pushed and half dragged along in their midst. The shower mob escorted him up the stairs to the shower and told him to take off his clothes. He protested that he didn't need a bath, but they gave him his choice—either take off his clothes and shower or shower with his clothes on.

He removed his uniform and stepped into the shower. When the cold water hit him, he bounced right back out like a tennis ball. The mob pushed him back into the water and made him stay there until he had washed off a four day accumulation of Colorado soil. He jumped out of the shower and made a very profound statement. He yelled out, "Man, we can't get water that cold by putting ice in it at Corpus Christi." I was inclined to agree with him.

We had been warned before going to the jamboree that we would have some problems keeping our tents standing. It seems that the jamboree site soil was left when a glacier had plowed its way through here a million or so years ago. The soil looked firm, but an ordinary twelve inch stake would pull right out of the ground. We had thirty inch stakes made from reinforcing steel about one inch in diameter. The top was bent so that the stakes looked like steel walking canes. We used bungee or elastic cord in our guy lines to allow them to give a little without breaking or pulling the stakes out of the ground. We did not have a single tent to blow down at the jamboree, but many others were not so lucky.

About the same time every afternoon, a wind would come from the north down through the valley which was the site of the jamboree. You would hear a pop and look up to see a tent or dining fly sailing through the air. One group used tents made of parachutes, and they had a few problems. Our jamboree gateway wasn't very tall because of the danger of getting blown down and demolished. Some troops had brought large gateways and suffered the consequences. They were blown down and ended up being used as campfire material for the troop and section campfires.

We did some sight-seeing at Seven Falls, Cave of the Winds and went to Elich's Garden Amusement Park in Denver. One of the highlights of this jamboree was President Eisenhower's visit to the jamboree. Most of the Scouts and I had never seen a president of the United States so close up and we were very thrilled.

The jamboree ended, and we boarded the buses for our trip home. We were to spend the night at the Clovis, New Mexico, Air Base. When we drove up to the main gate, we could see that something was in the air. The young man who was our liaison officer boarded the bus and explained to me what was happening. I had noticed that all of the military personnel at the front gate were carrying rifles and most of them were carrying side arms.

This was the time they were having the Cuban crisis, and this air base had been put on "Red Alert." We were going to eat at the dining hall and then go to the big gym, where we were to spend the night. He suggested that, if we decided to go to the movie, after we ate, if any guard challenged us, to remind the boys not to give some "smart aleck" answer. He said every one was very jumpy, and we might end up with bullet holes in various portions of our anatomy.

After we ate and went back to the gym, the other leaders and I decided that it was too risky for our Scouts to be roaming around on the base. We told everyone the situation and they accepted it very well. We played volley ball and basket ball and decided that these two games, even the way they were played by the Scouts, was not quite as dangerous as roaming around a darkened Air Force installation, with a bunch of trigger-happy G.I.'s ready to blow holes in our posteriors.

We made it home with no problems and were welcomed by a large group of parents and the news media. From the welcome we received, one might have thought we had conquered Pike's Peak and annexed Colorado as a part of West Texas.

Once again, I was selected as tour group leader for the 1964 Jamboree. Our jamboree group had decided to fly to Newark, New Jersey, in order to give us more sight-seeing time at the World's Fair and in New York. Some of the parents were concerned about the kids missing all the scenery, but I assured them that boys that age could care less about scenery. A special plane came to San Angelo to pick up most of our group from the local airport. Part of our group, from the lower part of our council, went to Dallas by bus and flew on a commercial airliner to Newark.

When we left San Angelo, we flew to Atlanta, Georgia. We flew at about 23,000 feet and the ride was very smooth. We went from Atlanta to Philadelphia, where some members of the section staff who were going to have to be in camp a little earlier met us. When we flew from Philadelphia to Newark, we flew very low, about 3500 feet, and the ride was very rough and bumpy.

There was a large oval-shaped section in the tail portion of the DC-9 plane which would hold about thirty-five Scouts. According to the Scouts, this particular section was the very choice section of the plane and the ones lucky enough to get a seat there felt like they were a bunch of V.I.P.'s.

As we flew to Newark, the ride got rougher and more bumpy. The kids in the oval section could feel the bumps more, and one got the same sensation you get in a rough ocean, where your boat is picked up by a giant wave, and then seems to fall out from under you as your boat falls down in the trough between the waves.

When the plane would hit a bump and suddenly rise, you could hear the Scouts in the oval section give a great gasp in unison. Then, as the plane seemed to fall out from under them, you could hear another sound—it was the sound of several Scouts, who were getting rid of their suppers, dinners and maybe even a few breakfasts.

Quite a few in our section had become airsick, and, in a very short time, the "up-chuck" bags were becoming difficult to find—especially the unused ones. The three stewardesses on the plane surely did an outstanding job with all the sick kids. For a while the score read: Airsick Scouts—40, Stewardesses—3. These gals got wet towels and bathed the kids' faces and helped to make them a little more presentable. When we finally got off the plane at the Newark Airport, most of the people there realized that we were Boy Scouts and not some displaced people from one of the countries behind the Iron Curtain.

One little Scout, Robert, who sat across the aisle from me complained all the way to Philadelphia, about the fact that he had to sit in a seat away from the window. Of course, there wasn't much to see, since we were flying at night, but he griped anyway.

When we started to Newark and the ride got bumpy, he could have cared less. He was one of the sicker ones on the plane and used every airsick bag we could find in our portion of the plane. When I questioned him about what he had eaten for supper, he told me that he ate a good meal before he came to the airport. However, while we were waiting for the plane, he decided that he might get hungry before we could eat again, so he ate three hot dogs at the airport. I pointed out to him that he had lost his supper, his three hot dogs, and most of the food he consumed for the past two days. He would just nod in agreement and motion for us to hand him another barf bag.

We went by bus into New York and checked into a hotel in downtown New York City. There were about six hundred Scouts in this hotel with two or three Scouts assigned to each room, depending on the room size.

We had hardly checked into our rooms when we had a serious problem. One of our party, a Scout from a neighboring town in our council, had gotten sick very suddenly. We called a doctor who examined the boy and told us that he had a serious case of appendicitis and needed to have an operation as soon as possible. We put the boy in a hospital and then set about trying to find his parents to inform them of their son's condition, and to get their permission to go ahead with the operation.

We called the home of the parents but got no answer. We called several people in their town, but no one could shed any light on their whereabouts. The hospital called and said that they must operate in a very short time or there was danger the appendix would rupture.

Since I was the tour group leader, I told the other leaders I would take sole responsibility for the operation. But the other men in our contingent would have none of that. They decided that we would all take the responsibility and share equally. This action certainly made me feel a lot better, because I wasn't too keen on being the one to tell the hospital to go ahead with the operation without the parent's permission. We had gone to the hospital to sign the necessary papers in order that they might proceed with the operation. One of the other leaders in our group came running in with some good news. They had located the parents of the sick boy—and guess where they were? After their son left to go to the jamboree, they had decided that this would be a good time to attend the World's Fair and to visit their son at the jamboree. The parents had come to New York and were staying in a hotel about five blocks from where our hotel was. They had been contacted and were on their way to the hospital.

I must admit that I heaved a sigh of relief at this good news. This emergency operation was a very serious crisis and I was glad I didn't have to make the final decision. The operation was a success and the Scout came through in fine fashion though his parents decided that he had better go with them and not attend the jamboree.

We went back to our hotel and were sitting in the lobby, letting our nerves unwind, when someone came running into the lobby and said that a Boy Scout had fallen out of a window of the hotel. As we ran out of the door and down the sidewalk to where a crowd had gathered, I think I prayed, "Dear God, please let it not be one of ours." We pushed through the crowd and saw a Scout lying on the sidewalk. As the other leaders and I arrived, the boy was trying to sit up. I could see that he was not one of our contingent but was from a different council.

We told him to lie still until we could get a doctor or medic to examine him for possible fractures. He kept saying that he was OK and wanted to get up. While we were locating a doctor who was staying at the hotel, we checked to find out what had happened. It seems that the boy was jumping on his bed, which was very near the window of his second story room. The window was open, and as he jumped, he hit the bed at an angle, which propelled him right out the window. A canvas awning broke his fall, and about all the damage he suffered was having the wind knocked out of him and suffering a blow to his dignity.

After the doctor checked him, it was decided that he should go to the hospital where they could make some x-rays. After a thorough check, it was found that all the damage he sustained was some pretty good bruises on his posterior where he crashed through the awning and landed on the sidewalk.

After this latest incident, things settled back down to "normal" and we did a little sight-seeing in New York City and planned to attend the fair the next day.

The day after we went to the fair, we had a full day of sight-seeing. In the morning, we went to the Statue of Liberty and several other places of interest. That afternoon, we made the boat trip around Manhattan Island and really had a ball. We returned to our hotel late in the afternoon and ate supper. Some of the lucky Scouts had been able to get tickets to the New York Yankees vs. the Baltimore Orioles baseball game at Yankee Stadium. They were going to ride the subway to the game and were excited about their first subway ride.

We got back to our hotel from the boat ride about 6:00 p.m. The Scouts going to the ball game had left shortly after that and the rest of us sat around in the hotel lobby and visited. I had gone to my room to do a little reading when someone knocked on the door. When I opened it, there was one of my Scouts with some more disturbing news. He told me that he had looked everywhere for Greg, his roommate, and couldn't find him anywhere. I asked the boy if Greg had gone to the baseball game, but he was sure that Greg didn't have a ticket.

He told me that the last time he saw the missing boy was when they were coming back to the hotel from the boat trip. I decided that we had better start a search party and try to find the lost boy.

I alerted the other leaders and we started going from door to door in the hotel. I thought Greg might have gone to some other room and fallen asleep. We checked every room in the hotel with no luck. I remembered that some of the Scouts had been going up to the roof of the hotel where there were some telescopes for viewing New York City. We looked on the rooftop—but no Greg.

In 1964, the year of the jamboree, there had been some riots in the city, and we had talked about the possibility of some Scouts becoming involved in the civil disturbances. We hadn't had any trouble, but, I must admit, I was worried that Greg might have become involved in some sort of trouble and might have been tossed off the top of the hotel.

We decided to go down and check the alley back of the hotel. We were wandering around in the alley, moving garbage cans and looking behind boxes of trash. Some employees of the hotel saw us and decided to call the police. The first thing we knew, there were patrol cars blocking the alley, and we were told to stand up.

When we explained what we were doing in the alley, the cops were very understanding. We asked them for suggestions to help us in our search for the missing Scout, and they promised to help in any way they could. It was about 10:30, now, and the Scouts should be returning from the baseball game about 11:45. If Greg wasn't with them, we were to call the police station and they would put out an all points bulletin.

The other leaders and I waited outside the hotel to catch the first glimpse of our Scouts returning from the ball game. About 12:00, here they came, straggling down the street. I went running over to check to see if our missing boy was with them. The boys told me that they didn't remember seeing Greg, but that part of our group was going to be a little late.

It seems that part of the boys didn't get off the subway when they were supposed to, and that they must go out to Coney Island before returning to our hotel. When I checked, I found that this group of Scouts would not make it back before 2:30 in the morning.

I kept questioning the Scouts about seeing Greg. All assured me that they hadn't seen him, and didn't think he had a ticket to the baseball game.

As I paced, waiting for the last group to arrive, I kept thinking—where do you look for a fourteen-year-old boy at 2:30 in the morning in New York City? All sorts of terrible possibilities raced through my mind—but the worst part was my helplessness. There was just nothing I could do to help the situation, and all I could do was wait until the last Scouts returned.

About 2:45 a.m., here came our group of wandering Scouts. I was torn between two urges. I wanted to run to check on Greg, but I was afraid that they would tell me that he wasn't with them. As they got a little nearer to the hotel, I was very sure that I could see Greg with them. Sure enough, there he was. I had an impulse to hug him and to strangle him at the same time. When I asked him why he hadn't told anyone that he was going to the ball game, he said that he thought he had told someone, but he couldn't remember just who it was.

I told him that he had caused us to arouse everyone in the hotel and we almost got thrown in the pokey for loitering in the back alley among the garbage cans. He seemed genuinely sorry for all of the trouble he had caused, but this penitence lasted for almost three minutes, because he wanted to know if I thought it was too late for him to go across the street to get something to eat.

I warned him that if he even got out of his room without telling me, I was going to lock him in his room and just let him out about twice a day for a breath of fresh air.

After our stay in New York, we went on to the jamboree where we set up our camp. Our site was very near a big parking lot, and our camp was the first one the visitors saw. We had lots of people in our campsite at all hours of the day—and sometimes night, and this situation caused us to suffer from a strange malady. It was called "Tent Whiplash." You could be in your tent, changing your uniform, when some lady would pull back the flap from your tent, or stick her head into your tent and demand to know where a certain portion of the jamboree was located. To guard against being caught with your trousers at half-mast, as you dressed, you had to constantly move your head from side to side to avoid being trapped. This constant wear and tear on your neck finally caused you to suffer the classic symptoms of "Tent Whiplash," red, bloodshot eyes, caused by nervously trying to look in two directions at the same time, and "charley-horses" in the neck, brought on by too much wear and tear of the neck muscles.

You know, we had some excellent doctors in our section, but they never were able to come up with any sort of antidote for "Tent Whiplash."

Being camped so near a parking lot, we had another problem which was a bad situation. People took things such as cameras, binoculars, knives or anything which wasn't nailed down. Some of the more valuable items, we would take to section headquarters where we had a place we could lock them up. Visitors would steal patches—either loose ones or which they would cut off your shirt, if you left it hanging where they could get to it. People would take jackets and shirts with patches on them and some Scouts lost all the patches they had which they had placed in a box for safe keeping.

There were a lot of professional "patch traders," who would come to the jamboree and cheat the kids our of their patches. The leaders in the various sections finally got a line on some of the characters and made them leave the jamboree grounds. But a lot of kids got gypped out of valuable patches by these vultures.

At most of the jamborees I had attended before the one in 1964, we had carried cots to sleep on. Since we flew this time, our space was limited, and the kids slept on the ground.

The leaders had been briefed, and we, in turn, had told the Scouts about a small beetle, which had a habit of getting in the Scouts' ears. We issued cotton balls each night and made sure the Scouts put them in their ears. The boys had joked and laughed about any beetle crawling into their ears, and let us know they thought we were pulling their legs.

About the third morning of the jamboree, just as our Scouts were cooking breakfast, we heard all this screaming. Two adults were half-dragging, half-carrying a Scout who was obviously in great pain. They carried the boy to the hospital tent, where we found out that he hadn't used the cotton in his ears the night before, and one of the pesky beetles had crawled in his ear.

After that, we had no trouble getting the boys to use the cotton balls. In fact, when we were passing out the cotton, if we missed someone, he made sure that he got his protection against the beetles.

We had used Baker tents at this jamboree and I had painted animals, birds, and reptiles on the flaps. Most of the wild life I used was native to West Texas, but some of the kids had chosen some animals which had never seen West

Texas. Two of my Scouts had decided that they would have a little fun with their tent flap, and had me paint a rhinoceros on their tent. They told visitors that it was a West Texas Doodlebug, and I was amazed that so many people believed them.

One little Scout, Randy, and his older brother asked me to paint the head of a longhorn steer on their tent. I put cattle brands all over the tent surrounding the steer's head. Right between the horns of the animal, I painted a brand which had caused a lot of embarrassment for Randy. The brand was a 2, a 2 on its side, and a P. The way you read the brand is: two, lazy two, p. Randy was the youngest Scout in our unit and he appointed himself official guide for people visiting our camp. He would take them around and point out the various birds, reptiles and animals painted on the tent flaps. He had worked up quite a spiel and was a very interesting and knowledgeable guide. It was very funny, though, when he would show the visitors his tent with the head of the longhorn steer painted on the flap. He would explain all the cattle brands surrounding the animal's head, but would somehow overlook the embarrassing brand. Invariably, the visitors would ask what that particular brand meant, and Randy's face would turn red, and he would stammer and stutter. When he would finally manage to blurt out the meaning of the brand, the visitors would really laugh. Randy confessed to me that he very seriously considered taking a black marker and obliterating the offending brand.

I told him that some day he could look back on his embarrassment and be able to laugh at his own discomfiture. He is a doctor now and, when we get together, we can look back and laugh at that poor little red-faced Scout trying to explain the brand to our jamboree visitors.

All too soon, the jamboree came to a close and we went to Washington to do a little sight-seeing. We got to see all of the monuments and spent quite a lot of time at the Smithsonian Institute. We went to Mt. Vernon which was very impressive to most of the Scouts. As one boy expressed his feelings about Mt. Vernon, I found myself experiencing the same feelings. He said, "You know, when you read about George Washington in our school books, you get the feeling that this period in our history was something that happened a long time ago and was just a story. But when you come to Mt. Vernon and see where Washington lived and the things he used in his daily life, the whole story comes alive and you feel a little closer to Washington."

Another thing which impressed me was when groups of Scouts would walk down the hill to Washington's tomb. On the way there the boys would be laughing and chattering as boys will, but when they were standing outside the iron grill, silence would fall over the group. You could almost feel the awe and reverence the boys felt as they stood there. As I stood watching the Scouts, I had a positive feeling of confidence about our younger generation. I felt that we old "dodo's" were very lucky to be able to place our country's

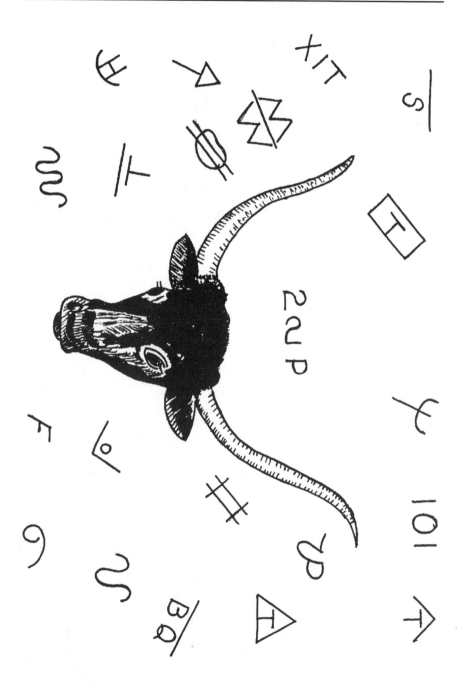

*Our 1964 Gateway was made to resemble a bobcat.
You walked through the mouth to enter our campsite.*

future in the hands of fine young men and boys like these. They were stronger, smarter and their love for their country was just as strong as ours. They were Boy Scouts.

After leaving Mt. Vernon, we returned to our hotel and got ready to leave Washington. We were to fly to Atlanta, Georgia, and then home to Texas. When we reached the airport, we got on the plane and were trying to get everyone settled for our long flight home. Robert, the little Scout who was so sick on the flight to Newark, New Jersey, once more sat across from my seat. He told the Scout in the seat next to him, "You got the window coming up here, so I get to sit by the window going home." The other Scout agreed and they changed seats. I couldn't see that it made much difference, since we would be flying at night, and there was not much to see out of the window.

The other leaders and I decided that we didn't want to go through the "mass air sickness" thing again, so we had checked with the doctor who was flying back with us. He suggested that we give the Scouts tranquilizers and tell them they were Dramamine or air sickness pills. After we were airborne, we gave each Scout the tranquilizers, and the effect was miraculous. Most of the kids went to sleep and didn't even wake up when we stopped in Atlanta to refuel.

Poor Robert, the little kid who was so obsessed with sitting by the window, went to sleep shortly out of Washington, and never woke up until we were landing in San Angelo. He sort of grinned and said, "Well, at least I got to sit by the window coming back."

A large crowd of parents and well-wishers was on hand to greet us. From the welcome signs and all of the fuss, you might have thought that we had returned from conquering Mt. Everest and maybe finding the lost Ark. I was glad to get home without any more kids falling out of windows, having emergency appendix operations, or looking for lost Scouts in New York City at 2:30 in the morning.

The author at four years old with his dog, Ring.
"My Soldier Boy" is in his Grandmother's hand.

The author, age 13 years, caught in the act of tossing a piece of lead up in the air at Scout Camp, Junction, TX, 1928.

At seven years of age in Toyah, Texas. Later he went in his room and smashed his clarinet to pieces. He wanted only to be a Boy Scout.

Never before published photo of L[
Robert Baden-Powell founder of th
world-wide Scouting movement. (19
Photo courtesy of Carl Cummins[

Author as a Scout ,about 14 years old,
with C. B. Foster, Asst. Scout Executive,
Concho Valley Council.

Again with C. B. Foster and his camera
that got "ruined" when hiking
down "700 Springs" and fell
into a hole up to his neck!

Author as a Scout atop cliffs at Paint Rock, Texas, where there are many ancient drawings by Native Americans. (Photo 1928)

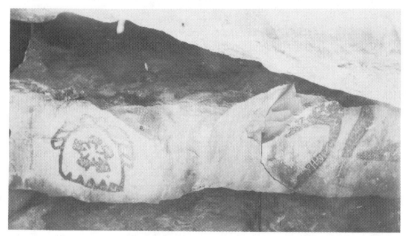

Some of the ancient cliff drawings at Paint Rock, Texas are estimated to be 10,000 years old. (Photo by author - 1928)

Fellow Scouts on a hike to "700 Springs", Junction , Texas. Photo by author. 1929.

Author with his wife, Vivian, on their
50th Wedding Anniversary.

Eddie Whitaker,
where are you?

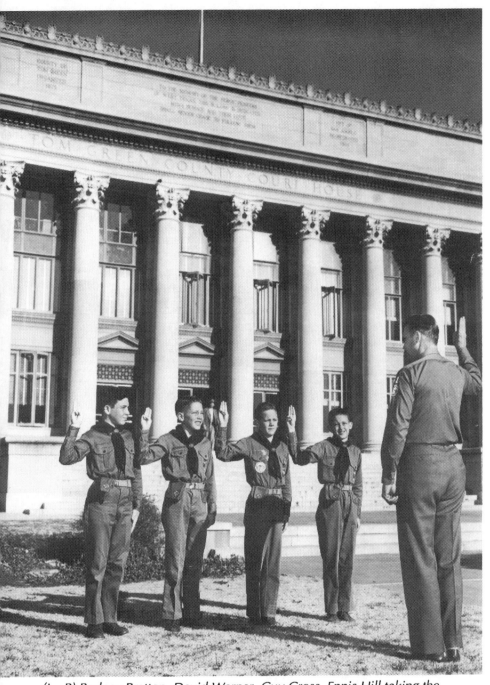

(L - R) Rodney Bratton, David Warner, Guy Gross, Ennis Hill taking the Scout Oath on the Courthouse lawn, Tom Green County in the early 50's. J. T. Henderson, Scoutmaster.

Scouts fishing on the banks of the San Saba River at Camp Sol Mayer.

(L - R) David Warner, Stan Alford, Bob Butner, keep the fire burning at Camp Sol Mayer.

Troop 1 had several members of this jamboree troop who attended the National Jamboree in 1953, at Irvine Ranch near Santa Anna, California.

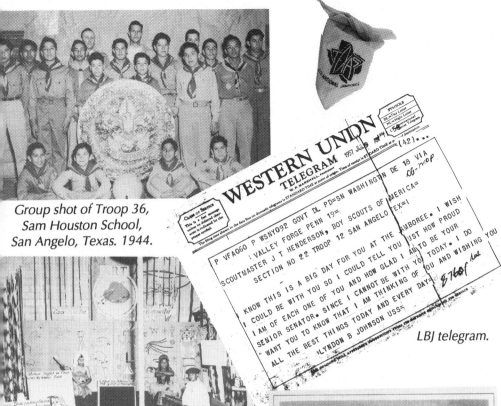

Group shot of Troop 36, Sam Houston School, San Angelo, Texas. 1944.

LBJ telegram.

Scouts of Troop 36 demonstrating Art Merit Badge at Boy Scout exposition. Note center—famous "Black Cat Sitting on a Pile of Coal at Midnight."

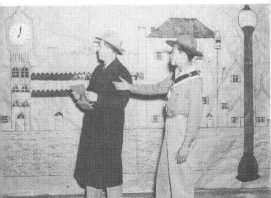

1957 poster. (Reprinted courtesy of BSA.)

Scout Alberto Hernandez and adult Scouter, Bill Warner, doing skit of "Unknown Scout in England" that helped bring Scouting to America.

Allen Byars gives a "Horned Toad" to a grateful boy at the 1957 jamboree.

Visiting the U. S. Capitol, Washington, D. C., 1957. (Look who's riding drag.)

Johnny Fields and Bob Wyatt at Mt. Vernon, 1957 jamboree, Valley Forge, Pennsylvania.

John Simpson and Bill Bivens "fakin out the tourists" at Valley Forge.

1957 group shot of Concho Valley Jamboree Troop at Valley Forge.

Bob Butner takes time to "write home." Valley Forge, Pennsylvania, 1957.

"WOW, New York City!"

Five Eagles: John Troilinger, Clint Johnson,
Bob Rogers, Alan Byars, David Warner.

Barry Rountree,
outstanding scout of Troop 1.

Troop 1 camp, Camp Sol Mayer. (Look who's way in back.)

Several members of Troop 1 are in this group attending Philmont. Second from right, top row is Dick Wyatt.

Author made this display for one of the Concho Valley Council's Annual Dinners.

Several members of Troop 1 were in this group, from the Concho Valley Council, on this canoe expedition. Author is top row center.

Author is with Larry Seibert and Chris Herschberger and one of the tents he painted for the 1960 National Jamboree at Colorado Springs, Colorado.

1960 Concho Valley Council shot, National Jamboree, Colorado Springs, Colorado.

Concho Valley Council Jamboree Troop Camp, Colorado Springs, Colorado, 1960.

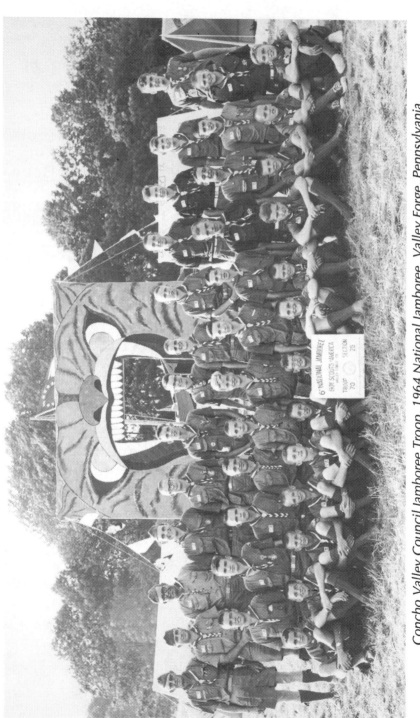

Concho Valley Council Jamboree Troop, 1964 National Jamboree, Valley Forge, Pennsylvania. (26 members from Troop 1.)

Jimmy Kalaitzes receives his Religious Award from the Eastern Orthodox Church.

Six Scouts from Troop 1 got their Eagle. 2nd row, 2nd from left: Alan Goldberg, Robert Wood, Steve Weaver. Three Scouts kneeling are the Cates brothers. This was the first time three Scouts from one family received their Eagle at the same time.

Camp Ranger, Buddy Wyman leads singing at dining hall, Camp Sol Mayer.

Scouts Troop 1, about 1967, with some Eagles.

More Scouts and Eagles.

Four more Eagles.

Some Committeemen from Troop 1.

Easy going on the Rio Grande.
1973

Rio Grande Raft Trip #2, Big Bend National Park.

(Above)
Emerging from
Santa Elena
Canyon.

Don
Borger

"KER-SPLASH!"

Making camp on Rio Grande Trip #2.

Grizzly Ada- . . . er . . . J. T. is coming home from #3.

We're back from #3 and we didn't drown.
1975

With Randy Rountree, Another Troop 1
outstanding scout on receiving
his Eagle Award.
1965

" . . . Boys in Scouting
are boys first."

Author J. T. Henderson, 1991.

(SAST photo Cade White)

Chapter 17
Philmont

The first Scouts from our troop to attend the Philmont Scout Ranch in northeast New Mexico went in 1951. At that time the Scout Ranch functioned a little differently from the way it now operates. A crew had to carry most of their supplies for the entire trip, instead of being able to carry enough food for a few days and then to replenish it at the various base camps.

We impressed on the Scouts the importance of not wasting any food or we might be on short rations before we could make it to the next base camp.

One of our crew, Tom, was a tall, lanky, red-headed kid, who could eat more than even four average teenagers. He took the food situation very seriously, and asked me if I thought that we might have trouble with bears trying to get our food. I told him there was always that possibility but not to worry about it.

At night, we would put our food supply on a tarp on the ground, and fold the corners over to completely cover our supplies. We would place our pots and pans on the tarp—not to prevent the bears from getting to the food; but to warn us in case of a "bear invasion."

After eating supper one night, we had gone to bed pretty early, and I was just about to go to sleep, when I was jolted out of my sleeping bag by this loud clanging noise. I rolled over and looked out my tent door, to locate the source of all the uproar. Sure enough, there in the beam of my flashlight, was one of our furry, hairy bear visitors. He was standing on his hind legs and was swinging his paws like a boxer. With every swipe of his paws he was sending the pots and pans flying in all directions.

I was a little hesitant as to the proper procedure of separating a big bear from his intended meal; but the final decision as to what action to take was made by Tom, our chow hound, who just couldn't stand to see a bear eating his precious food. Tom was in the tent next to mine, and I heard him let out a scream of rage at the audacity of that uninvited bear about to gobble up his food. As I watched in shocked silence, Tom came bounding out of his tent. He had a flashlight in one hand and was dressed in long-handled underwear which he used to sleep in at night. He ran straight at the bear, flashing his light and yelling at the top of his voice. The raiding bear took one look at this terrible apparition coming toward him out of the night, tucked his tail between his legs, and ran as fast as he could to the safety of the woods.

After the bear had gone, I asked Tom, "What would you have done if the bear hadn't retreated?" He sort of grinned and said, "All that I could think about was that durned bear eating all my food, and I just couldn't stand to see that happen." We told our crew that we were lucky to have run into a cowardly bear, but the next time the bears decided to eat our food—just let them. It would be a lot easier to obtain some more food, rather than try to glue together some brave, but foolhardy Scout who had been bear chawed.

After we had several Scouts to attend Philmont, we had learned a lot about the type of equipment which was best—such as sleeping bags, packs and packframes, and hiking boots. After our first couple of Philmont expeditions, we found that a lot of equipment we had carried was not needed, and some other items were needed to make the hiking more enjoyable.

We had planned a Philmont expedition with most of the Scouts coming from our own troop. Bill, one of the leaders, and I had discussed the trip very thoroughly and were a little worried about three of the boys who were going. These Scouts were not very big and were slender in build. We thought that they might have a little difficulty keeping up with the rest of the crew. We had talked to the Scout who was to be our crew chief about our misgivings, and he assured us that he would help them out, if necessary.

On the first day of hiking, our crew was going over Clear Creek Mountain. The path was steep, and our crew would hike five minutes and then rest one minute. The boys were doing just fine and the three smaller kids were having no trouble at all. When we got up above the 8500 foot level, our troubles started.

It wasn't the Scouts who were having difficulties, it was Bill, our leader, who started having all sorts of problems. He started having altitude headaches, and the higher we went, the worse they were. The crew had changed the plan for hiking. Instead of hiking five minutes and resting one, the boys were hiking one minute and resting five. Bill's headaches were very painful, but there wasn't a whole lot we could do. Some of the kids suggested that the crew might just turn around and go back down the mountain, but Bill insisted that he could make it.

As the crew struggled along, various Scouts would come up to Bill and

*Tom ran straight at the marauding bear,
yelling and waving his flashlight.*

take part of his load to help ease his pain. When the bunch finally reached the top, it was found that the only thing Bill was carrying was just his empty pack and packframe. The three little kids we worried about were not only carrying their own gear but were carrying the biggest part of Bill's too. After that, we didn't worry any more about the three little ones making it. We decided that, if anyone survived the trip, it would be these three.

We had several Scouts from our troop, who served as camp rangers at Philmont for a number of years. We had some Scouts who were in charge of base camps and who served in other positions on the Philmont staff.

One thing we always cautioned the Scouts about was the importance of having the proper type of footwear. We would suggest that the kids get their boots a long time before leaving for Philmont, in order that they might be broken in properly. We warned them about rubbing blisters on their feet, and the fact that, since your traveled on your feet, if they hurt, you were in big trouble.

One summer we had a complete crew from our troop going to Philmont. One of the boys had big feet. He was a big Scout, and he wore a size 16 boot. His parents had ordered some boots for him since no one in our town stocked boots that large. As it got nearer to the date for their departure for Philmont, I would call Barry to find out if his boots had arrived. He would check with the store, and they would assure him that the boots would arrive in time. The day finally arrived for them to start their trip. Still, no boots! It was decided that he would take a couple of pairs of athletic shoes, to at least have something to hike in. The boots arrived the next day, but his parents and I decided that there was no way we could get the boots to Barry before the crew left on their trip. Also, I reminded his parents that the boots needed some breaking in before he started wearing them for long periods of time. So, it was decided that we wouldn't send the boots and hope that the Scout could make the trip in his tennis shoes. Barry made the trip in great shape, and said the athletic shoes were very comfortable. So much for all our worries and agonizing over the poor kid hiking around Philmont in a pair of tennis shoes.

One summer we had a crew from our troop who went on a very interesting Philmont expedition. Instead of having to use backpacks and manpower to transport their gear over the Philmont trails, they used donkeys to carry the loads. Before the crew left from home, at some of our troop meetings, the "mule-trainers" were bragging about how much easier their trip was going to be. No more totin' heavy packs over the trails. The little donkeys would carry all the load, securely and expertly, lashed to their pack saddles with a diamond hitch, while our Scouts walked along with no worry on their minds and no load on their backs. They even suggested that, as they walked daintily along, they might even stop to sniff a wild flower. One of our former Philmont expeditioners told the bragging crew that this was going to be a different type

*Here is a Scout earning his "Philmont Dragon Award."
This is earned by dragging a reluctant donkey
over the trails of Philmont.*

*The Scout earning his "Philmont Dragon Award," said
that he would have fared better if he had carried the load,
instead of the donkey carrying the equipment.*

of expedition. On this particular trip the four-legged jackasses were going to do all the work, while the two legged variety goofed off.

When the bunch returned from Philmont, we were all anxious to find out about their trip. For some unknown reason, the boys didn't seem very anxious to talk much about their trip. Finally, their outrage overcame their reluctance to talk, and we finally got the whole story. It seems that the donkeys didn't care anything about the beauties of Philmont, other than the area surrounding their pasture. To get them to go to other areas, you had to literally drag them along. One Scout said it was uncanny the way the donkeys could untie the diamond hitches used to lash the gear on the animal. The crew would top a hill and look back and see the pots, pans, sleeping bags and tents strung out along the trail. One boy insisted that it was always the last donkey in the train which threw its pack so that you never noticed the missing gear until you stopped to take a breather and happened to look back along the trail.

One kid said that he was supposed to get two "Fifty Miler Awards" for his efforts. He thought he should get one for himself and another for dragging the donkey over the trip. One boy came up with a great idea. He suggested writing to Philmont and having them come up with a new award. It was to be called "The Dragon Award" but it was to be spelled "draggin'" award. He thought that this would be a very appropriate award in as much as he had dragged that stubborn donkey over 120 miles of Philmont trails.

We never did hear much more from the mule skinners, as to how much smarter they were than the poor jokers who carried their packs on their own backs.

We still have Scouts going to Philmont almost every summer. It is a great adventure for a boy to hike around in the country and feel that he is rubbing elbows with some of the great mountain men of our western heritage. When a Scout returns from Philmont, he is a little more poised and has more confidence in his own abilities. He comes home talking a little like a mountain man, looking a little like a mountain man, and sometimes smelling a little like a mountain man.

Chapter 18
Canoe Trips

The Charles Sommers Canoe base begins near Ely, Minnesota and extends into Canada. The first year I went on a canoe trip at this base, our council had planned on three crews of ten boys each. At the last moment, one of the leaders could not go and three boys dropped out as their fathers were being transferred to another military base. The other leader, Phil Robbins, and I talked it over and decided that we could handle the larger crews. This meant that, with the guide, there would be fifteen in one crew and sixteen in the other.

When we arrived at the canoe base and talked to the people in charge, we were told that we might run into some difficulty with the large crews. They said that most of the camping areas were designed for a crew of eight boys, a guide and leader. Since there was nothing else we could do at this late moment, we would just have to chance it.

We met our guide, drew our equipment, were measured for paddles and decided just where we were going to tame the wilderness. I must confess that I was a little disappointed when I first met our guide. In my mind, I had pictured a guide as being a huge man, who weighed about three pounds less than a horse and had a voice that would put the bellow of a bull moose to shame. He would also have a head of wild red hair and a flaming beard to match.

Ken, our guide, did have a beard but the similarity ceased there. He was very quiet-spoken, was tall and slender, and his hair was cut neatly.

In my crew, we had five boys who had been on the canoe trip once before and were the largest and most muscular Scouts in the crew. We also had three little skinny kids, who probably didn't weigh 125 pounds soaking wet.

My idea was to put the smaller boys each in a canoe with a couple of the larger kids, but the little ones protested. They wanted to be with their friends, and all three wanted to be in one canoe together. In my great "wisdom," I was going to order the kids to go along with my seating arrangement in the canoes.

Ken, the guide, drew me aside and said, "Let the little ones go in one canoe. If they think they are doing it their way, they will try a lot harder to make it work."

I still worried about this arrangement, but decided to heed Ken's advice. I was in the canoe with the guide, and we had been paddling about half an hour, when a sudden thought hit me. I asked our guide where were we supposed to get drinking water? In dry West Texas, water is always a problem, and you have to be careful about the water you drink. Ken pointed to the lake and said, "Help yourself. The water in these lakes is probably better water than you get from your kitchen faucet at home."

Most of the Scouts in our crew had very little experience in a canoe. As we paddled along that first morning, we would meet crews coming in to the base camp after they had been on the trip for several days. Their canoes were traveling in a straight line, while ours looked as if we were doing a zig-zag route. One of our Scouts remarked that our crew looked as if it might be following the trail of a drunk snake. Our guide told the boys "not to worry—It wouldn't be long before we, too, could paddle in a straight line."

As we met the incoming crews, our guide would yell out, "Whole Rye! Whole Rye!" The other crew would answer back, "Whole Rye! Whole Rye!" Our guide explained that this was greeting used between crews from the Sommers Canoe Base. Whole rye was a type of bread used on the trips by canoeists. This bread looked like a cracker and tasted like it was made from old cardboard and a poor grade of wallpaper paste.

I was paddling in the bow of the guide's canoe, and as we approached the first portage, I asked him what was the proper procedure. He said you didn't run the canoes into the shore, if possible, to prevent damage to your craft. When we got close to the shore, I was to stand up, step out of the canoe, onto a rock or the bottom of the lake, and steady the canoe.

As we came in close, I stood up and stepped over the side into what, I thought, was about twelve inches of water. The clear water fooled me. Instead of twelve inches of water, I had stepped into water about six feet deep. There I was, one leg hanging over into the canoe, and the other leg frantically, reaching for the bottom. The guide was paddling like mad to keep me from overturning the canoe. I might have been able to touch the bottom, except for one thing—I wasn't eight feet tall. Ken yelled for me to let go of the canoe, so he could keep it upright. I let go with my leg and he righted the canoe. My dignity suffered a severe blow and my pride was dampened—literally.

When all the canoes came in to shore, I had to endure the slurs concern-

As we came in close, I stood up and stepped over the side into what I thought was about 12 inches of water. The clear water fooled me. Instead of a foot of water, I had stepped into water about six feet deep.

ing my great exhibition of canoeing expertise as we got ready to go across the first portage. When you come to a portage, one Scout usually carries the canoe by himself. One Scout carries the personal gear pack, containing sleeping bags and all personal gear to be used by the three boys in the canoe. The other boy carries a food pack, a cooking gear pack, or a tent and tools used by the crew.

As we were getting ready to start across the portage, I was watching the three little kids in the canoe by themselves. As the boy who was to carry the canoe tried to hoist it to his shoulders, his foot slipped, and he fell into the water, with the canoe resting on top of him. I went rushing over, fearing that the kid might drown, but when I got there and pulled the canoe away, the boy looked up at me and said, "Oh, well, I guess that I needed a bath anyway." I was about ready to go back to my original plan, but the other two little Scouts assured me that they had everything under control. They helped the boy hoist the canoe to his shoulders and we were on our way.

Our first portage was very short in length, and the crew was struggling across. As we were about half-way across, we heard the cry, "Man on the portage." This was a signal for our crew to get out of the way of the people coming across the portage. As we backed into the brush and trees lining the trail on the portage, here came the people on the portage. They were girls. They weren't walking or plodding across the portage like we were—oh no! They were trotting. Our poor kids stared at them in wonderment. One boy said, "They looked like girls, but they sure didn't act like girls." Our guide assured them that, they too, could go trotting across a portage, after they had been out for a few days.

I was in the canoe with the guide and we would go across the portage first. We would sit in the canoe and wait for the rest of the crew to come across. I would sit there, biting my nails, listening to the boys on the portage. You could hear crashes and the sound of canoes being banged into rocks, trees and other canoes. I would want to go back to help them, but the guide would tell me not to worry—that the boys would make it OK.

In the United States, the portages are nicely marked with the name of the portage and the distance. In Canada, they purposely leave the trails as wild as possible, with very few, if any, improvements. After you get into Canada, you may find trees fallen across the portage, which makes it a little difficult at times.

When we came to a portage, our guide would carry his canoe, which I shared with him. I carried a food pack, which weighed about 110 pounds. These packs, which I believe were called "Duluth Packs" were not designed to be used like a hiker's backpack where your backpack puts the weight on your shoulders. The Duluth pack was designed to carry heavy weights for a short distance. The weight in these packs was further down on your back, which made you feel a little top-heavy.

One day, as we were crossing a portage in Canada, there was a downed tree right across the trail. Our guide had gone on ahead, and I started to step over the trunk of the tree. As I did, I lost my balance and fell over on my back. I was attempting to get up with the pack, but just couldn't raise straight up. I was thrashing around and felt like some oversized beetle which had gotten on his back and couldn't turn over. About this time, I heard Ken say, "Roll over on your hands and knees and you can get up." I tried his method and got to my feet. I was thankful that none of the boys had seen me in this predicament, because I was certain that my great image as a voyager might have lost a little more of its luster.

When we first started our canoe trip, I asked our guide about the possibility of our running into a belligerent bear. Ken looked at me and said, "As big as you are you couldn't climb a tree a bear couldn't climb. You could not run as fast as a bear through the underbrush, and you can't swim as fast as a bear. You might be able to paddle a canoe faster than a bear can swim—provided that you can get a canoe." I assured him that I wouldn't try to climb a tree to escape a mad bear, but I sure might try outrunning him through the underbrush.

We saw several bears along the shores of the lakes, but didn't see any very near to us. One morning, we were going across a portage and heard a loud crashing noise in the brush along the trail ahead of us. When we reached the water, we saw several big bear tracks which were very fresh. It appeared that the bear was more frightened of us than we were of him. I was glad that the bear had run off without our confronting him. I was afraid that my image of the "Great North-woodsman" might have lost a little more of its luster if the kids had seen me running frantically through the dense underbrush, knocking down small trees, with a mad bear on my tail.

Ken, our guide, had told us that there were no snakes in Canada. All of us had been raised in West Texas which has all four poisonous species of snakes. It was comforting, though, to know that, when it was necessary to get out of your canoe to push it through one of these "pot-holes," filled with black water and reeds, you didn't have to worry about a cottonmouth water moccasin crawling up your pants leg. One day I was down by the lake washing out some socks, when this "thing" came swimming through the water. It was a foot long and, at first glance, I thought it was a snake.

I yelled for our guide to come check it out. When he saw it, he laughed and told me it was a "leech." It was a chocolate brown color with some orange spots. We had leeches in the waters at home, but nothing like this huge specimen. I called for the boys to come see this thing. We kidded some of the smaller ones about being carried away by the leech and eaten. The guide assured us that these large ones hardly ever bothered human beings, and that the ones we would have to contend with were the small leeches found lurking in those "pot-holes."

The tents we used were small and meant to hold two people or three at the most. Since our crew was so large, fifteen total, sleeping at night presented a few problems. Most of the campsites were so small we could only put up three tents at night. This meant that five people were sleeping in a tent designed for three campers. This was a test for true "togetherness." When someone turned over at night, we all had to turn in unison.

Several of the boys in my tent had a tendency to snore when sleeping on their backs. When they all got to going at once, the volume compared favorably with the Mormon Tabernacle Choir, but the harmony was awful.

One of the boys in my tent was known to walk in his sleep. I slept next to the door, which was covered with mosquito-proof mesh. The idea was, if the boy started walking in his sleep, he would have to crawl out over me and would wake me up.

One night I was lying there trying to go to sleep, but it was broad daylight outside. In Canada, where we were, it didn't get dark until about 12 o'clock at night. For once, the kids were sleeping peacefully with no snoring, but I was having a hard time trying to doze off.

Suddenly, I became aware of this noise like a distant airplane. I listened but the noise didn't seem to grow any louder. I decided to go outside to check it out. When I opened the tent flap, I discovered the source of the noise. Right outside our door, covered by the mosquito netting, was a humongous cloud of mosquitoes. The noise, which I thought was a distant plane, was made by their buzzing, and their sheer numbers blocked out the light coming in our doorway.

I lay there for a few minutes watching this cloud of bloodthirsty predators. I hoped that none of my boys would have to get up to go tinkle because, once the mosquito mesh was opened, we would be engulfed by about a jillion mosquitoes coming into our tent. None of my tentmates had to avail themselves of the latrine, that night. I finally decided that they were all blessed with exceptional kidneys, or just maybe, they weren't going outside to tinkle. Several mornings, there were strange puddles in our tent, but when I checked them out with the boys, they assured me that the puddles were caused by the condensation from our breath inside the tightly closed tent—I'll never know!

The mosquitoes were bad, but the biting flies were terrible. There were three sizes of these pests—one was about the size of a housefly, the middle-sized one was about the size of a yellow jacket, and the large economy size was a black and white spotted monster about the size of a large wasp. When this last one bit you it brought blood. Once you were out on the lake away from the trees, the mosquitoes left you alone—Not so, with these pesky flies. They had the uncanny ability to land on a spot on your back, which was impossible to reach from the side, over your shoulder, or reaching up from your belt.

When you couldn't reach the fly, you had to call on your buddy, sitting in the canoe behind you, to give you a little aid and comfort. This was usually accomplished by his swatting the biting fly with his paddle. Since this was done, quite often, with more force than finesse, your ended up getting rid of the fly but having the breath knocked out of you.

Our second day out from the base camp was a rough one. We went over fifteen portages. Some of these were about fifty yards long, and some were much longer. One of these portages had been named "Yum Yum," by some joker with a sadistic sense of humor. This portage was one of the worst I had ever encountered on canoe trips and float trips down the Rio Grande. The only portage worse than "Yum Yum" is one called the "Rock Slide" in Santa Elena Canyon in the Big Bend National Park.

On this second day there was an eclipse of the sun. Our guide had thoughtfully brought along some pieces of film negative and some tinted glass through which to look at the sun. As we lay there in the canoes, looking at the sun, our tired muscles were aching and we were being slowly devoured by clouds of mosquitoes and biting flies. One of the boys expressed my sentiments exactly. He remarked, "I am so tired that the only thing which could impress me would be if the sun fell completely out of the sky."

Con Mee was to be our layover stop. We really enjoyed camping there as we could relax after several days of pushing ourselves. We did a little laundry and a lot of fishing.

There was a coffee can nailed to a tree and in it were lots of messages written by crews who had stayed at Con Mee over the past several years. We found some names of our own troop members, who had gone on the canoe trip several years before. The messages would tell about their fishing luck and some of the adventures they experienced in getting to Con Mee.

About the time of my first canoe trip, the television show "Candid Camera" was very popular. Since we swam in the buff, a bathing suit was just one more useless item to carry, you were fair game for anyone with a camera. As you stood there, flexing your muscles, preparing to dive into the clear waters of the lake, you would hear someone say sweetly, "Smile! You're on Candid Camera." The click of the shutter closing was bad enough, but the more terrifying sound was the gentle whirring noise as they recorded your every move on a movie camera.

This got to be so bad that several members of our crew were stricken with a new disease, which our guide named "Camera-Phobia." The symptoms were very easy to spot. The victims complained of tight, stiff neck muscles, caused by constantly turning your head from side to side, and the gradual wearing away of your spinal cord. This last was caused by revolving your head like a

S-M-I-L-E!
You're on <u>CANDID CAMERA!</u>

beacon as you tried to spot some sneaky devil, with a camera, as he came slithering through the brush to take your picture.

Not too long ago, I saw a television special of the best of "Candid Camera" reruns taken through the years. Frankly, I was a little disappointed. I felt that many of the pictures taken on our canoe trip were just as interesting and funny as any of those old reruns. Maybe the world just isn't ready for great photography like we shared on the canoe trip.

It was at Con Mee that I had my first experience with "gunnel jumping." This is done by standing on the stern of the canoe and moving your weight up and down. This causes the canoe to move through the water, and with a little practice, you can turn the canoe by shifting your weight.

One of our best pictures taken on the canoe trip of my crew chief, Jim, a very muscular young man, as he engaged in a little "gunnel jumping." He was not wearing anything but a broad smile and a red and white polkadotted cap. The smile was one of contentment and accomplishment as he finally mastered the art of "gunnel jumping."

We left Con Mee and started over to the Horse River country. One day my boys came to me and wanted to paddle into the town of Ely, Minnesota. I reminded them we didn't have any money with us, and I just couldn't see paddling the extra sixty miles into town and back with no money to spend. They persisted so I told them, "I have two one dollar bills with me. If you can raise $5 by pooling your money along with my money, we'll go into Ely." They got all of the money together and could only come up with $3.65, so I told them the trip to Ely was out of the question.

We had an unusual situation in our crew. Out of the thirteen boys in our group, five were named Bill. When I yelled for Bill I always got some response. Never 100%, but three out of five isn't too bad. One of the Bills in our group was one of the larger kids, and had an appetite and a bad case of laziness to match his size. He had a bad habit which was causing a lot of grumbling among the other members of our crew. Each afternoon, when we pulled in to spend the night, all members had a job to do. The two boys, who were our permanent cooks, along with our guide, got ready to prepare supper. Some of the crew put up the tents and some collected wood for the cook fires. Two Scouts were assigned to wash dishes after the meal and one was given the job of making the latrine.

Our lazy Bill had a cute trick. As soon as we hit the shore, he would grab his fishing rod and go off fishing. He would usually return just in time to eat. This had been going on for several days, when the crew chief and assistant crew chief came to me. They said they were tired of Bill not doing his job and wanted my permission to try a little disciplinary action. I told them I just finished building the latrine, which was Bill's job, and, anything short of tying a rock around his neck and tossing him into the lake, was fine with me.

That evening, we lined up to eat and our lazy one was first in line. Our crew chief walked up to him and said, "Bill, you're not going to eat supper. You haven't been doing your job, and no work—no eat." Bill bristled up and said that he'd eat anyway.

Our crew chief told him he was going to have to whip him first. Then the assistant crew chief told him he was going to have to whip him second. Then George, one of the largest, most muscular kids in the crew, told Bill, "After you get through with them, I'll be waiting."

Bill decided in a hurry, that muscles wouldn't get him anything except a few contusions and abrasions, and that he had better try a little diplomacy. He came to me whining about the fact that they wouldn't let him eat, and wanted me to do something about it. I told him that I had to dig the latrine, which was his job, and that I really didn't care whether he ever got anything to eat.

Bill decided that, in talking to me, his plea was falling on deaf ears. He decided to appeal to Ken, our guide. Ken told him that he was hired to guide us on our trip and see that we got back safely. Any disciplinary action to be taken was the business of the members of the crew and their advisor.

So, our lazy one didn't get to eat that night. The next morning, our crew chief told him that if he didn't do his job that day, he could expect the same treatment. It was amazing what a change was visible in Bill. He did his job and did it well. We decided that his love of eating was stronger than his dislike for work. That was the last and only time we had any problems with discipline on the entire trip.

One day we paddled up to this trading post out in the wilds of Canada. It was operated by a family from Oklahoma. They would keep it open until the weather got bad and then close it up for the winter. They showed us a spot on the flagpole which represented the average level of the snow in the wintertime. This spot was about 20 feet up the pole, which made us West Texas boys decide that the few piddling snows we had didn't amount to much when compared to the blizzards they had. The family told us that they spent the winters in Oklahoma, and returned to Canada when the snows had melted in the spring.

Remember, I told you that the entire crew had only $3.65, and two dollars of this amount was mine. We all managed to get a Coke or a piece of candy, but it didn't take long to deplete our funds. The kids wandered around in the trading post, drooling over all of the stuff on display. One item which all of the kids wanted was a red beret. They thought this would make them look like French Voyagers and would add to their image as northwoodsmen. The owner of the trading post overheard some of the boys expressing a desire to buy these items. He came to me, but I told him that we didn't have any money on the trip.

He told us to pick out what we wanted and send him a money order when we got back to the first post office. I reminded him that he didn't know us and that he was taking a chance trusting us. He sort of grinned and told me, "If I can't trust Boy Scouts, I guess that there isn't anyone I can trust." I told the boys and they started doing their shopping. When they had finished, the bill was over $80. I had made a list as the boys piled their purchases on the counter, and asked the owner to check the list with me. He said that wasn't necessary and accepted my figures.

When we left the trading post with all of our goodies, I pointed out to the boys the good name of Scouting. Here was a man, who had never seen us before, but trusted us to the tune of more than $80, just because we were Boy Scouts.

When we got to Ely, Minnesota on our return trip, I made sure that he received the money order for items we bought. I used to get a Christmas card from the owner and his family each Christmas. The last one I got said that he was selling the trading post and returning to Oklahoma for good. It's sort of refreshing to find that there are still people in the world who have an abiding faith in the goodness of their fellow man.

As we started our long swing back to the Southeast to return to the canoe base, I had something happen one day which really startled me. One canoe, with three of the older Scouts, who had been up here the previous summer, had got ahead of us, and was about half a mile in front. As the guide and I paddled around the neck of land sticking out into the lake, I saw a sight which really blew my mind. The canoe had disappeared and two of the boys were standing on top of the water, literally. When we got a little nearer to the water walkers, I could see how they managed this. When they were up here the summer before, the boys had found this spot where the rocks come up to a few inches below the surface of the water. The two had sent the third boy and the canoe to hide in some convenient brush along the shore.

When we first spotted them, they were yelling for help and waving their arms. I couldn't figure what had happened to the canoe, or how these two had suddenly acquired enough faith to allow them to walk on the water. We had a good laugh and the guide marked the rocks on his map to warn the people back at the canoe base. He thought it might be a good idea to prevent someone from crashing into the rocks and ruining a canoe.

The latrines we constructed on the canoe trip were works of art. The appointed latrine builder would first find two convenient trees with forks about two feet from the ground. He would dig the hole and then place a strong pole in the forks of the trees, so that it went over the hole in the ground. Here you could sit in comfort, surveying the beauties of nature, while going about your business. On this particular canoe trip, we had three tragic or humorous accidents concerning our latrine.

Three times, the latrine builder had chosen a pole which was rotten, was partially eaten through by the bugs, or just wasn't strong enough to support a person doing the heavy thinking. When the pole broke, it was tragic if you happened to be the one using the latrine. It was humorous if you happened to be one of the onlookers. After the third accident, we all tested the latrine pole to make sure it would hold up under the most serious thinking.

We returned to the canoe base with no further mishaps, where we checked in our equipment and enjoyed a bath in the sauna. A delicious meal of turkey and dressing and all of the fixings, really hit the spot.

At night, all of the canoe crews get together to report on their trips and put on a few skits. There is always a lot of rivalry among the crews to see which one had gone on the longest trip to set a new record.

Several crews had reported when Jim, our crew chief got up and announced, "You'll be happy to know that our crew just set a new record." Immediately, all the other crews wanted to know how far we traveled and where we went. Jim held up his hand for silence and with a straight face announced, "We had more people fall in the latrine than ever before on a canoe trip. Three of our crew paid the penalty of having a faulty latrine maker." The other crews started laughing and yelling, and Jim's announcement just about broke up the meeting.

After an uneventful trip we returned home to dry West Texas. We wished for just a few of those lakes we had seen in Canada and Minnesota. A large crowd of parents was on hand to greet us and we received a hero's welcome. We casually mentioned portaging, gunnel jumping and whole rye. To hear us tell it, we were a combination of the French Voyagers, members of the Lewis and Clark Expedition, with a little bit of Hiawatha thrown in for good measure.

Chapter 19
Order of the Arrow

In case you didn't know, the Order of the Arrow is an honor campers' society based on Indian lore. To become a member of this select group, one must be voted into the organization by the members of your own unit. A candidate is tapped out, usually at a council fire presided over by the Order of the Arrow. After being tapped out, the person must go through an arduous series of tests known as the "Ordeal Ceremony."

The Order of the Arrow is often called "The Brotherhood of Cheerful Service." O. A. members have given many hours of service in good-turn projects which helped their units, their community and their council.

The members of this group take great pride in the fact that they have helped to preserve our great Indian heritage. This is done mainly through their costumes, dances and ceremonies. Order of the Arrow members spend many hours making authentic Indian costumes, using the same materials the Native Americans used.

Since this is a very serious organization, the ceremonies are conducted in such a manner as to leave no place for humor. Because of the very seriousness of these ceremonies, any goof-up which happened, seemed to be more humorous than one in a less serious ceremony. O. A. members flubbing their lines, or a council fire which refused to be lit, always brought chuckles and giggles from the audience.

Through the years I have seen many beautiful Order of the Arrow ceremonies. I have also seen many ceremonies where something unexpected forced the O. A. members to make a radical departure from the original script. I would like to share with you some of these more humorous events. This is not to poke fun at the O. A , because, after one of these unfortunate things had taken place, the members, themselves, had a good laugh over the foul-up in their ceremony.

After I became Scoutmaster of Troop 1, our first summer camp was at Camp Sol Mayer, on the San Saba River. The council ring, at that time, was located near the swimming area in the river. Near the council ring, a small hill with a road, sloped gently away from the river, up to the higher ground where the first aid station and the training lodge were located.

This first council fire was presided over by the O. A., even though this was not their night for the "Tap-out" ceremony. The Indian group had gone through a fire lighting ceremony and the council fire was burning brightly.

The camp director was in the midst of his speech in which he welcomed the boys to camp, and hoped they enjoyed the week to come. Just as he was finishing his speech, we heard this terrible Comanche war whoop from the top of the hill. We all looked up and saw this Comanche warrior sitting on a beautiful palomino horse. The Indian was dressed in a full war bonnet of white feathers, leather leggings and mocassins, and a decorated leather vest completed his costume.

Even as we sat there in awe, the Indian came galloping down the hill, uttering war whoops at every jump, and rode into the council ring. His face and chest were streaked with war paint and he had a very fierce appearance.

When he rode into the council ring, I could see that this wild Indian was our beloved camp ranger, Buddy Wyman, and his beautiful horse. He spoke a few words of welcome to the few remaining Scouts and then galloped up the hill into the darkness.

When he first came charging down the hill, we lost the biggest part of our audience. The kids had scattered like a bunch of quail and were out in the darkness, peering around trees and up over the river bank. Even the O. A. members admitted that Buddy had taken them by surprise.

We finally coaxed all the Scouts back to the council fire, but you could tell that they were still a little uneasy. The boys kept glancing up to the top of the hill, and one little Scout told me that he wouldn't have been surprised at all to see a herd of wild buffalo come charging over the hill.

Buddy usually led the singing after the meals in the dining hall. He told me that several Scouts came up to him and asked him if he had played the part of the Indian on the horse. When he admitted that he was the one, they would look him up and down and say, "You sure don't look like that guy who was wearing all the war paint."

The second year I took my troop to camp, I was tapped out by the O. A. My family came down to camp and were at the council fire. I was sitting with my family when the O. A. members came around and yanked me to my feet. I was tapped on the shoulder and a wreath, made of cedar branches, was placed around my neck. I was shoved, none too gently, to the center of the council ring, where I was pushed to the ground.

My little daughter, Jan, was only four at the time. She couldn't stand to see her daddy treated like this. She jerked away from my wife and other daughter Judy and came running out to where the Lodge Chief was standing over me. She began beating him on the legs with her tiny fists, and all the time she was yelling, "You leave my Daddy alone! Don't hurt my Daddy!"

All around the council ring people were laughing, and the chief's face got redder than the war paint he was wearing. Jan continued to beat on the chief's legs and kept on yelling at him not to hurt me.

Finally my wife came out and rescued the chief by pulling my daughter away and explaining to her that this ceremony was only a game. Jan was pacified, but the chief stayed away from where my wife and daughters were sitting.

The boy, who was Chief of the lodge at that time, later admitted to me that this was the only time in his life he had been beaten up by a four year old girl.

One year at summer camp, several members of our troop were candidates for the Order of the Arrow. After the Tap-out, the boys were placed on silence. They came to our campsite where they got a blanket or their sleeping bags and reported back to the O. A. members. Each boy had to spend the night alone in the woods, and had to keep a fire burning all night.

During the Ordeal Ceremony, each boy had to maintain silence for twenty-four hours. If a candidate forgot and spoke three words or more, an additional hour of silence was the penalty. Some of the boys came up with an idea to help them maintain silence.

A bit, like a horse's bit, was made from a small branch of a tree. This was secured in the boy's mouth by tying a piece of string to one end of the bit, passing it around the back of the head, and tying it to the other end of the bit. This held the bit in place and was supposed to prevent the candidate from talking.

After spending the night in the open, the Scouts worked on various service projects, which were part of the Ordeal Ceremony. At noon we saw them when they came to the dining hall for their very meager meal. They took their bits out when eating, but most of them were wearing them around their necks so that they could be returned to their mouths after eating.

Late in the afternoon, I was going down the trail which led to the council ring. One of my Scouts, Frank, who was one of the O. A. candidates, was sitting by the side of the trail. He had his head down and I asked him if he felt bad. When he raised his head I could see what was the matter. His face and lips were so swollen that he could hardly see. I rushed him up to the hospital building and the medic checked him over to see what was causing the swelling. Suddenly I had an idea as to the cause of all his misery. The medic and I checked the bit he was wearing, and found that the Scout had made one slight error.

He had picked up a stick along the trail to make his bit and had accidentally chosen a piece of poison ivy vine. Wearing the bit in his mouth for almost twenty-four hours had caused quite a severe case of poison ivy.

We put Frank in the hospital where he spent the next two days. He never did get in the Order of the Arrow. Later he jokingly told me that his experience during the Ordeal Ceremony had "poisoned" his desire to ever become a member of the O. A.

One year at summer camp the Order of the Arrow members had planned quite an elaborate ceremony for the tap-out. There were to be several dances and the event was to begin with a spectacular lighting of the council fire.

We had a new council ring that year and the facilities of the new ring were so much better than the old one. Giant pecan and live oak trees surrounded the area which was very near the river. As you sat in the council ring, you could look across the river and see the road, which crossed the river at a low water crossing, curving slightly as it climbed to the top of a low hill several hundred yards away.

It was the year of the Olympics and the O. A. boys had decided to have several runners to carry a flaming torch until the final runner would run into the council ring and light the fire.

After it got dark you could see the first runner light the torch at the top of the hill and start his run. Each runner was to run about 100 yards and then pass the torch to the next man.

The first runner ran his course and passed the torch on to the next man. The second runner came on down the road and gave the torch to a man who was standing near the shallow crossing. He took the torch and splashed across the river.

The people in the council ring could watch the passage of the torch, and it was an impressive sight. Each runner was dressed in his Indian costume and you could see him plainly in the glaring light from the torch. As the runners got nearer the council ring, you could even hear the tinkling of the bells attached to their costumes.

The next to last runner traveled up the road, which ran almost parallel to the council ring, and then crossed over to the house where the Camp Ranger lived. The last runner was to receive the torch and run down the hill into the council ring and light the fire.

All eyes were on the final runner as he started down the hill to the council ring, and this was about the spot where fate took over. You know how you can start running down a hill, and, if you're not careful, your body seems to get ahead of your legs and you usually wind up taking a nasty spill.

This is exactly what happened to our last runner with the torch. He came barrelling down the hill and started losing his balance. Just as he reached the edge of the council ring, he fell—and horrors of horrors — the torch went out.

No one seemed to know just what to do. One of the visiting parents had the answer to the problem. He was sitting near the spot where the boy and torch hit the ground. The visitor got up, walked over to the boy and asked him about any possible injuries. The only injury to the O. A. member was a severe case of bruised dignity and a couple of skinned knees. The man picked up the torch, took out his cigarette lighter and relit the torch.

The runner limped down to the fire lay, and got the council fire started. There was a lot of applause and cheering for the runner and for the quick thinking visitor.

The Chief of the Lodge later told me that when the torch went out, he didn't know just what to do. He said there certainly were no pockets in his breech cloth where he might have a few matches stashed away.

After the council fire, we checked with the man who had come to the rescue with his cigarette lighter. We found out that he was a former member of the Order of the Arrow, and had experienced a few difficulties when putting on ceremonies back in his Scouting days. We told him that we felt that his quick thinking had saved the whole ceremony from becoming a disaster.

Another fire-lighting scheme in this same council ring almost ended in a tragedy. A wire had been run from a limb high up in one of the trees surrounding the council ring. The wire stretched from the limb down to the fire lay in the ring. A large wad of rags and string had been wound around the wire to form a ball. This ball had been very generously saturated with Boy Scout water, kerosene to you.

The idea behind this plan was as the Medicine Man danced around the fire lay and implored the spirits to send down fire from heaven, the boy in the tree was to light the ball of rags. After it was well lit, he was to give it a push and it was supposed to slide down the wire into the fire lay and start the council fire.

Everything went as planned —for a while. The Medicine Man asked the spirits for fire from heaven, the boy in the tree lit the kerosene soaked rags and the fireball blazed up brightly. But when the boy tried to push the blazing ball down the wire, it refused to move.

When we looked up in the tree the boy was sitting on the limb with the flames all around him. He was trying to protect his face and hands from the fire, all the while frantically kicking at the burning rags, trying to get the fire ball to slip down the wire.

He finally managed to get the blazing rags to slip down the wire a few feet, where it stopped again. However, this was far enough to avoid the danger of his being roasted alive, and we told him to stay in the tree until we could send him some help.

A couple of O.A. members, carrying ropes, climbed up the where our almost barbecued Scout sat. He assured them that he was OK but they decided not to take any chances with his injuries. They tied a rope around his chest and lowered him to the ground. The camp medic examined him and found that his burns were not serious. His eyebrows and eyelashes were singed, as was the hair at the front of his head. He had a couple of small burns on his hands, and a slight burn on one of his feet. This was caused by his kicking the fireball and one of his moccasins was scorched. This was the last time the O.A. used the "fireball from heaven" method for lighting a council fire.

Another method which was tried in lighting the council fire was the flaming arrow. A wire was stretched from outside the council ring to where the fire lay was placed. An arrow, to which was fastened a ball of flammable material, was attached to the wire.

The idea was to light the flammable material and then shoot the arrow along the wire into the fire lay. This had worked well in practice, and the O.A. members felt they had a very impressive way of lighting their council fire.

That evening, as the Chief of the Lodge danced around the ring, imploring the gods to send down fire, the O.A. member lit the arrow and sent it speeding toward the fire lay. The arrow stuck in the wood but the ball of fire kept on going and lay on the ground, several feet from the stack of wood.

The chief was equal to the occasion. Without missing a step, the chief danced over to where the fire ball lay blazing on the ground, scooped up the fire and pitched it into the fire lay. It was done so gracefully that many of the audience thought it was part of the plan.

After the ceremony was over, I suggested to the chief, that before they used the flaming arrow bit again, he had better flame-proof his costume. With all of the feathers in his costume, picking up a ball of fire in his hands might result in his tail feathers becoming slightly singed.

When I was going through the Ordeal Ceremony, I had spent the night in the woods alone, had maintained twenty-four hours of silence, and had worked hard on the service projects dreamed up by the members of the O.A. We had been fed a good meal and had been allowed to break silence for about an hour. We went back on silence again and were taken to the small, secret Order of the Arrow council ring. We were blindfolded and ordered to sit on the ground in a line. The night before, as we were taken to the spot to spend the night, the O.A. members told us to look into the burning fire and do some deep soul-searching. We were instructed to make vows to lead a better life, to be of more service to our community and to set a better example for the other Scouts.

Since the O.A. council ring was very small, we candidates could hear everything which was said. The O.A. members would lead the blindfolded candidate into the council ring, where he was instructed to kneel in front of the Lodge Chief. The chief would ask each one to repeat his vows, and admonish him to try to live up to these vows. The boy, who was in front of me in line, was very nervous. When we were allowed to break silence, earlier in the afternoon, he had confessed to me that he just knew that he was going to make some stupid mistake which would ruin his chances of getting into the Order of the Arrow. When it came time for him to go in to the chief, I could hear the bells on the moccasins of the O.A. members as they escorted him into the council ring. He was told to kneel before the Lodge Chief. The chief said, "Candidate Sawyer, what are your vows?" The boy answered, "A—E—I—O—U and sometimes Y." In his nervousness, I suppose the boy misunderstood him and thought the chief said "vowels."

When I heard his answer, I just fell over on the ground and started laughing. I just had to laugh even if it meant not getting into the O.A. I found that I wasn't the only one who got a charge out of the boy's answer. Even the chief had to struggle to keep from laughing. Incidentally, the boy did make it into the O.A. but every time I hear anyone mention vows, I think back to that poor nervous kid, trying so hard to make the O.A., and his answer, which was a classic.

The Camp Ranger had constructed a huge arrow which was to be used in Order of the Arrow ceremonies. The arrow, made from three inch pipe welded together set at about a forty-five degree angle and had four legs made from the same type of pipe. This piece of equipment was very sturdy, but it took four husky O.A. members to move it. Usually the arrow was wrapped in burlap, and doused thoroughly in kerosene. It was lighted during the Tap-out ceremony and made quite a spectacular display.

One summer camp, the boys in the O.A. decided that the arrow would show up much better if it was placed out in the shallow water of the river. After wrapping the arrow with burlap, and tying the material in place, the boys carried the arrow out into the river, where the water was about three feet deep. They drenched the burlap with kerosene and decided that everything was in readiness.

Everyone was assembled in the council ring. The ceremony was to begin with an archer, standing on the shore, shooting a flaming arrow at the big arrow in the river. This was to light the big arrow, which was the signal for the ceremony to begin. The archer lit the ball of flammable material on his arrow and sent it flying through the night sky to where the big arrow stood in the river. He hit the large arrow, but the burlap didn't ignite. He tried again and the same thing happened. The archer tried and tried until he had exhausted his supply of arrows—still no fire on the big arrow.

In desperation, finally, an O.A. member waded out to the arrow in the

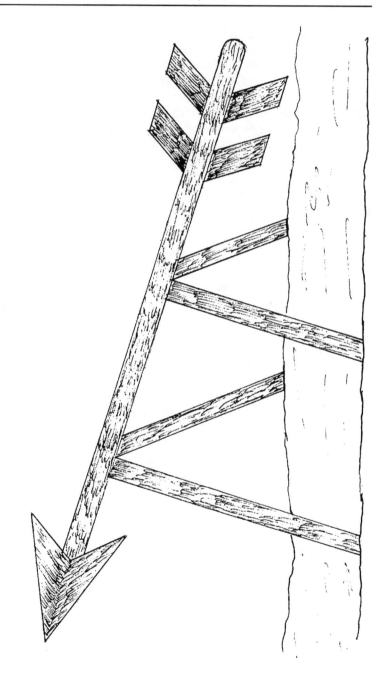

The Order of the Arrow had made a huge arrow out of pieces of three inch pipe. This piece of equipment was very impressive when used as part of the Indian ceremonies.

river and tried to light it with a match. He couldn't even light it with a match. We decided later that the burlap had soaked up enough moisture, rising up from the river, to make the burlap almost fire proof. At least, the burlap was immune to our puny efforts using flaming arrows and matches. The arrow still stood in the river the next day as a silent reminder that sometimes, even the best laid plans go awry.

I have witnessed several O.A. ceremonies in which snakes of the non-poisonous variety were used. Most of the time bull snakes were used, because they grow very large and make an impressive sight.

One night we had a large number of visitors, who had come to camp for the Order of the Arrow Tap-Out. The Chief of the Lodge, followed by several O.A. members was stalking around the council ring. He would stop in front of a candidate, who was pulled to his feet by two O.A. members. The brave, carrying the big Bull Snake, would shove it into the face of the candidate and he would receive the taps on the shoulders to symbolize the tap-out portion of the ceremony.

The ceremony was going quite well until the snake managed to wriggle free from the grasp of the brave. The reptile hit the ground and started crawl- ing swiftly to where most of our audience was seated. We had instant panic. Women were screaming, little children were crying, and a few brave men were seen climbing up on the seats of the folding chairs, in which they had been seated. The chief was trying to restore order by telling the guests that the snake was harmless. Most of the women were of the opinion that they didn't care to have any kind of snake crawling around their legs.

We finally got the audience settled down a little. This was accomplished by moving all the people, who had been sitting on the side where the snake was headed, to the opposite side of the council ring. This mass exodus didn't completely calm them down. For the rest of the ceremony, if a bug landed on someone's arm or neck or a blade of grass touched their leg, there were muffled screams. They just knew that monstrous snake was about to pounce on them. We never did find the poor snake. One O.A. member suggested that, when all of the screaming started, the poor snake became so frightened that he was probably still running—crawling, that is.

One summer, the Camp director and the members of the Order of the Arrow decided to move the council ring across the river from the present location. A series of rock ledges, almost like steps, sloped gently away from the river, and made a natural amphitheater for the ceremonies. The council fire was usually built just a few feet from the edge of the river, and the flames created a beautiful reflection in the water.

On this particular night, all of the guests were seated, and the troops of Scouts had found their places around the council ring. A member of the O.A. had lit the council fire and soon, the flames spread in the fire lay. Around a bend in the river one could hear the muffled drumbeats. As the sound of the drums increased, the first canoes came in sight. They were traveling single file, and were paddled by the O.A. members in all of their Indian finery. It was quite an impressive sight. There were no sounds at all except the beat of the drums.

The lead canoe really made a hit with the audience. One lone brave paddled the craft, while the chief stood in the bow on the canoe, with his arms folded across his chest. He had a scowl on his face and was decked out in all his glory, complete with feathered war bonnet. A light had been placed in the bow of the canoe so that it shone on the chief. Before the canoe got near the light from the council fire, the chief stood bathed in the rays of the light in the canoe and the rest of the canoe was in darkness.

It made it appear that the chief was gliding across the surface of the water. The audience appreciated this bit of showmanship, and one could hear appreciative murmurs and "ooohs" and "aaahs" as the people reacted to this spectacle. All went well until the chief's canoe arrived near the spot where the chief was to step from the canoe onto the river bank and then proceed to the council ring.

The brave paddling the canoe suddenly realized that he had gone too far past the landing spot. He made an abrupt turn in the river and the chief went sailing out of the canoe. The water wasn't very deep at this spot, about four feet, and the chief stood up and started wading ashore. As he squished into the council ring, an expression my grandmother used to say flashed through my mind. "Mad as a wet hen" was her saying, and I felt it very appropriate on this occasion, because the chief resembled a wet hen. The feathers of his beautiful war bonnet hung down around his face and his whole appearance was a little bedraggled. The water, running down his legs and into his moccasins, made a squishing noise with each step he took. It sounded sort of like a cow pulling her hoof out of a mudhole.

But you have to give the chief credit for overcoming a very embarrassing situation. After he came into the council ring, he went ahead with the ceremony, as if nothing had happened. When he had finished the ceremony, a parent in the audience stood up and said, "I think we should give the chief a round of applause. This young man demonstrated the spirit of Scouting by completing his duty in the face of great adversity."

Everyone must have agreed—they gave him a standing ovation. As he stood there with the audience clapping and cheering, it was great to notice that he even managed a small grin. Later, he was able to laugh at what must have been one of the most embarrassing events in his life.

Through the years, the Order of the Arrow has provided great ceremonies for Scout camps, camporees, Scout expositions and circuses, and courts of honor. Through their dedication to the O.A., its members have helped us

The chief stood in the bow of the canoe with a light shining on him. He looked as if he were gliding across the surface of the river.

to appreciate our great Indian heritage. The Order of the Arrow, by means of its costumes, dances and customs, has helped us to remember the great Indian tribes which once roamed our part of the United States.

And if you think the O.A. doesn't make an impression on the young campers, ask any first year camper about his memories of summer camp. High up on his list will be "Those Indian guys who danced around carrying snakes in their hands."

So, to the Order of the Arrow: May your "Brotherhood of Cheerful Service" live forever. In this day and age, it is very refreshing to find an organization whose main goal is service to others. Keep up the good work.

Chapter 20
Swim Meets

At one time Swim Meets were a very important part of the program of our council. At the district level, Boy Scout troops, Explorer posts, and sometimes, even Cub Scout packs competed against one another in their own age bracket. The winners in each event went to the Council Swim Meet where they competed against the winners from each district.

Our troop was blessed with a number of excellent swimmers through the years and won more than our share of the district meets. We were able to send a number of Scouts to the council meets, where we fared very well.

One summer, the council meet was to be held in Junction, Texas. The event itself was to be held in the Llano River. The swimming events were to take place in a very wide portion of the river, where there was little current. The races were designed to be run upstream, except in the case of the relay races, in which two members would have to swim upstream, and two would get to swim downstream.

One of my Scouts, George, who had qualified for the finals in the freestyle, came to me with this idea of his. He decided that, if he swam nearer the bank, the current would be less, and this would give him a decided advantage.

I pointed out to him that the current was almost negligible, and I didn't think it would make any difference. He insisted that his theory was correct and wanted my permission to try it. I told him that it was OK with me, but to check with the people who were in charge of the meet.

George checked with them and they told him he could swim anywhere in the river. When the swimmers lined up for the start of the 100 yard freestyle race, our boy was about thirty feet away from his nearest competitor.

The other boys in the race kidded George about his wanting to be alone. He assured them that he had a plan which would assure him first place in the race.

When the gun sounded, our boy was away like a flash. At the halfway mark he was about twenty feet ahead of his nearest competitor. I had decided that maybe he had a point about this swimming near the bank to get away from the current. I was watching George when suddenly he came to a shuddering halt and then stood up in the water. The water there was about four feet deep, and when he turned around, I could see what had caused him to come to such a sudden stop. He had run into a rock which was sticking up in the river almost to the surface. He had plowed into this slight obstacle and had cut his nose and forehead, and had loosened a couple of his front teeth. We hauled him out of the river and had a doctor examine him. It was soon evident that the only permanent damage was that suffered by the rock when it was in collision with his hard head. George later went on a canoe trip with our troop, and the other kids used to kid him about being sure to paddle next to the bank to get out of the current.

One summer the Council Swim Meet was held in San Angelo at the Central High School indoor pool. We had qualified several boys and two relay teams for the finals. One kid, Sam, was a very good swimmer and was to swim in the freestyle race and on one of the relay teams. He was a tall lanky boy who was very narrow in the hips.

The bathing suits back then were quite different from the ones used now. Those used today look and fit more like a second skin. The ones used then were more like P.E. shorts, with a drawstring to hold them on you.

In this race, the swimmers had to swim the length of the pool twice. Sam started off well and was about fifteen feet ahead of the boy swimming in second place. When Sam made the last turn and started up the length of the pool, I was standing about halfway up the pool. It was evident our boy was having some difficulty. He had slowed down, and I thought that maybe he was just getting tired.

When he passed by where I was standing by the pool, I understood his problem. The drawstring in his trunks had broken, and the trunks had slipped completely down around his ankles. He was swimming mainly with his arms because he couldn't kick his legs with the trunks acting like a hobble.

As he swam, his bare bottom bounced up and down in the water, and you could hear people laughing sitting in the stands. Sam went on to win the race. When he got to the end of the pool, he ducked under the water, pulled up his trunks and ran to the dressing room. We couldn't even get him to come out to receive his award.

At the Council Swim Meet in Fort Stockton, we had something to happen in one of the relay races which was the funniest incident ever in a swim meet. This humorous occurrence cost us the race, but our whole team laughed about it all the way home from the event.

This particular race was the Medley Relay. If you are not familiar with the rules, it goes like this: the first swimmer swims the breast stroke; the second swimmer swims the side stroke; the third swimmer swims the back stroke; and the last one swims the freestyle.

In Boy Scout swim meets, the swimmers are not allowed to dive to start their races. In the relay race, the first two swimmers were in the water on opposite sides of this large pool, about 40 yards across. The other two swimmers sat on the edge of the pool directly behind the boys in the water.

When the gun sounded, the first swimmer crossed the pool and touched the second swimmer. As the first two were swimming, the other two boys slipped into the pool and waited while their team members crossed the pool. When he was touched, the third swimmer swam across the pool where he touched the last swimmer on the team.

The last swimmer on our relay team was Richard, who was to swim the freestyle leg of the race. As he slipped into the water and waited, he was nervously playing with the cord used to mark the lanes of the pool.

Since this was just a temporary set-up in the pool for the swim meet, the council had used rather small cord to mark the swimming lanes. In fact, the cord used was cotton and was about 1/8 inch in diameter. The lines had not been pulled very tight, so that there was quite a bit of slack in the cord.

As Richard nervously watched his team member swimming across the pool, he wound his finger in the cord marking off the lanes. When the third swimmer tagged Richard, our team had a very good lead. Richard was struggling with something in the water, and we were yelling, "Go Man Go!!!" By this time the other teams had caught up and passed us, and Richard still hadn't started his swim across the pool.

When the race was over, I went over to see what had happened. Our swimmer explained that, in his nervousness, he had wound the cord around his finger. When he was tagged and was supposed to start his leg of the race, he couldn't get his finger loose from the cord. The more he struggled the tighter it seemed to get. When the other kids from our troop saw what had happened, they almost fell in the pool, they were laughing so hard. Instead of blaming Richard, they thought the whole thing was hilarious.

All of the way back to San Angelo, all 170 miles of it, the kids would doze off and the car would get pretty quiet. Then, all of a sudden, you would hear this giggle and the whole car would erupt in laughter. By this time, even Richard could manage a smile or two, especially after he found out that the other members of our troop were not planning to make him the guest of honor at a lynching, even if he had caused us to lose the race.

Chapter 21
Expositions and Scout Circuses

Expositions and Scout Circuses were always fun-type events in Scouting. The Expositions were booth-type shows in which units usually demonstrated some merit badge, while the circus was usually performed on the floor of a coliseum, with units putting on various acts of skill.

One year our council was planning a huge circus for the entire council. Boy Scout troops, Explorer posts and Cub packs were invited to participate in this Circus. Since there was quite a number of events or demonstrations, each event was scheduled to last only five minutes.

Most of the Cubs came dressed as animals, Indians, cowboys and clowns. They would put on their shows while the big demonstrations were being set up on the coliseum floor.

There were five main events in which the troops and Explorer posts were involved. They were: The Bicycle Event; the Chariot Race; the Physical Fitness Demonstration; the Disaster Drill; and the Pioneering Event.

Our troop had about 100 members at this time, so we had planned to enter all the main events except the Chariot Race. By entering four events, we felt that every member of our troop would be given an opportunity to participate.

The Bicycle Event consisted mainly of the cyclists performing drills on bicycles, jumping over ramps, and a few boys doing some trick riding. We had one boy in our unit who was very good on the unicycle, and had been asked to ride in this event.

The Physical Fitness event had Scouts and Explorers doing a number of things which had to do with physical fitness. There were tumblers, boys doing gymnastics and a few doing weight lifting. There were some boys performing on the parallel bars and the single high bar. A vaulting horse was set up, and quite a few Scouts demonstrated vaulting to the audience.

The Chariot Race was a fun event. The chariot was built to resemble the old Roman chariots and held one rider. The vehicle was pulled by four strong horses (boys), and rolled on bicycle wheels. The chariots were quite fancy and usually sported a banner or flag, proclaiming that this unit was sponsored by this troop or that Explorer post.

At the sound of the starter's gun, the great chariot race was on. The chariots, with their riders, had to circle the coliseum floor twice. A course had been set up on the floor and was marked plainly with flags and bales of hay.

This race was almost as wild as the one in *Ben Hur*. Chariots would lock wheels and there would be a humongous crash, with parts of the chariots sailing in all directions, along with the riders. Some of the horses just gave out and ended their race in a very slow trot instead of a high gallop.

Many of the bicycle wheels on the chariots just couldn't take the strain. As the chariot went around the curve the outside wheel would collapse. One chariot got a lot of applause from the audience. When the wheel collapsed, the rider balanced his weight on the opposite side over the good wheel. With the horses helping to keep the chariot from overturning, the rider, with his chariot, was able to make it across the finish line.

A few riders suffered skinned elbows and knees, where they hit the coliseum floor. Luckily, no one was trampled by the horses like you saw in the movie of *Ben Hur*.

The Disaster Drill was quite a spectacle. A small town had been built on the floor of the coliseum. The town had streets and houses and people going about their business. Suddenly, you heard the sounds of bombers and machine gun and cannon fire. The P.A. system played a tape with all of the sounds you would associate with a town under attack. There were loud explosions and bursts of flame as exploding bombs were simulated.

When the first bombs had hit, the lights in the coliseum went out. In the darkened building, the noise and the bright bursts of light actually made this seem very real. When the lights came on the town was leveled. The houses and buildings had been constructed with hinged walls, and when the bombing started, the boys in the buildings and houses simply undid the fasteners and let the walls fall flat. It was very effective and the town looked as if it had been hit by a disaster.

Firemen, policemen, sheriff's deputies, the Emergency Corps, medics from the local Air Force Base, and Explorers, who were trained in emergency preparedness, all manned fire trucks and ambulances which rushed to the town.

There was even a Coast Guard unit from the Corpus Christi Naval Base which rigged up a "breeches buoy" to help rescue victims. In a very few minutes, all of the victims were gone, the flattened town had been hauled away, and the coliseum floor was clean as a whistle, with nothing remaining but the memories of a spectacular event.

We had wanted to do something for the Pioneering Event, but just couldn't come up with any good ideas. Fess Parker, the star of movies and television, was a former member of Troop 2, one of the local Boy Scout troops. He had been asked to attend the circus as the guest of honor, and we knew that he would help his old troop in the Pioneering Event.

This troop was going to build a log cabin in the allotted five minutes. This wasn't to be just a model of a log cabin. It was to be a full 12 X 14 feet in size. The logs had been pre-cut and numbered, so that it was quite a lot like building something from "Lincoln Logs," the toy building set.

Our council Scout Executive had two sons in our troop. I was talking to him one day about wanting to do something out of the ordinary for the Pioneering Event. He challenged us to build a monkey bridge across the coliseum. Not only were we to build it, but it had to be strong enough to support a person crossing the bridge to span the coliseum floor.

We went out to the coliseum to look over the prospects and problems involved in building such a structure. Now remember, this bridge had to be built in five minutes or less, since that was all the time allotted to each event.

When we checked out the coliseum, we saw that we were going to have several problems. There was no way we could anchor the bridge to the floor of the building. The only place we could find something to anchor to was a column under the seats on either side.

The seats nearest the floor were about 8 feet above the arena. There were doors leading back under the floor supporting the seats so we could anchor to the columns with no trouble.

However, when we measured the distance we would have to span with the monkey bridge, we were a little shocked. The bridge would have to be about 170 feet long. Not only was the distance a problem, but the bridge would have to be built lying on its side and then raised into position. To span 170 feet, the timbers holding up the ends of the bridge would have to be at least ten feet tall. Since we had no giants or basketball players in our troop, the bridge would have to be constructed, tied all together, and then raised into position.

We had one more slight problem. We could not practice building the bridge in the coliseum—not even once. The building was in use almost every night, and there just wasn't any way we could practice our bridge building. We marked off an area by our Scout cabin using the exact measurements we would be facing in the coliseum. Since there were no columns we could use as anchors, we used a convenient telephone pole and the front bumper of my pickup truck.

I told the kids how important team work was, with each person doing his job in the right sequence. We practiced every meeting night, and had a few sessions on some nights other than meeting nights. We had finally handled the stiff ropes enough to wear off some of the new, which helped them to become soft and pliable. We reached the point where we could complete the bridge in about three minutes, but there was that nagging worry in the back of my mind that we might have overlooked some small detail.

When we lined up for the Pioneering Event, our troop was next to Troop 2 which was going to build the cabin. Sure enough, Fess Parker, with his coat off, was standing by, ready to help his old troop. Our boys were a little awed, being so near so famous a person, but we told them to close their mouths and get ready to build that doggone bridge.

When the gun sounded, everything went very well. We had a little trouble with the block and tackle getting the ropes tight enough, but that was taken care of in a very short time. We took about four minutes to build the bridge, and then we sent one of our Scouts, Mike, to travel across the coliseum using our structure. About halfway across, Mike got tangled up in the ropes holding the side-rails to the walkway rope. He was hanging upside down about ten feet off the floor. Luckily, we had chosen him for his agility, and he was able to right himself and continue across the coliseum.

The circus had two performances. One was in the afternoon and one at night. Between the shows, we got together and worked out our problems with the afternoon event. That night we built that 170 foot monkey bridge in three minutes flat. Mike had no trouble crossing the bridge—in fact, he did a little show boating on the way across this time.

Our troop had always been very interested in ropes and knot tying. This probably came about through my interest in knot tying, since I had been a member of the Knot Tying Patrol in the Exhibition Troop in the early days on our council. One year our unit had been trying to come up with some new event which would be interesting and would make an impression on our audience. We decided that we were going to do some "King Size Knot Tying."

As this was to be done on the floor of the coliseum, we felt that we needed a rope large enough to be seen by the people sitting in the stands. We decided that we needed a nylon rope 100 feet long and six inches in diameter.

We wrote to one of the leading rope manufacturers and asked about the possibility of obtaining a rope this size. They answered that, unless we were planning to move the rope around with a Jeep, they were sure that we couldn't handle it. A piece of rope this size would weigh about 1500 pounds, and the price for a rope like this was about $25 per foot or $2,500 for whole piece. Very quickly, we decided that we couldn't handle that rope either physically or financially. We must find some other rope which didn't weigh as much or cost as much.

Our District Executive called to say that he had found a piece of four inch rope about eighty feet long. He said that the rope was new but had been stored in an oil drum for about twenty years. He thought that the rope looked good, but it would need some cleaning to get rid of the accumulation of dirt and dust which had settled on the rope for the last twenty years.

I asked him how much the oil company wanted for the rope. He said we could have it for free since it was for a Boy Scout Troop. I asked him to bring it back, and we would get started cleaning it.

The rope was sisal and was stiff from being stored in the drum so long. We stretched it out and started working on it with detergent and some good scrub brushes. As the dirt and grime were washed away, the rope became more pliable, and we knew that we had a good rope for our "King Size Knot Tying." We whipped the ends of the rope to keep it from unraveling and came up with another idea to make the rope more visible to the audience.

We were going to use colored plastic tape, which was about one inch wide, and had bought the tape in red, white and blue rolls. We ran a ring of red tape around the rope and then skipped about a foot and put a ring of white tape. We moved down the rope about a foot and then put a ring of blue tape on the rope. When we finished, we had an eighty foot piece of rope with rings of red, white and blue the full length of the little piece of knot tying rope. Now we were sure the audience wouldn't have any trouble following the rope as it was twisted, turned and pushed through loops to form the knots.

The kids decided that they were going to tie the knots which might be a little more familiar to the audience. These were the knots they decided on: Square, Sheet Bend, Bowline, Sheepshank, Tautline Hitch and Spanish Bowline.

After many hours of practice, the day of the Scout Circus finally arrived. The kids put on a demonstration which was very well received—in fact, they got so many compliments on their "King Size Knot Tying" that they decided to take their big rope to the 1964 Jamboree. In our section, the boys demonstrated their skills and were so impressive that several more sections asked them to come show their expertise in knot tying. Some of the Scouts from other states suggested that they might change the name from "King Size Knot Tying" to "Texas Size Knot Tying." By this time our Scouts had worked up a little audience participation. They would ask a few of the boys from the audience to come up and help tie the knots. The visitors seem to get a kick out of crawling through and under the rope to tie the old familiar tenderfoot knots. Several troops from other parts of the country said, that when they got back home, they were going to get a big rope too and do some "King Size Knot Tying" for their folks back home.

Expositions were always a lot of fun for our troop. This is a booth-type show in which Scout troops and Explorer posts usually choose some merit badge to demonstrate. Some merit badges, like Camping, First Aid, Cooking, Pioneering and Safety were good action badges, which helped you to keep something going in your booth at all times.

One year, when the Russian "Sputnik" had been put into orbit and was circling the earth, our troop decided that many people might be more interested in Astronomy. We decided that Astronomy would be the merit badge to demonstrate in our booth. We covered the top of the booth with a large piece of dark blue cloth. In this we had punched holes to simulate the stars. We had lights up above the cloth shining down to add the illusion of a starlit sky. We had gone to a lot of trouble to find the position of the stars in our area for that particular time of year, and had punched the holes in the cloth to duplicate their position in the sky. We had charts and a revolving display of our solar system showing our Earth, Sun, Moon and all of the planets. We had made a moving mock-up of the Earth showing "Sputnik" orbiting around it and had pictures and diagrams of "Sputnik."

As a gag, we had constructed a very large telescope. It must have been about ten feet long, and was painted black with simulated brass fittings. We had a sign on the telescope which read: "Five Cents To See The Shooting Star." When you looked through the scope, you saw a lighted picture of Hopalong Cassidy, the western movie star, complete with two guns blazing. We hadn't really intended to charge for looking through the scope, but it was taken out of our hands. People would come up, pitch a nickel on the counter and peer into the scope. Most of them would burst out laughing and then walk away grinning. Many would leave and then come back with a friend in tow. They would suggest that the friend should look into the scope to see a spectacular sight. This went on the entire time of the show. When it was over, we had more than $7 taken in by our gag telescope.

We had several Scouts in our unit who were very promising artists, so it was only natural that one year it was decided that we were going to use Art Merit Badge for our demonstration in the exposition. In our booth, we had displays showing the various types of supplies necessary for working in oils, watercolors, and India ink. We also showed easels, palettes, and various types of materials on which the paints might be used.

We had an authentic display of cave man art. The originals were taken from a cave in France and were supposed to be 25,000 years old. To demonstrate these we had one of our Scouts dressed in the latest cave man style which was worn 25,000 years ago. Our cave man had a mop of black hair, literally made from a mop, which had been dyed black. He sported a huge club, and was dressed in a garment made from a pair of leather, fleece lined flying pants with the hair or fleece side turned out. He made a very credible cave man — because—who was going to argue about what the well dressed cave man wore

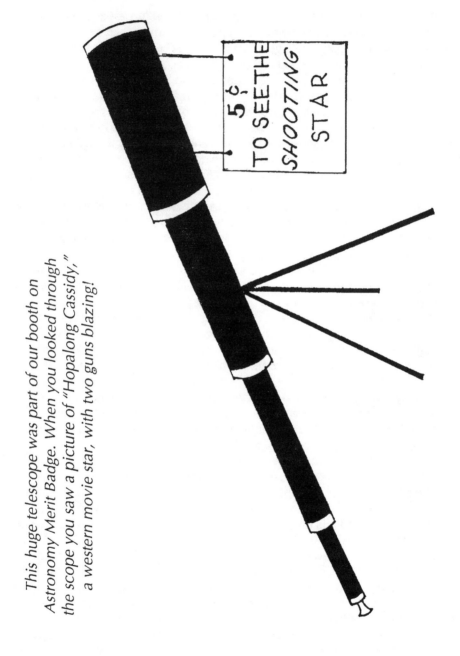

5¢ TO SEE THE *SHOOTING* STAR

This huge telescope was part of our booth on Astronomy Merit Badge. When you looked through the scope you saw a picture of "Hopalong Cassidy," a western movie star, with two guns blazing!

25,000 years ago! He pointed out the meaning behind the figures and explained what type of materials had been used to paint these figures on the walls of the cave.

We had a display of Indian art with a brave in full war bonnet and war paint to tell the people about the Indian art shown in our booth. We had authentic drawings and sketches made from pictures painted by real Indian artists from the many tribes which lived in our part of the Southwest. We had many pictures and sketches of Indian paintings taken from the cliffs near Paint Rock, Texas. These cliffs run for several hundred yards and are covered with many Indian pictures. Most of these remain a mystery to this day, as to who painted them and their meaning.

We had a display of modern art. One of our Scouts was dressed in an artist's white smock and wore a beret. In this display we had put a few gag pictures to have a little fun with the onlookers. I had taken one of Picasso's paintings and duplicated it on a large piece of white poster board. This picture was named *Woman Seated In Chair* and was one of those Picasso paintings in which you can see the front view and the profile view of the head at the same time. We had it expertly framed and called it *Woman Seated In Chair or Oh! My Aching Back.*

We had an example of modern art which was named *Nude Descending The Stairs.* This was just a series of diagonal lines which ran from the upper left hand corner of the painting to the lower right hand corner. We had framed this picture, which I had painted on poster board, but we decided that the word "nude" might be offensive to some of our parents. We changed the name to *Woman Descending The Stairs or Explosion In A Shingle Factory.*

There was one painting in our display of modern art which drew the most comments. I had taken a very large piece of black poster board and had put an expensive looking frame around it. There was absolutely nothing painted on the black poster board but some of our audience were sure they could make out something painted there.

We called our black picture: *Black Cat Sitting On A Pile Of Coal At Midnight.* Some members of our audience would come up and peer at the picture from different angles. One professor from the art department of our local college was sure that she could make out the outline of a cat. I didn't have the heart or the guts to tell her that there was nothing painted on the black poster board.

For our exposition merit badge demonstration one year, our troop decided to do a combination of Camping and Pioneering merit badges. We used two booths to give us a little more room, and I had painted outdoor scenes which completely covered the backs and sides of the booths. The outdoor scenes sort of gave you the impression you were looking at the places where you might practice most of your camping and pioneering activities.

Nicely framed, a plain black piece of poster board was called, "Black Cat Sitting on a Pile of Coal at Midnight." It was the center of a lot of fun as people visited our "art booth" and looked at the picture from different angles, trying to spot the elusive cat.

The Camping Booth had models of several different types of tents. The boys in the booth explained the advantages and disadvantages of each model. There were models of many types of fires. The Scouts showed how each fire was built and how each fire was used in camping for cooking or heating purposes.

There was a display showing a model campsite, with the Scouts explaining how to arrange tents, latrines and other facilities to get the best use for a certain campsite. They also pointed out the importance of placing your tents where you were shielded from the wind, and how not to pitch your tents in some low area where you might wake up, after a rain, to find the river flowing through your tent.

There were displays showing packs and how to pack them. There were menus to be used and a display showing how to make a comfortable ground bed.

The Pioneering portion of our booths showed a display of several different types of ropes. The Scouts pointed out how the strength of the ropes varied according to the material used in the ropes. There were models of bridges, towers and all sorts of pioneering projects. The boys showed the lashings used in different parts of these structures and how to tie them.

We had several Knot Boards showing about seventy-five different knots and splices. Many of the audience would come up and pick out a certain knot which was used in their profession. We were surprised to learn that two of the knots, which are used by firemen, are the bowline and the sheepshank. Many men, who had been in the Navy during the war, would tell us about using a certain knot and proceed to tie it.

There were several Scouts in our troop who were the best knot tiers I ever saw. These boys could tie five knots in about ten seconds. These were not the simple, easy knots which they tied. They were the square, sheet bend, bowline, sheepshank and clove hitch. As people would come up to our booth, the kids would challenge them to a knot tying contest. The Scouts were so good that they would tie the knots blindfolded, or tie them behind their backs.

We had one boy who could do a trick which I have never seen duplicated. Mike would tie a rope to an overhead beam or rafter, and let the rope hang to within three feet of the floor. He would jump up, grab the rope and support his body with one arm. He would use the other arm to tie a bowline around his waist with one hand. When he had tied the bowline, he would release the rope and hang there, suspended by the bowline around his chest. Through the years, I used to offer the Scouts in my unit $10 if they could do this little stunt. To this day, I have never had to pay off.

One year, our troop's plans for the exposition were very ambitious. We were going to do "First Aid," but had planned to do it a little differently from most Exposition First Aid booths. We had asked for and received three booths in a row. We used one booth for our props and a makeup room. The sides were completely covered and we had benches around the wall for the victims to sit on as they awaited their cue to appear on stage. Two long tables in the center of the booth contained our extra blood and all of the First Aid supplies needed to take care of the victims' injuries.

We had ordered those "Plastifoil Wound Replicas" from England, and they were very real in appearance. These wounds were made of soft, pliable plastic and were held in place with spirit gum, which is used by actors to attach beards and mustaches to their faces. One of the wounds used was a large wound about the size of a small plate. It was a burn and showed all three types of burns; first, second, and third degree. It was very gruesome looking and the kids loved it. It even had some small pieces of material sticking out of the burn. To add to the illusion of the victim suffering a bad burn, we had taken an old pair of blue jeans and burned a large hole above the knee of the jeans. This hole was placed over the wound replica and led the audience to believe the victim was badly burned when he fell into the campfire.

The booth next to the makeup booth was called "First Aid Theatre." We had built up a stage and covered it with artificial grass. I had painted outdoor scenes on the panels covering the sides and back wall of the booth. We had a flickering campfire and an appropriate log or two lying around. We had made a prop which looked like the front of a tent. It only stuck out about a foot from the back wall, but added to the illusion of an outdoor camp scene. Curtains, which could be drawn back, covered the front of the booth. These were kept closed until our Scouts were ready to show the audience how to care for the victim of an injury.

The third booth was filled with all types of first aid equipment. There were four different types of snake bite kits, including a "homemade" one you could make from things around the house. There was a display showing all types of band-aids, or bandages. We used colored poster board to show all types of gauze pads from the small ones for a minor cut to the huge ones used by the military for a large chest or stomach wound. We displayed all types of splints, including the new inflatable ones. We also showed items which might be used to make emergency splints such as blankets, pillows, magazines or limbs cut from trees.

This is the way our booths operated. We had two boys who served as Masters of Ceremonies. One boy would talk for about two hours and then the other boy would take over. These boys ran the whole operation. They were chosen because they had very good speaking voices and were able to "ad lib" if we had some foul-up in our show.

The M.C. would tell the audience that the boys in the equipment booth were going to tell about poisonous snakes in our area and the proper treatment for snake bite. After the Scouts had shown pictures of the poisonous snakes and told about the snake bite kits, the M.C. would ask them to direct their attention to the First Aid Theatre.

When the curtains were opened, they saw a victim suffering from snake bite. We had used morticians' wax to make a huge swollen place on the calf of the victim's leg. We had hollowed out a place in the swollen area and had put a cotton ball soaked in grape juice in the hole. Also, we had smoothed the morticians' wax to cover the hole and made a couple of fang marks directly over the cotton ball. When the first aiders, who were treating the snake bite victim, made their cuts over the fang marks, the purple grape juice oozed out and looked like poisoned blood. As the victim was being treated, the Master of Ceremonies was telling the audience all about each phase of the treatment.

After the "first aiders" had finished taking care of the victim, the M.C. would thank the audience for watching our show. He would ask them to direct their attention to the equipment booth where the Scouts would tell about fractures, both simple and compound. The curtains of the "First Aid Theatre" would be closed and the Scouts in the other booth would take over. They would tell about the different types of fractures and would show the equipment needed in their treatment.

When they had finished, the curtains would open and you could see a victim suffering from a compound fracture of the upper leg. The "plastifoil wound" was very realistic inasmuch as it showed a large bloody area with the end of the bone protruding through the flesh. The M.C. would tell each step in the treatment of such an injury, while the first aiders expertly placed the splints in place and treated the victim for shock. After they had finished, the M.C. would ask if there were any questions.

The audience would then be asked to watch the other booth where the Scouts would tell about all types of burns and how to treat them.

This is the way our show worked all day. One of my older boys and I worked in the makeup booth getting the victims ready and trying to stay about three victims ahead of the M.C. After a victim had been treated, there was usually some touch up work needed to replace blood or re-stick the wounds.

Our booth drew a great many people. Each time before we opened the curtains of the "First Aid Theatre," we had a portable police siren we would sound to draw the crowds. The people would come scurrying from all directions, especially the Cub Scouts.

When we started our show, the first victim was shown suffering from snake bite. There were several Cubs in the front row of spectators, and one little boy was standing about two feet away from where our Scouts were getting ready to make the cuts on the fang marks. He stood there with his eyes riveted on the cutting tool. When our Scouts made their cuts over the fang marks and the grape juice started oozing out—he fainted dead away.

I looked up and here came some of my Scouts carrying him into the booth where we were making up the victims. I told them that if he came to and saw all of the broken bones and cuts on the boys sitting around, he would probably pass out again. They hustled him out of the booth, and tried a little real first aid on the Cub. They soon had him up and about, and he was in the audience when the curtains opened again. The resilience of kids never ceases to amaze me.

We had two more fainting victims during our show. A teenage girl fainted when we were demonstrating the treatment of burns. Once again, they brought the victim into the makeup booth. I yelled at them to get her outside where she could get some fresh air, and she wouldn't come to with all of those horrible wounds staring her in the face.

Our booth caused one more person to faint. This time it was an adult woman, who fainted when we were demonstrating arterial bleeding. In this scene, our victim was seen half reclining on one arm. There was a very large, deep cut on the wrist of this arm. A pump type oil can, filled with red cake coloring, was taped inside the victim's jacket. A piece of rubber tubing ran down the arm from the oil can to the cut in the wrist. The tubing was hidden by covering it with morticians' wax.

When the victim pumped the oil can, a bright stream of blood gushed out of the wound and covered the victim's hand. The victim could regulate the timing of the squirts of blood so that it looked as if a pumping heart were forcing the blood from the cut.

It was very realistic—in fact, it was too real looking. This woman was watching the demonstration and passed out completely. This time they didn't bring her into the makeup booth but administered a little first aid to bring her around outside the booth.

The first aid show proved to be a great success. Several people told us that it was the best first aid show that they had ever seen. It was a lot of fun, but it took many hours of practice to make it successful and timing was very important.

One more note—as the show progressed the victims had a little contest going among themselves. Each victim tried to out do the others by showing more pain and giving out with a few more realistic groans. I don't think any of them would have won an Oscar or an Emmy for the great performances, but they had a lot of fun trying.

Chapter 22
Good Turns

I tried to impress on my Scouts the importance of the good turn in Scouting. The ideals of the Scout Oath and the Twelve Parts of the Scout Law, combine with the Good Turn to make Scouting so much more meaningful than the Y.M.C.A., the Red Cross and the Boy's Clubs, which seemed to exist just for their own pleasure. The Scouting Good Turn helped a boy to become a better citizen in his own community. He learned, that by helping others, he was helping himself.

Through the years our troop gave thousands of hours in helping out on community projects. Some of these civic good turns were ones which we did every year. A few were special projects which we worked on only once. Many of these projects are the same ones, which Scouts all over the United States have participated in. A few are special to our own part of the Southwest.

Here is a list of some of our Good Turn projects:

March of Dimes drives
Community Council drives
Tuberculosis Campaign and Christmas Seal project
Heart Fund drive
Cleaned out the building where the Lighthouse for the Blind was to be located
Helped gather items to be repaired by the Lighthouse for the Blind
Earned money to be donated the West Texas Boys' Ranch
Earned money to be given to the Boy Scout Tribute fund
Earned money to make several donations to the World Friendship fund
Helped rework items for display at the Fort Concho Museum

Had several Scouts who repaired radios for patients at the San Angelo
Center, a Mental Health - Mental Retardation unit at Carlsbad, TX.
Served as guides for the Fiesta del Concho
Distributed programs for the Fiesta del Concho
Served as Color Guards for many conventions in our city
Manned the kettles at Christmas time for the Salvation Army
Earned money and made a sizeable donation to the Salvation Army
Distributed programs and acted as ushers for the Miss Wool of America
Pageant
Ushered at high school football games
Collected toys for "Toys for Tots" program
Organized and participated in clean-up at Camp Louis Farr
Did painting and built a sidewalk at Camp Sol Mayer
Helped plant trees at Camp Sol Mayer
Delivered breakfast notices to finance workers in Boy Scout Finance drive
Collected books and magazines for La Academia, an organization to help
illiterate adults to learn to read and write
Collected books and magazines for the men at McKnight Tuberculosis
Sanatorium
Helped to provide equipment used at Girl Scout Day Camp
Older Scouts served as judges for Girl Scout Camporees
Delivered circulars and placed placards in store windows to help
promote downtown San Angelo
Spent one weekend in a clean-up job of Mission San Saba, located near
Menard, Texas
Built and sponsored a float for the Christmas parade
Worked on many clean-up, paint-up campaigns in our city
Earned money to help a needy family at Christmas. This was done for
several years by our troop.

Most of the above good turns have been done by many troops throughout the United States. Our troop did several special good turns, which are a
little out of the ordinary, and were unique in several ways.

For instance, our Scout troop sponsored a little Indian boy through the
Christian Children's Fund. Ellis was adopted by our troop and we took care
of him for seven years. We paid the regular fee which helped him with a few
necessities and sent him some extra money every once in a while to help him
to buy some of the things he wanted.

At Christmas and on his birthday, we would either send some extra money
or buy him something as a present. I'll always remember one letter he sent to
the troop in which he told how he liked to fish. He mentioned that he only
had one fish hook, and that he had lost that one. His letter made our Scouts
feel so badly that they decided to do something about it. We had made some

On my honor, I will do my best:
to help other people at all times!

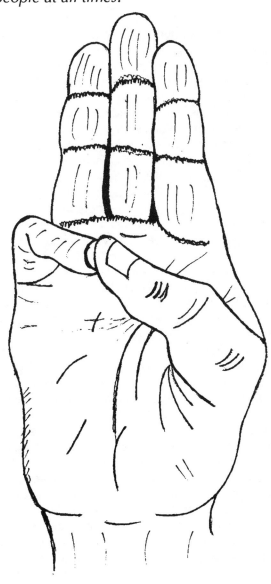

money delivering circulars, and the boys voted to use it to send Ellis some fishing tackle.

They bought a fishing tackle box and proceeded to fill it with all kinds of fishing goodies. There were several types of hooks, a good supply of sinkers and many sizes of floats. There were wire leaders and a couple of extra spools of fishing line. The boys put many more kinds of fishing gear in the tackle box, including quite a few artificial lures. There was some money left so the kids decided to buy Ellis something that he had never had before. They bought him a nice rod and reel, and decided that they had taken care of his fishing needs for a while.

I still have the letter from Ellis after he had received the fishing supplies. He was so thankful and surprised to think that anyone cared enough to do something like this for him. The teacher at the Indian school wrote a little note to say that Ellis was so proud of his present, they had a little trouble keeping him from sleeping with his new fishing gear.

A former Scout from San Angelo was a volunteer in the Peace Corps in Ethiopia. Pat had not been a member of our troop, but I had known his dad for years in Scouting, and Pat had been a member of our troop in the 1953 Jamboree. He had come home on leave and had visited our troop meeting one night.

He told us some very interesting stories about the Boy Scout troop which he had started in Ethiopia. He said that, when his troop went out on a week-end camp, the members did not carry much in the way of food. They would carry a little salt and some flour. The meat that they ate was provided by the game that they killed on the campout.

At first, Pat said it was strange to see his Scout troop carrying spears and bows and arrows on their campout. He was afraid that someone would get skewered by an arrow or end up with a large hole in some part of his anatomy. Pat said his fears were groundless as most of his Scouts had been hunting all their lives and were very careful with their weapons.

He came to our meeting to ask our help on a little project he had in mind. It seems that Emperor Haile Selassie, the ruler of Ethiopia, was paying a call to the town where Pat worked. The townspeople were very excited about the ruler's impending visit and were planning quite a celebration to welcome him.

Pat had been an excellent musician in high school and college, and he decided that his Scout troop would form a Drum and Bugle Corps to welcome the guest of honor. Drums were no problem as many of the boys in his troop had played drums all of their lives. Bugles were a little different matter and were not available in Ethiopia. He had decided that the Drum and Bugle Corps would need as many as eight bugles. He had come to our troop to see if we would take on the job of supplying him with the required bugles. Our troop had earned some money which we had decided would be used on some good turn project. The troop took a vote and decided that we would take on the "Bugles for Ethiopia Project." Pat was going to return to Ethiopia in about two weeks and wanted to take the bugles back with him, if possible.

A friend of mine owned a music store, and I went to him with my problem. I told him we needed eight bugles as soon as possible, and could he help us? He got on the phone, contacted his supplier in Dallas, and had the bugles shipped by motor truck line. We received them the next afternoon and presented them to Pat in a little ceremony. We asked him to tell Emperor Haile Selassie that the Drum and Bugle Corps came about as a result of a Boy Scout troop in Texas just doing a good turn, as usual.

The South Side Neighborhood Center was a non-profit organization which provided a place for working mothers to leave their pre-school children. The Center was not funded by any city, county or national organization. It had to depend on donations from individuals and civic groups along with some churches. The Center was located in a neighborhood which was largely Hispanic, and most of the families using the Center were very poor. The building was an old, two-story barracks building, which provided plenty of room for the little kids.

A friend of mine, Mrs. Rodgers, had seen the need for such a center, and she and some other Anglo ladies had decided to start the program. As I had said, there were no regular funds available, and they had a pretty rough time trying to scrounge enough needed equipment. They had been in operation for some time when Mrs. Rodgers contacted me to see if my Scout troop would like to take on a project to help out the Center. I told her that our troop was always looking for some good turn project, and that we would be glad to help her out.

This was her plan for the project. The Center desperately needed toys to keep the little kids occupied. She also said they needed picture books or coloring books which would be suitable for the pre-schoolers. Each child brought his own lunch to the Center, but since the families were so poor, the lunch in many cases was not very adequate. Mrs. Rodgers had the idea that, if each child could be given a bowl of hot soup, it would really help supplement the meager lunches the kids brought. She asked me if I thought our troop might be able to help out with the toys and books and especially the soup. I told her I would bring it before the troop and let them decide.

When I told the Scouts at our next troop meeting, they were very enthusiastic about taking on "Project Soup." I met with the Patrol Leaders and they suggested each Scout would contact the people in his neighborhood and ask for donations of toys, books and soup. The Patrol Leaders also suggested that grocery stores, supermarkets and convenience stores might be contacted to ask if some slow-moving soups might be donated.

We decided to make an inter-patrol contest out of this to see which patrol could gather the most soup. We ran the contest for two weeks and the results were astounding. The boys had collected a great number of toys, many of them brand new, and the rest in excellent condition. We had all kinds of stuffed toys such as bears, rabbits, dogs, cats and even an elephant or two. There were quite a few wheeled toys such as cars, trucks, and even a tricycle and a little red wagon. The Scouts had collected more than two hundred books, which guaranteed keeping the little kids busy on the days they couldn't play outside.

But the soup collection was the thing which made me so proud of my Scouts. In two drives, they had collected more than 2,000 cans of soup. I was sure the ladies who ran the center would be most pleased with this donation.

I had borrowed a truck to haul the toys, books, and soup to the Center. Mrs. Rodgers wasn't there that day when we arrived at the building. I had carried some of my Patrol Leaders with me to help haul in the loot. As I walked in, I told this lady I had some soup for the center and asked where she wanted us to put it. She had no idea how much soup we had collected, so she told us "to just put it on the kitchen cabinet." We started bringing in case after case, box after box of soup. With each load her eyes got bigger and bigger as the pile of boxes containing the soup grew higher and wider. We brought in all of the toys and books and added them to the big pile of soup. When we left, the lady was still in shock. All she could do was to mumble a few words of thanks, and then she started wondering where in the world she was going to store all of the soup.

Mrs. Rodgers called later and was so appreciative of all the work the Scouts had done. She said their good turn would assure that the little kids would get their hot bowl of soup for a long time. That was the end of "Project Soup."

One of my former Senior Patrol Leaders, Dick Wyatt, was attending school at Missouri Valley College. Dick, who was planning to enter professional Scouting, sent me a most interesting letter one day. In this letter, he said that he had been working as Assistant Scoutmaster for a Boy Scout troop at the Marshall State School and Hospital in Marshall, Missouri. Dick said that there had been no state funds set aside for the troop, and they were in desperate need of some used Scout handbooks. He thought that our troop might have some old handbooks lying around and asked me to send them to him if I found any.

I talked to the troop and read Dick's letter. The boys decided that we could do a little better than just some old used handbooks. We had some money in our "good turn fund" and decided that this would be a most opportune time to spend it. We sent cook kits, canteens, hatchets, picks, shovels, compasses, a first aid kit, two tents, and some new handbooks. We enclosed a note to Dick which read, "Here are some handbooks—and a few more items."

This happened about the time Alaska was taken into the United States as a state and Texas had lost its rating as the largest state. The people at the state school sent us a copy of their school paper called *The Bugle*. In the paper was an article which went like this: "Texas may have lost their title as the biggest state in the Union, but to the boys of Scout Troop #43 here at Marshall State School, Texas is still #1." Our troop received a nice letter from Boy Scout Troop 43. Each boy had signed it, and they expressed their thanks for the Scouting equipment. My Scouts felt very proud that they had helped in a small way to make Scouting more meaningful for a group of kids in Missouri.

One day the council Boy Scout office called me about an unusual letter which they had received. The letter was from a young Italian man, Ernesto Barba, who had been a Scout in Italy, and had attended the World Jamboree in Austria in the early 50's. After the jamboree, he had returned to his home in Rome where he was very active in Scouting.

After some time, he became ill and found that he was suffering from tuberculosis. He was sent to Sondalo, Italy, where there was a sanatorium for the treatment of tuberculosis. There were quite a few boys in this hospital, and Ernesto decided that he would organize a Scout troop. Scouting would help to keep the boys interested and would help to get them to spend more time in the out-of-doors. He needed some help as he had no funds to start this troop. He decided to write to the United States and ask for help. Of all places, he chose San Angelo, Texas, because, he explained in one of his later letters, he thought that San Angelo was an Italian-sounding name.

I picked up the letter from the Scout office and took it to our troop meeting. The boys were enthusiastic about helping to start a troop in Italy. We voted to help them out but needed to find out more about their needs. This was the beginning of several exchanges of letters between Ernesto and myself. He was the only one in the proposed troop who could speak and read English. Some of the first letters he sent were sort of funny in the way he expressed himself.

He told us that the boys could get Scout uniforms, so that was an item which they didn't need. Ernesto expressed a need for camping equipment such as tents, shovels, hatchets, rope, canteens, cook kits, a first aid kit, pocket knives, compasses, and any other equipment needed for camping.

In one of his first letters, Ernesto said that the Italian boys would really like to have some labor pants. We couldn't figure out what he meant by this expression, and it took another letter to find out that the Italian Scouts wanted blue jeans. We got the boys' sizes, and we sent each boy a blue jean jacket and a pair of jeans. I think the Italian kids were more thrilled with these items than any other thing we sent.

We sent some handbooks and a year's subscription to *Boys' Life*. Ernesto said that the handbooks could be used even if the Scouts couldn't read English. The picture and illustrations were self-explanatory. He also told us that he would read *Boys' Life* to the kids.

When we had bought everything which we thought they needed, we had a rude awakening one day. After spending nearly all our funds on equipment, we didn't have any way to send the stuff to Sondalo, Italy. We had four footlockers of equipment, but no way of getting it to the boys in Italy.

I called the Commander of Goodfellow Air Force Base to see if he had any ideas about shipping the loot to Italy. His son had been in our unit, and the Colonel was most helpful. He told me to call a Colonel Karmony, who was attached to the base hospital and who had just returned from a tour of duty in Italy.

I called Colonel Karmony and he gave me a good lead on getting the equipment to Italy. He had a good friend, General Cassidy, who was the Military Attache at the Embassy in Rome. He felt that the General could come up with some solution to our problem.

I was beginning to think I was getting the old "buck passing" treatment, but I decided to try to contact General Cassidy. I sent a cablegram to him and explained our problem. I was very pessimistic about a busy man like the General taking time out to even answer my cablegram. Wonder of wonders —I received an answer from the General, and he had the perfect solution to our problem.

He told me to ship the equipment to his APO address in New York, and the items would be sent to him in Rome. He would see to it that the footlockers containing the gear would get to Sondalo. We shipped the stuff to New York by motor freight—which just about cleaned out our "good turn fund." True to his word, when the General received the equipment, he sent a truck to carry the items to the boys in Sondalo, Italy. I still have some copies of the newspapers, in English and Italian, telling about our "Equipment Across the Sea" good turn.

In our cabin, there is still a nice plaque, beautifully done, showing hands clasped in the Scout Handclasp, with a Texas flag in the background. This was sent to us by the Italian Scouts. They also told us that they had named their troop "The Lone Star Troop" in honor of our troop from Texas.

Through the years, our troop has been very proud of their good turn record. Not only have our Scouts given many hours in community service, but they feel they had a small part in helping a Scout troop in Marshall, Missouri, sending bugles to a troop in Ethiopia, helping the Scouts in Italy, and helping Scouting in many countries by contributing to the World Friendship Fund.

Many of our former Scouts live in and around San Angelo. They are grown now, and many take a very active part in the many civic affairs designed to make our community a better place in which to live. I like to think that just maybe it all started back in our old troop with the idea of the importance of "doing a good turn."

Chapter 23
Courts of Honor

A Court of Honor is a meeting attended by Scouts, their parents and friends, at which time public recognition is given to the boys for their advancement in Scouting.

Some troops have their own Court of Honor, but some districts may have such a meeting for all of the troops in the district. In some of the larger towns in our council, a Court of Honor may involve all of the troops in that town. Our troop always seemed to enjoy the Courts of Honor because there were so many more people involved, and a Scout felt it more impressive to receive his awards before a large crowd.

Also, usually on the district level, the Order of the Arrow would take part in the event and add to the ceremony. The Scouts would see what other boys in other units were doing in advancement and this sometimes would be an incentive to work a little harder.

We participated in many impressive Courts of Honor, and were in a few where someone blew their lines or where there was a foul-up in the awards to be given. One of my most embarrassing moments came during a Court of Honor when Mr. Roe Bartle was in our city and had consented to award the Eagle Scout badges at this event. Mr. Roe Bartle was an internationally known Scouter, and it was quite an honor to have this gentleman participate in our Court of Honor.

This was a district Court of Honor and was taking place at the main auditorium at Angelo State College. The Order of the Arrow had been put in charge of the program and everything had gone very smoothly. The O.A. had put on a dance just before the awarding of the Eagle badges, and the stage was set to show an Indian scene with a couple of teepees, a council fire, some drums and other equipment. The white lights had been replaced with red and blue lights to further accent the costumes of the dancers. The only bad thing about the colored lights was the fact that you couldn't see as well as you might with the white lights.

The Scouts were to receive their Eagle awards from Mr. Bartle. One boy was from my troop and his parents and I were standing with him. My Scout, Stan, had very poor eyesight and wore thick glasses. The other Scout received his badge first and our group stood nervously by awaiting our part in the ceremony.

Stan's mother pinned his Eagle badge on him and then it was time for Stan to pin the miniature Eagle pin on his mother. In his nervousness, he dropped the pin on the floor. As I mentioned it was sort of dark on the stage and we couldn't find the pin. Stan, his parents and I were down on our hands and knees feeling around trying to locate the elusive pin. Mr. Bartle stood there, graciously smiling, while we crawled around on the floor. We never did find the pin and the Scout Executive came to our rescue when he announced that he would see to it that a pin was delivered to Stan's mother.

We had really tried to impress Mr. Bartle, but I always wondered what his impression of West Texas was. To this day, I cringe when I think how it must have looked to see three adults and one Boy Scout, down on their hands and knees, frantically searching for that little pin. From all of the nice things I heard about Mr. Roe Bartle, I wouldn't have been at all surprised to find that he might have been just a little amused at viewing such a spectacle.

In our troop, for years, I used to kid my Scouts about a mythical award. It was called "The Purple Durkle With The Mesquite Cluster." To earn this award one had to accomplish some great feat like Paul Bunyon or Pecos Bill might do. I told my boys I was the only one in the world to have ever received this award, but when they asked to see the award, I told them it had been lost in the flood of 1936.

"The Purple Durkle With The Mesquite Cluster" was a joke in our troop for a long time. If a Scout did something outstanding, the other boys would tell him that he just missed qualifying for this honor. Boys who had been in our troop years before, would return home and visit our troop meeting. Invariably they would ask if anyone, besides myself, had ever earned this great honor.

We were having a troop Court of Honor just before school started in the fall. Our troop had attended summer camp, and had earned a great number of merit badges and many advancements in rank. We expected a large turnout of parents and friends and were going all out to make this a very impressive Court of Honor. We did have a large group of people attend the Court of Honor, and the crowd filled the banquet hall at the church which sponsors our troop. Everything went smoothly and we had presented two Scouts with their Eagle awards. This presentation was usually done last as we always considered this the high point of the Court of Honor.

However, on this particular night, our Senior Patrol Leader stood and made an announcement which caught me by surprise. He told the audience that, "Tonight we were pleased to make a very special award to one of our members." I didn't know of any special award to be presented and couldn't understand what he was talking about. He asked me and my wife to please come and stand at the front of the room. When we got there, my Senior Patrol Leader, David, made a flowery speech and had my wife pin the "Purple Durkle With The Mesquite Cluster" to my uniform. For once in my life, I was speechless.

The kids had sent off and had this beautiful medal made to order. A gold bar at the top had the word "Durkle" engraved on it. A purple ribbon was suspended from the gold bar and supported a round gold medallion with my initials in the center. Around the edge of this medallion were engraved clusters of leaves. I had finally received the "Purple Durkle With The Mesquite Cluster." David told the crowd that, now when people asked to see the famous award, I would have one to show them and wouldn't have to use the excuse that it had been lost in the flood of 1936.

Our troop had many Scouts to earn their Eagle award. We put a lot of emphasis on advancement and spent part of each troop meeting working on various merit badges and rank advancement. When we went on a weekend camp, we always planned to work on several merit badges which had to do with camping and the out-of-doors.

As a result of our concentration on advancement, our unit had between 150 and 200 boys earn their Eagle. We had three Scouts from one family to be presented with their Eagle Awards at one Court of Honor. We had twelve Scouts at one time from our troop to receive their Eagle Scout badges.

One of the saddest experiences in my Scouting career had to do with a young Scout in our troop. Jim Horton was Patrol Leader of one of our outstanding patrols and had completed his Eagle requirements and the requirements for his God and Country Award. He was an outstanding student and had been elected to serve on the Student Council of his school for the coming school year. Jim was a very good athlete and had the ability to get along well with other people. His dad and I had been in Scouts when we were boys, so our friendship went back a long way. Jim's older brother was a member of our troop and his younger brother was planning to join our unit.

Jim died quite suddenly before he was awarded his Eagle and God and Country awards. His parents and I asked the council office to check with the National Office to see about the possibility of making the awards posthumously. The National Office wrote that this was permissible and asked the local council office to take care of the ceremony.

Jim's Eagle was presented to his parents at a Court of Honor, as I stood with them. It was one of the most difficult things I ever had to do. Later, the God and Country award was presented to his parents at a church service.

A very unusual story came out of this tragedy. After Jim's death, the members of his patrol vowed that they would all earn their Eagle in honor of their Patrol Leader. All ten members did earn their Eagle to keep their promise, and several went on to earn their God and Country award, also.

Our troop always stressed the importance of a Scout earning the religious award in the church of his faith. During my tenure as Scoutmaster, our unit had many boys who qualified for the God and Country Award. We were very proud of the fact that these awards were earned in many different denominations and faiths: Methodist, Baptist, First Christian, Presbyterian, Catholic, Episcopal, Church of Christ, Lutheran, Jewish and Eastern Orthodox.

In looking back over forty-nine years of Scouting, I find that Courts of Honor were some of the most memorable events which helped to emphasize the high ideals of Scouting.

Chapter 24
Rio Grande Raft Trips

Several of our Scouts participated in the "200 Mile Bicycle Trip," many more were members of Philmont expeditions and canoe trips into Canada from the Charles Sommers Canoe Base in Minnesota. As exciting as these were, I believe that our raft trips down the Rio Grande were tops in high adventure Scouting.

Members of our troop made four different trips through the canyons of the Rio Grande. One of these was a trip from Presidio, Texas, through Colorado Canyon, to the town of Lajitas. This is a good canyon to try for your first rafting experience. There are some nice rapids through here, but if you should overturn and lose all your gear, it is possible to walk out since this is the only canyon where the road runs along the river bank.

On our first trip we had decided on a rather ambitious journey. We planned to travel the Rio Grande for the full length of Big Bend National Park. This is a distance of almost 100 miles through some of the wildest, most spectacular scenery in the United States.

Thirty-one members of our troop were going on this trip. When I checked the roster, I was a little shocked to find that we had eleven Scouts who were eleven years old. Four of these had never been on an overnight camp. Our crew included seven boys who were twelve years old, and eight more Scouts who were in the thirteen, fourteen and fifteen year age bracket. Counting the five adults who went, there were only nine in the over-sixteen age group.

For our trip, we used six-man rubber rafts, with each having a capacity of 1,500 pounds. There were eight of these rafts, and we had divided the Scouts so that there were four rafts with four Scouts and one adult in each. There were three with three Scouts in each of them and one raft, a supply raft, which

We paddled down the Rio Grande in our rafts, usually carrying four or five river rats. Much of the time we rode the raft with one foot dangling in the water.

was manned by two of our older boys.

Before the trip, we spent one weekend on a "shakedown camp" at the lake. We inflated the rafts and learned that they were quite different from handling a canoe. The rafts could not be turned as quickly and were more difficult to handle when the wind was blowing. The boys came up with the best technique for paddling the cumbersome rafts. The Scouts sat on the sides of the raft, one foot dangling in the water and the other foot inside the raft. By paddling in unison, the boys soon learned to control the rafts and to go where they wanted to go, instead of where the wind blew them.

On a trip like this, you must plan to carry all of the equipment you need, since there is no place to obtain any more. In the Big Bend National Park, the distances are so great and the lack of communication are such as to make it impossible to obtain any sort of help, including medical attention, in under six hours. This is a conservative estimate, because in some parts of the park it might take a couple of days to get any help. So, you carry everything you need and heed the advice of a veteran professional river guide, "Don't break no legs!"

We carried extra paddles, both wood and plastic ones, and plenty of half inch nylon rope. There was 100 feet of rope in each raft and the supply raft had about 400 more feet of this line. The Rio Grande is almost always muddy, about the color of hot chocolate, and we knew that we couldn't carry enough water to last on our trip of seven days. There were no springs along the river in this section, and drinking the untreated river water brings on a bad case of diarrhea, known as "Montezuma's Revenge" in this part of the Southwest.

We had put our drinking water supply in one-gallon plastic jugs. This made it easier to handle, and the small containers were perfect for storing in the rafts. We started out with 100 gallons of water, but knew that we would have to boil and purify the river water for drinking, before we completed our raft trip.

Our equipment included three fifteen gallon aluminum stock pots, like the military used. These had lids and would be used to boil the river water to make it safe to drink. We had Halazon Water Purification Tablets, which were used in boiled water, also, to make it fit for human consumption.

One of the pieces of equipment, into which I put a lot of thought, was our first aid kit. Since medical help was so far away, our crew had to "be prepared" for almost every type of emergency. Our kit included inflatable splints, slings, several types of burn ointment, all sizes of adhesive bandages, many types of gauze compresses, eye patches, eye medicine such as "Visine" and "Murine," and even medicine for an aching tooth.

The area through which we would be traveling, had its share of poisonous snakes. I carried two types of "Cutter Snake Bite Kits," a "Freeze Type kit," and an "Anti-venom Snake Bite Kit." We also carried about twenty-four packages of "instant ice," like the athletic trainers use. These packages are about the size of a cigarette package but twice as thick. They contain a chemical, which when the package is squeezed and the chemical released, turns to ice. We thought that this "instant ice" might help to slow the spread of poison in case of snake bite, since it might take several hours to get medical attention.

Besides the snakes, there were several other poisonous "critters" along the Rio Grande. There were scorpions, tarantulas, centipedes, spiders and vinegerones, the whip-tailed scorpion. Our first aid kit contained an assortment of salves and sprays which were supposed to relieve the pain caused by any of the above "critters."

We also carried needles, tweezers and a couple of magnifying glasses to remove cactus thorns, in case any of our crew managed to fall into a cactus patch or brush up against some of these pesky plants.

I felt that we had the necessary equipment to take care of cuts, bruises, sunburn, broken bones and even snake bite, but I worried about the possibility of some boy coming up with an attack of appendicitis. I knew that in this remote area, it could be several hours or even days before we might get medical help.

I know now that all of my worrying was for nothing. In our four trips through the canyons of the Rio Grande, we had some sunburn, a few small cuts and scratches, one "stubbed toe" caused by a Scout running around with no shoes on, and one good case of diarrhea—but that's another story.

We divided our group into three crews: the Red crew, the White crew and the Blue crew. Our food, mostly freeze dried trail food and some canned items, was packed into plastic bags inside canvas bags. We carried lots of snacks such as raisins, dried fruit, Snack Packs, which are individual cans of pudding, and quite a lot of jerky. The leaders, remembering the thirteenth part of the Scout Law: "A Scout is Hungry," felt that these snacks would relieve the pangs of hunger between meals.

Our food was packed in bags marked for each crew and each meal. This way, the cooks would not have to open several bags to find the food needed for a certain meal. Menus for the complete trip were given to each crew so that there wouldn't be any questions as to what they were going to have for each meal.

Early one August morning, we assembled at the Scout cabin to load all of our gear onto a chartered bus. All of the parents and families of the boys were there, and after many tearful farewells, we boarded the bus for the beginning of our Great Adventure. Since we had so many little Scouts going on this trip—remember, of the thirty-one people there were fifteen boys who were twelve and under—I am sure there were many parents who believed that this was the last time they would ever see their son.

After a long trip, about 360 miles, we arrived at the little town of Lajitas, Texas. This town was about eleven miles above the river entrance to Big Bend National Park, and this was where we would put our rafts in the river for a journey of about 100 miles.

Lajitas, a town of about 100 population, is located on high banks above the river. About 300 yards up the river, the Rio Grande splits into two streams. The main stream, about 200 yards from Lajitas across a low island, is about thirty yards wide at this point, and has a good current. The smaller stream, which split away from the main part of the river, is almost like a small creek. It curves around and runs almost under the high banks of Lajitas. The water was shallow, about ankle deep, and we carried all of our equipment across this "creek" to make our camp on the low island. This island is very large and is made when the "creek" flows back into the main Rio Grande. This island is only about four or five feet above the river, and I made a mental note to keep a close watch to see that we weren't caught in any sudden walls of water coming unexpectedly down the river.

We made our camp and inflated our rafts. Because of the weight problem, our plan was to not carry any tents. So, our camp making was very simple. Each crew got all their equipment in one area and unrolled their sleeping bags. We cooked supper and everything seemed to be going smoothly.

Late in the afternoon, we had a meeting of all the crews. I pointed out to them that I had been watching the clouds, and far up the river it looked as if it might be raining. I reminded them that we were only a few feet above the river, and any sort of rise could put the water up into our camp. The other leaders and I decided that we might have to move back across the "creek" where we would be out of danger on the high banks.

We went to bed, but I didn't go to sleep. I kept watching the lightning, far up the river, and it seemed to be getting nearer. About 1:30, I woke everyone up, and told them to prepare for some rain. We suggested that the sleeping bags be rolled up to keep them from getting wet.

Some of the kids decided that, in case it started raining, they might get under the rafts and keep from getting wet. I told them that the water would probably run under the rafts, and they would get wet anyway.

Well, about 2:15 it started to rain. It was coming down in buckets, and it didn't take long for us to decide that our perch on that low island might become a trifle damp. I told the leaders to start moving our equipment back across the shallow creek to the banks near Lajitas.

We started carrying our gear back across to Lajitas, and it was one big mess. It was raining so hard it was difficult to breathe, and the sandy soil had turned into gooey mud. The footing underneath was bad and we slipped, stumbled and slithered as we toted our stuff back across the creek.

We had to make several trips to move all the equipment, and by this time the water was beginning to rise in the creek. When we first crossed in the afternoon, the water was only ankle deep, but had risen to where the water was about three and a half to four feet deep.

We yelled at the smaller kids to stay on the bank, not to try to cross the creek any more. The leaders and some of the older Scouts were carrying the last bags of food across the creek. I was the last one across and I was carrying a canvas bag of food.

Just as I got to the center of the creek, the water was about up to my waist. The current was running pretty good and it was difficult to try to force your way through the water. I stumbled over a big, round rock and the current knocked me down.

I was floundering around, trying to get up, and the food bag was floating down the creek. The kids yelled, "Don't lose the food! Somebody grab the sack!" It was then I found out how I really rated with the boys. Here I was, about to drown in the creek, and no one—and I mean no one—even paid one bit of attention to their leader caught in the grip of the raging torrent. All they were worried about was making sure the food was safe.

We were wet and cold and it was impossible to start a fire. Most of the kids had ponchos and we told them to get together and share a little body heat. After about another hour, it stopped raining, and it seemed to become a little warmer. I finally got so tired, I just wrapped my poncho around me and went to sleep, lying in the mud.

When it finally got to be daylight the next morning, we were a sad looking bunch. We were wet and muddy and looked like a bunch of wet chickens which hadn't quite made it to the hen house. Once again, I was amazed at the speed which kids can overcome seeming disasters. Here we had spent one of the worst nights in all my camping experiences, and the boys seemed to take it in stride. As one kid put it, "Aw shucks! It was pretty bad but no one got drowned!"

We finally managed to start a fire and whipped up some breakfast. After a little warm food in them, the kids perked up even more. They wanted to know how soon we could start our raft trip. The leaders and I decided that, if there was no more evidence of the river rising, we might try to start about noon.

We watched the river and found that it wasn't coming up any more. In fact, it seemed to be falling a little. About noon we decided to try it and started carrying our gear back across the island to the main Rio Grande. We loaded our rafts, and decided to eat after we had made a few miles on the river.

After loading our rafts, we checked to make sure that everyone was present, and then embarked on our first great raft trip. The first few miles on the river were rather hectic. We were having a little difficulty in paddling our unwieldy craft just where we wished to go. The first few times we went through

"Just as I got to the center of the creek, the water was about up to my waist. The current was running pretty good and it was difficult to try to force your way through the water. I stumbled over a big round rock and the current knocked me down.

I was floundering around, trying to get up, and the food bag was floating down the creek. The kids yelled, "Don't lose the food! Somebody grab the sack!"

some small rapids, some of the rafts got turned around and the crews were going through stern first. But after a short time, we learned to control the rafts better, and also learned to read the river a little better. By reading the river, we learned to know that certain patterns in the water indicated hidden rocks or maybe a stump or two lurking beneath the surface.

After about five miles of river we decided to pull in and have lunch. It was here that we made a very disheartening discovery. When we opened the food bags for that first meal, we found that most of our bread supply was ruined. Between the downpour of rain and the plastic bags inside the canvas bags, our bread was such a mess, one kid suggested that we could drink the bread. Inside the plastic bags, the moisture had accumulated to the point that everything in the food bags was wet.

Luckily, most of the food was packed in waterproof containers, but some items like the bread and jerky had gotten very wet. We discarded the bread but decided to try to salvage the jerky. We had several cartons of crackers and some hard tack, a sort of survival bread, and felt we could make it with quite a few cartons of shoe-string potatoes.

When we first started our trip, my raft had four boys in it, two on each side. I was in the front and tried the old canoeing position of kneeling in the raft. There were three large inflatable cushions which covered the bottom of the raft. I used one of these to kneel on but quickly discovered that the kneeling position was not very practical. As long as the water was deep enough, my knees did fine, but when the river became shallow, you could hear and I could feel my knees bumping against the rocks. After the kids in my raft complained about the noise caused by my knees making contact with the rocks, I thought that I had better try something else.

Since the boys rode in the raft with one foot inside and one dragging in the water, I decided that I would sit on the front of the raft with both feet in the water. This position seemed to work very well, and with a few hours of rafting under our belts, we had reached the point where we considered ourselves real experienced river rats.

All went well until we came to our first big rapids. I told the kids to put both feet inside the raft and to get ready to paddle like crazy when I yelled the instructions as we traversed the rapids. We were just approaching the first waves, and I turned around to make sure my crew was all set. As I turned around to look, the raft where I was sitting had become wet from the first waves and was very slick. I lost my balance and fell over backwards in the raft with my feet sticking up in the air like an enormous bug, struggling on its back. The waves from the rapids were tossing the raft about, and the kids couldn't take time to help me regain my balance as they were too busy trying to avoid the rocks.

We went completely through the rapids before I could get up and regain my position on the front of the raft. There was a rope which encircled the raft and had a piece at the front of the raft to tie it up to the bank. After my embarrassing performance, whenever we approached some rapids, I would hold to the rope like a bareback bronc rider or a bull rider in the rodeo.

I might add that my crew was not very impressed with my expertise and knowledge as to the proper way to ride a raft through the rapids. As I remember, some slurring remarks and quite a few ill-concealed giggles were in evidence when someone mentioned my great leadership in guiding them through the rapids.

The rest of the rafts made it through OK and we continued on down the river to where we were going to camp right outside Santa Elena Canyon. Right before the river starts through the canyon, it makes a big sweeping "S" curve and there are some good rapids here. We all managed to negotiate the "hay stacks," (rapids) and pulled in to the shore where we planned to camp.

Each crew set up their camp and we started spreading out the gear and food to see if we could dry it out some. We came to the conclusion that, plastic bags inside canvas bags, was not the ideal way to pack our equipment, especially the food. One of my bright crew members came up with the observation that the plastic bags and canvas bags created their own weather, and when the sun was shining outside, it was raining inside the plastic bags. I was inclined to agree with him.

We ate supper and went to bed very early. I told the crews that tomorrow was going to be a very dangerous and very tiring day. We planned to go through Santa Elena Canyon and would have to make a long portage over the "rock slide" in the canyon. As I lay in my wet sleeping bag, I thought about all of the little kids we had in our crews, and I started to worry about how they would do in the canyon.

I mentioned the rapids right before the river starts through the canyon, and I could hear the water roaring through the first walls of the cut which takes you into the canyon. These walls are several hundred feet high, and rise straight up from the very banks of the river. Further into the canyon, the walls are 1500 to 1800 feet high and give you the impression that the walls are wider at the bottom than they are at the top.

You seem to feel that the walls are about to topple over on you. After you start through the canyon, the river is very crooked and you must make sharp turns to keep from being thrown into the walls of the canyon. The hydraulics of the water is so strong that each person in a raft has to be alert to keep the raft from crashing into the rocks.

From where you first start into the canyon, there is about a mile of very swift water. The river falls rapidly until you reach the "rock slide." This slide occurred about ten thousand years ago, when a large portion of the canyon wall on the Mexican side crumbled away and fell into the river. Boulders as large as houses block portions of the river and make a very hazardous trip if you try to run the rapids. Through the years, the water has hollowed out holes under the huge rocks and created "suck holes." A large log or even a canoe or raft could be pulled under by the current and lodged under the rocks.

Since we had so many little boys, we thought that we had better portage around the "rock slide." I mentioned in the chapter on canoe trips that this "rock slide" was the worst portage I was ever on, and many other canoeists and river rats will agree.

You start out on the portage by climbing over, around and under some of those house-sized boulders. You start up a very steep incline with the wall at your elbow rising some four or five hundred feet above your head. On the other side, the rocks and debris slope very sharply down to the river bank, about five hundred feet below. There isn't much of a trail and, in some places it is so narrow that we had to let the air out of our rafts to negotiate the turns. The trail keeps climbing higher and higher until you finally reach the point where you have to start your descent to the river bank. Getting back down to river level is quite a chore. The trail is very steep, and you have to be careful not to step on loose rocks, which might propel you several hundred feet into the chocolate colored Rio Grande. Outside of a few minor cuts and scratches and a bruise or two, everyone made it back down to the river bank.

We inflated our rafts and started preparing lunch. As we were eating, some of the kids wondered if the rapids at the "rock slide" were really as bad as we had been told. To answer their question, I pointed to a large bundle hanging from a tree limb. This is placed there by the Park Rangers and contained a raft and a small amount of food. This was to be used in an emergency by someone trying to run the rapids and ending up losing their raft and food supply. There is no way you can get out of the canyon at this point unless you are a bird. It is impossible to go back up the river the way you came in because of the very strong current. You would have to go on through the canyon, about another nine miles, and a raft is mandatory. You might be able to swim it but it would be very hazardous.

One Easter, when there are always many visitors to the Big Bend National Park, the Mexican government decided to release a large amount of water from a dam in old Mexico. There were many people on the river, in canoes and rafts, between Lajitas and Santa Elena Canyon. They were caught by surprise by the wall of water and were washed down the river to the rocks of the "rock slide." Many suffered broken arms, legs and other bones and quite a few had severe cuts. Most of the people were in shock, and were clinging desperately to the rocks. The Park Rangers had to come up the river from the lower end of the canyon in air boats. These are boats which are propelled through the water from the thrust of an airplane propeller mounted on the back of the craft. Since there is no propeller in the water, the air boat can go through water only a few inches deep.

I told the kids that several people had drowned at the "rock slide" and that it was as bad as its reputation. Also, from where we sat eating lunch, I showed them several pieces of rafts and canoes along the river bank where people had tried to run the "rock slide" instead of portaging around it. I mentioned that many rafters and canoeists had lost their food supply in the rapids and were forced to go hungry. When I mentioned the possibility of losing the food, this was the clincher in my argument as to why we did not run the rapids. Boys may not seem to understand a lot of reasons as to why you do or do not do certain things, but when you mention the possible loss of their food, you are reaching them on a level they understand.

We traveled on through the canyon and came to the end about five o'clock in the afternoon. Our crews passed by the "Cottonwood Campgrounds," a beautiful camping spot. There were quite a few people here and there just wasn't enough room for our thirty-one river rats. We were able to replenish our water supply and went on down the river about a mile, where we made camp.

After we had eaten, I was talking to my son-in-law, who was one of the leaders in our expedition. We were laughing about the boys wearing their life jackets. We had repeated over and over that no one—and we did mean no one—was to get in a raft without wearing his life jacket. When we got out to eat at noon, sometimes the temperature was hovering over 100 degrees, and the kids were still wearing the life jackets. I told Ted that I would bet that some of the little boys would probably sleep in their life jackets, if we hadn't told them to remove them.

Before we started our trip, and were back home in the planning stages, I had worried about some sort of communication system. Radios would not operate in the deep canyons, but transmitters might be able to send a message to an airplane, if it were flying directly overhead. One of my ex-Scouts was an instructor in the Border Patrol. I mentioned to him about my communication problem, and he offered to let us borrow a transceiver from the Border Patrol. In the course of the conversation, he casually mentioned that these things cost about $500 each. I could just picture a raft overturning and the piece of radio equipment being lost in the muddy waters of the Rio Grande.

I declined his offer and he came up with another idea to signal for help in case of an emergency. He said that their patrol planes flew along the river twice a day looking for "wetbacks," illegal aliens trying to enter the United States. His idea was—as the planes flew overhead at a low altitude, if everything was OK, all the people in the rafts were to stick their paddles out of the right side. If anything was wrong and we needed help, we were to stick the paddles out of the left side of the raft. This seemed like a simple, foolproof procedure and I had spent quite a lot of time briefing the boys and the leaders on this means of communication. I warned them about some joker thinking it would be cute to stick his paddle out of the left side of the raft. I also reminded them about the little boy who cried, "Wolf!", and could not get any help when he really needed it. I pointed out to them that if they fooled the Border Patrol into thinking we needed help, and they sent a helicopter from Alpine, Texas, someone was going to pay for this joke, to the tune of $500.

What was so funny about this whole bit about the paddles on the right or left sides was the feeling of security it gave us. Actually on our whole seven day trip, we never saw one single Border Patrol plane. We found out later that most of the time the planes fly parallel to the river but about a half a mile away. Luckily, we never got into any serious trouble, but I imagine we could have worn holes in the rafts thrusting the paddles out of the left or right sides, before we got any help from the Border Patrol planes.

While camped that night, we took an inventory of our food supply. The bread was all lost but we had some crackers and hard tack. I felt that, in a pinch, we could use shoe-string potatoes as a substitute for bread. Our canned food was in good shape and we had an ample supply of Spam, canned roast, canned bacon and chicken loaf. Our jerky, which we had planned to use as snacks, was in sad condition. It had been very wet from the rain and the food bags making their own weather inside the plastic bags. Most of the jerky had a green coating of something which resembled penicillin. I wouldn't have eaten a piece of this stuff for any amount of money. One of my Scouts, Tom, would take a piece of the jerky covered with green mold and run it between his fingers to remove the mold. After he had eaten it and suffered no ill effects, some of the rest of the kids tried this green delicacy. To this day, I have never been able to eat another piece of jerky.

After an uneventful night except for a very large, very determined wood rat which tried to crawl into my sleeping bag, we arose to face another day of rafting on the river. As we were cooking breakfast, a Park Ranger came by and told us that we shouldn't have camped at this spot. I told him we were sorry for camping in an unauthorized spot, but we had no way of knowing that we were breaking the rules. I was afraid that maybe he was going to make us un-camp, and I wasn't sure just what was involved in such a procedure.

Just across the river from our camp, was the small Mexican town of Santa Elena. When we got ready to leave, the entire population came down to see us off. "Off" was a good word to describe what the natives thought of our rafting down the river. We kept yelling at them and motioning at them to come go with us. They kept yelling back, "Poco loco! Poco loco!" Some of the boys asked me what the words meant. I told them that the villagers thought we were a little crazy for going off down the river in those flimsy rafts.

Between Santa Elena Canyon and Mariscal Canyon there is a distance of about forty-two miles. The river banks are not very high and the terrain flattens out.

The banks of the river are covered with a thick growth of cane, twelve to fifteen feet high, and so thick in places that a snake would have difficulty crawling through it.

On this part of the river, we really had to paddle. The river was very wide and the current was sluggish. At times, the wind blew directly into our faces, which made paddling the rafts even more of a chore. It took two days of hard paddling to get across this part of the Park. One afternoon as we were paddling along, my raft was fourth in line. Suddenly the lead raft turned and started paddling feverishly for the shore and the other two rafts followed the lead raft and were headed for the river bank. I couldn't imagine what in the world was going on. When we got near enough to see what was causing all of the excitement, I nearly fell out of the raft, I was laughing so hard.

A few years before, Lady Bird Johnson, and a party of V.I.P.'s had been taken on a tour of Big Bend Park. The Park Service had constructed a comfort station to take care of the needs of the party, and there it sat, a lonely monument to civilization, in the wilds of Big Bend Park.

By this time, all of the rafts had arrived, and we were greeted with the spectacle of twenty little boys all trying to use the "john" at the same time. The kids could have gone right out in the open since there was no one within forty miles, except the members of our troop. When I asked one little kid why he used the "john," he said that it was like asking a mountain climber why he climbed a mountain. The mountaineer replied, "I climbed it because it was there." The little Scout replied that he felt obligated to use the comfort station because it was there. I couldn't argue with that logic.

On this trip between the canyons, we had another incident to occur which concerned a horse. Or, I should say, a mare and a little colt. We were floating along and the water was quite shallow in this part of the river. A mare and her colt were standing in the water, which was about three feet deep, when the lead raft came near the horses. I guess that the mare thought that the raft was about to harm the colt, and she went charging through the water, straight for the raft. For a moment or two I thought that the raft might take on another passenger, as the mare looked as if she were trying to climb into the raft. The boys waved their paddles and scared her away, but, as the rest of the rafts floated by where she stood, snorting and tossing her head, we kept a wary eye on her.

The remoteness of this area of Texas provides a wonderful opportunity for criminals to smuggle dope across the Rio Grande into the United States. Quite often you hear through the news media that law enforcement officials have confiscated a big haul, or that officers have fought a gun battle with the smugglers. The fact that this happens quite often gave me something else to worry about. I was afraid that we might stumble accidentally on a bunch of smugglers crossing the river, and that they might decide to do away with us to keep us from "talking."

Even though it was not supposed to be done, I carried a handgun with me on the raft trip. Of course, this was only a .22 caliber pistol, and was a little more effective than a "Daisy B-B" gun. About half the time it was so wet that there was a question in my mind as to whether or not it would fire. The other half of the time it was tucked away in my duffle bag in our raft, and would have been difficult to find in an emergency.

Between Santa Elena and Mariscal Canyons, there is a place on the river called the Loop Camp. The river makes almost a complete circle, and causes a little confusion to first time river rats. Most of our travel had been in an easterly or southeasterly direction, with the sun behind our backs in the afternoon. When we camped at the Loop Camp, we came ashore where the river is almost completing the circle and we are traveling west. I climbed out of the raft and thought that the sun had finally gotten to my brain. The way it appeared to me, the sun was sinking in the east. After we got out our maps, we could see that we were actually traveling west, instead of east as we had for the past few days.

We made camp in a big stand of salt cedars," a tree which grows along rivers and creeks, which have a high salt content. We cooked supper and decided that we must boil and treat the river water to replenish our supply. All three crews did their boiling bit and we covered the big aluminum stock pots to let the water stand overnight.

We went to bed and everything seemed to be in order until about 2:30 in the morning. Something woke me up and I listened to see where the sound was coming from. It sounded like someone was paddling a metal boat or canoe across the river from the Mexican side. The paddles hitting the metal sides made the noise which woke me up. The moon was shining very brightly and I went crawling through the brush to a point where I could see the boat crossing the river. It was only about thirty yards away from our camp, and I could make out the figures of two people in the craft. As I lay there watching the boat, someone put a hand on my shoulder and I almost came "un-glued." It was my Senior Patrol Leader who had also been awakened by the boat. He had come crawling through the brush to see what was going on and had spotted me.

When the boat reached our side of the river, a man stepped out of the brush along the bank and the men talked in low tones. One of the boaters handed the man a package, and he faded away into the cane. The boat people started back across the river. Randy, my S.P.L. whispered to me, "What do you think we ought to do?" I told him to be as quiet as possible, and hope that the smugglers didn't spot us. I was afraid one of our kids might make some noise to alert the men to our being there. We had paddled many a mile that day and I guess that everyone was so tired that they were all sleeping the sleep of the innocent.

The next morning, when I got up I wondered if I might have just dreamed the whole affair. I checked with Randy and he agreed that we weren' t dreaming. We walked up the river a short distance to see if we might see the boat. Sure enough, across the river in a little cove, we could see a crude boat made out of sheet iron. The smugglers had very carelessly covered the boat with cane, but we were able to find it easily. Randy could not understand why the men were so careless in hiding their boat, but I pointed out to him that this area was so remote, that it was unlikely to be found.

The evening before, when we first started making camp, one of the boys came to me and said he had diarrhea. I gave him a generous shot of Kaopectate and Pepto-Bismol, and reminded him that I wanted him to take some more before he went to bed. He confessed that he was a little sick at his stomach, and thought that it might have been caused by his eating some of that moldy jerky. I immediately gathered up all the jerky we had left, and threw it into a convenient fire. The kids sent up a howl of protest over the loss of their jerky. Several said that they had been eating it and their stomachs were OK.

I told the sick boy, Paul, to just eat some canned fruit for supper to see if we could clear up the nausea. Before we went to bed I gave him some more medicine, and told him to check with me in the morning. When we got up the next morning, Paul said that he still had a touch of diarrhea, but that he was not sick at his stomach, anymore. I told him that I wanted him to ride in the raft with two of the older boys, Randy, my S.P.L., and Stuffy. We started down the river, and after a few hours of paddling, were getting near the spot where we planned to eat lunch. My raft was about fifty yards behind the raft with Paul, Randy and Stuffy. All of a sudden, Paul went over the side of the raft and held on to the rope which encircled the craft. He made no effort to get back in the raft, but I thought that he might be having some trouble trying to get into the raft.

I yelled to him, "Paul, are you OK.?"

He answered back and said, "I am doing all right."

We floated on about another hundred yards, but Paul still hung on the side of the raft and made no effort to crawl back in.

I called to Randy, "Help Paul get back in the raft."

Randy yelled back, "We don't want Paul in the raft."

I couldn't understand his behavior at all, because Randy was always such a thoughtful person. I figured that maybe the sun and the river had finally gotten to him and he was suffering from an acute case of "river rat-itis."

When we pulled in to eat lunch, I immediately collared Randy and asked for an explanation for his "un-scout-like" behavior. When he had explained,

I almost cracked up laughing.

It seems as they were floating along, Paul said that he needed to go to the restroom. Randy told him we were going to stop for lunch in a little while, and couldn't he wait? Paul said that he couldn't wait, so Randy suggested that he just jump over the side of the raft, pull down his pants, and go to the bathroom. After they had floated along for about fifty yards, he asked Paul if everything was OK. Paul said he was doing just fine. Randy asked him if he had pulled down his pants. Paul said, "I didn't pull down my pants because I didn't need to—it was so thin it was just going through my pants." About the time Randy received this enlightening information, I had called to him telling him to help Paul back in the raft. This was when he yelled back that "They didn't want Paul back in the raft." When he told me about Paul's decision to not pull down his pants, I agreed that it was a wise decision to keep him out of the raft. So much for the "Great Diarrhea Caper."

We planned an early start after lunch, because we wanted to get through Mariscal Canyon before dark. This canyon is a lot like Santa Elena Canyon with walls rising 1,500 to 1,800 feet above the river. To me, Mariscal Canyon is darker and more gloomy than Santa Elena. The rocks are gray, and the canyon is so deep and narrow, there are many spots where the rays of the sun never penetrate to the bottom of the gorge. About the only time the sun ever reaches the canyon floor is when it is shining directly overhead. The river doesn't curve as much as Santa Elena, and the current, through most of the canyon, doesn't seem so strong.

Our eight rafts were moving through the canyon at a pretty good clip, with my raft third in line. We were about seventy-five yards behind the second raft when we came around a bend in the canyon. A huge wall of rocks, fifteen to twenty feet high, completely blocked the river except for a very narrow channel on the Mexican side of the bank. We had heard about this obstacle, but we had arrived there before we had planned.

The two front rafts had pulled in to the shore and their crews were standing along the river bank. The current had suddenly picked up speed, because the water was being forced through the narrow channel like water being forced through a pipe.

It suddenly dawned on me that we were too far out in the river to make it to shore before our raft was carried downstream and demolished against the rocks blocking the river. I threw a rope to the people on the shore and they really "set down on the rope" to prevent the weight of the raft from pulling the rope out of their hands.

When the raft hit the end of the rope, it flipped around like a line of kids playing "crack the whip." My little grandson was in the raft with me, and he was thrown into the swift current. I was on the front of the raft and didn't even know he had fallen out until the boys on the shore yelled.

Lee, one of the boys in my raft, was an older Scout and was very muscular. Lee was an outstanding football player for our high school and he and Dan, my grandson, had developed quite a friendship on the trip. When he saw my grandson flip out of the raft, Lee jumped out of the raft to try to get to Dan before he was swept into the rapids boiling around the rocks. By this time, I had jumped into the river to see if I could prevent them from being injured or drowned when they hit the rocks.

The water here was about up to my chest, but the pull of the current was terrific. We were washed down and pinned against the rocks by the force of the water. The current was so strong you could feel it washing the sand from beneath your feet.

Finally, the crews on the shore got some ropes to us and were able to pull us out of the river. At first, I thought that I wouldn't mention this little episode to my wife and daughter when we returned home, because they weren't too keen on letting Dan go on this trip. However, I figured that I had better tell them when we returned home, because, blabbermouth that he was, Dan would probably tell them as soon as he got off the bus. I could hear him telling the two women, "I got thrown out of the raft into the rapids, and Lee jumped in and saved my life." I decided that they had better hear it from me first.

By this time all of the rafts had arrived, and we were looking over the situation to see if we would have to portage around the rocks, or maybe take a chance and try to run the very narrow channel. As we stood there deciding on our course of action, I was amazed to see a figure come bounding down the rocks on the Mexican side. He was wearing a yellow, surplus "Mae West" life jacket, and as he bounded from rock to rock, the thought flashed through my mind that I was looking at a modern Robinson Crusoe.

He plunged into the river, swam across, and came up to where I was standing. He was a young man and, if his sudden appearance was startling, his first words were even more so. He asked me, "Did you bring my mail?" My first thought was that he was not playing with a full deck, and that he had been isolated in the canyon too long. He explained about his mail. Usually, when a rafting crew was getting their "float permit" from the Park headquarters, if the rangers knew that you planned to go through Mariscal Canyon, and they had any mail for this hermit, the rangers would ask you to deliver it to him.

The story behind this young man was quite interesting. He was from a town in East Texas and had spent some time in the Big Bend Park. He became interested in the Buddhist religion and decided that he needed to go some place where he could spend a lot of time in solitude and meditation. He chose Mariscal Canyon because there would be weeks or even months when he would see no one.

At the time we saw him, he had been in the canyon for about three months. He invited us to see where he lived, and once more, I was struck with the thought that here was a modern Robinson Crusoe. He was living in two caves and had built some crude furniture to furnish his home. He had even rigged up a deal where he could heat water and take a hot shower. About once a month, he would hike out of the canyon, and bring back a supply of canned vegetables.

We asked him about running the narrow channel and he gave us some information which made us decide to portage around the rocks. About a month before a family in two rafts was attempting to run the channel. Two teen-age girls in one raft were knocked out into the water and pulled under one of the large rocks. Luckily, they were carried completely under the big rock and popped up on the downstream side of the rapids.

This made up our minds for us and we chose the portage route. This portage was only about fifty yards long, and was a piece of cake, when compared with the "rock slide" in Santa Elena.

After we left the portage, we knew that it was a long haul to get out of the canyon. In fact, it took us almost five hours to get through to the lower end. It was late in the afternoon, and we knew that we had to make camp soon. The only good place to camp was on the Mexican side so we headed in to shore.

I told the kids in my raft that I would save them from getting their feet wet when we pulled in to the river bank. I was on the front of the raft and would jump out in the shallow water, and pull the raft to shore. I had been riding so long that my legs were cramped. When I jumped out of the raft, my legs gave way, the raft knocked me down and ran over me. I came up sputtering and gasping for air behind the raft. Four boys looked at me with disgusted looks and muttered something about what a great raftsman I was. I did remind them that my intentions were good, even if my action was deplorable.

We made camp and some of the kids asked me what would happen if the Mexicans found us camping on their side of the river. I kidded them a little by telling them that it would probably be "the wetback procedure" in reverse. We might all end up in jail until the Mexican authorities determined that we were not invading Mexico.

Since we had gotten in very late, it must have been about 9:30 when we finished eating. About 100 yards from our camp, there was a hill about four hundred feet high. Suddenly, one of my Scouts yelled, "Look up on the hill! There is someone up there with a light. They are coming to get us!" I checked to see what was causing all his concern. The planet Mars was just coming up over the hill, and it did look like someone was up there with a light. When we got everyone settled down again, I told the whole bunch we were going to have a meeting.

At the meeting, I told the boys that the other leaders and I had been talking and decided on a course of action. Since we had lost part of our food supply, we felt that we were running a little short on provisions. When we first planned the raft trip, we had thought that we would make a two day journey from Mariscal Canyon to Rio Grande Village, where we planned to end our trip. Because of the food shortage, we had decided to make this trip in one day. I warned that it was going to take a lot of hard paddling to accomplish this, but by getting up early, and really bending our backs to the paddles, I was sure we could do it. When I told the kids we would be able to buy more food when we reached Rio Grande Village, they were all for it.

After the meeting was over, one of our young Scouts, who had never been on an overnight camp before the raft trip, came bustling up to me and announced that he had to use a phone. I told him the nearest phone was about forty miles away in the Basin. When I asked him about the sudden emergency, he told me that he really needed to call his folks.

I suspected that he might be getting just a trifle homesick, but I explained that he might call when we reached Rio Grande Village the next afternoon. He seemed pacified and went back to the members of his crew.

We got up early the next morning and started paddling with vigor. All went well until it came time for our noon lunch break. All of the food for my raft and another one, carrying my son-in-law, was in a supply raft, manned by two older Scouts and two little boys.

The rest of the crews ate and offered to share their food with us, as our supply raft was nowhere in sight. We thanked them and told them we were sure that our food would be appearing shortly. I told the other rafts to go on and our group would wait a while for the erring raft.

We waited about an hour, and still no supply raft. I told the kids that we needed to go on before the other rafts got too far ahead of us. We started paddling down the river and by three o'clock, we were really getting hungry. The kids in my raft were looking at me like they might pull over to the river bank and have "barbecued leader." I told them to check the supply bags in our raft to see if, just maybe, there might be something edible we had overlooked.

One of my rafters gave a cry of delight and showed me two packages of dried apples. We started eating this dried fruit, and boy, did they taste good. The weather, which was very hot, along with the dried apples soon created a humongous thirst in our bodies. We drank quite a lot of water, and soon discovered that this was a mistake. When the dried apples were mixed with the water in our stomachs, something began to happen. This mass began to swell and soon one's stomach felt as tight as the head of a drum. Leave it to the kids to come up with some outdoor philosophy in a time like this. One of my crew members said that we didn't need to wear our life jackets any more. We had so much air in our stomachs, that we couldn't have sunk on a bet. After the natural digestion process took place, the pressure on our stomachs was less painful.

It was getting rather late in the afternoon and we had no idea how much farther it was to the Rio Grande Village. We saw two little Mexican boys and asked them how far it was to our "getting out point." None of us could speak much Spanish, and the little boys were at a loss to understand English. We thought that we finally made them understand by repeating over and over, "Rio Grande Village, Rio Grande Village, ..." At last one of the Mexican boys seemed to understand, but he gave us an answer that came as a shock. He said, "Fifteen kilometers, fifteen kilometers."

I was sure that we were very close to our destination, so the information nearly floored us. My crew said that it would be pitch dark before we got there. Again we had a sample of the words of wisdom from our outdoor philosopher. He told us that it would not be dark when we got there—oh no! It would take us all night to travel that distance and the sun should be just about ready to come up the next morning. We were just about ready to throw him overboard when we heard someone yelling at us. It was one of our Scouts, and he told us to pull over to where he was standing—we were there!

We pulled in to the shore, and I stepped out of the raft, in the middle of a patch of quicksand. At first, I didn't realize what it was. When I stepped out of the raft, I immediately sank in halfway to my knees. I reached back to retrieve my duffle bag from the raft and had sunk in over my knees. I thought that maybe I could get down on my hands and knees to relieve some of the pressure.

This was not the most brilliant idea in the world, as I was soon in mud up to my hips. I yelled at the kids to get a rope to pull me out. One of my trusted followers told the others to bring a camera. All the time I was sinking deeper into the sand, and I threatened all sorts of terrible things if they didn't pull me out. They pointed out to me that, if they didn't pull me out, there wasn't a whole lot I could do.

After they finally finished with their picture session, they hauled me out of the quicksand. The event sort of scared me and I wondered what a person would do if caught in this mess with no one around. One of my kids pointed out to me that you would probably end up like the livestock, which we had seen occasionally mired in the mud by the river. After a few days, when you ripened sufficiently, you become the main entree of a "buzzard banquet."

All of the rafts except our supply raft had come in to the Rio Grande Village. I was really getting worried about them, because it was going to be dark before they arrived. As we were camped about a hundred yards away from the river, I was worried that they might not see our fires and float on past in the dark.

We ate our supper, and I placed some boys with lights on big rocks near the river. I told them to keep flashing their lights on and off, and maybe our lost raft would spot the signal. I told the other leaders, that if the raft wasn't in by ten o'clock, that I was going to notify the Park Rangers. They could go up the river in their air boats to search for our missing crew.

We could see a storm building up in the Carmen mountains in old Mexico. We could hear the thunder and see the lightning, and we felt that there was a good chance that the storm might come into the Rio Grande Village. As I had mentioned earlier, our crews had no tents, so I figured there was a distinct possibility that we might get wet, in case of a rain.

I told the kids that we might use the deflated rafts to provide some emergency shelter, but we might have another experience like our first night on the river at Lajitas. My words of pending doom didn't seem to make much of an impression on the boys, as they assured me that they would be OK.

It was about 9:30 at night, and our raft was still missing. I suggested to the other leaders to pile all of our equipment together to prevent its blowing away in case of a hard blowing rain. I told them I was going down to the river to see if the boys with the lights had any news to report on the lost raft. I had decided to wait until 10 o'clock and then report the lost raft to the Park Rangers.

Just as I reached the rocks on which the boys were sitting, flashing their lights, we heard someone yelling at us from far up the river. After exchanging yells for a few minutes, we recognized Randy's voice and the other kids in the raft.

When they reached shore, we crowded around them to ask why they were so late. Randy and Stuffy, the two older Scouts, told us that they had run into some terrific headwinds caused by the storm in Mexico. It was blowing so hard and they were making such little headway that Stuffy, who was a lifeguard at one of our municipal pools and an excellent swimmer, decided to see if he could tow the raft and help the paddlers.

He tied one end of a nylon rope around his chest and was swimming about twenty feet in front of the raft. His pulling the raft seemed to help, and with the three boys in the raft paddling, they were moving a little better against the wind. After a while it began to get dark and since there was no flashlight in the raft, the two older boys worried about hitting a stump or crashing into a rock in the river. Stuffy thought that it might be better if he continued to swim in front of the raft, to prevent their "trashing out" on the rocks. The raft went through two pretty good rapids, but, luckily, they didn't run afoul of any obstacles lurking in the river. Stuffy said that he knew the water was getting shallow because his knees were banging against the rocks. After they went through the last rapids, the river got deeper and the wind seemed to be dying down a lot. Stuffy got back in the raft and they were paddling along, wondering where they were, when they saw our boys flashing their lights.

We helped them carry the gear up to where we were camped. When we got there, we could see the other leaders standing around, but there wasn't a boy in sight. I asked my son-in-law what had happened to the boys, and he just pointed to a very large restroom which was located near our campsite.

This "comfort station" was a large unit with the men's facilities on one side and the women's on the other. I went over and opened the men's side and discovered that we had a carpet of Scouts in their sleeping bags—wall to wall. When I had suggested that they find cover in the event of a storm, the boys did the obvious thing—they took cover in the nearest building.

I could see that all of our Scouts were not in the men's side, and frankly, I was afraid to ask where the rest of the boys were. I circled the building and carefully opened the door to the women's facilities. Sure enough, the rest of our river rats had taken over this side of the building. I asked these "squatters" what they would do if some female needed to use the facilities and found wall to wall boys. One of my boys, who later became a lawyer, pointed out to me the facts were as follows: there were no female campers in the area where we were camped, and since there were no females in our crew, no one would be using the restroom. I had to agree with his logic.

The storm never did materialize, and those of us, the leaders, who couldn't squeeze into the restrooms, had a nice night to sleep out in the open.

We had called home to tell the bus company to send our bus a day earlier than planned. After a quiet trip home, we were met at our cabin by a large crowd of parents and well-wishers. They had made a huge welcome sign, about twenty feet long, and my granddaughter had made individual diplomas to be presented to each of our river rats. Marcy, my granddaughter, had made a nice diploma of thanks to me for taking the kids on the raft trip. We all swaggered just a trifle as we casually mentioned portaging, reading the river, and running the rapids.

One further note to add to our trip. As we had so many little kids on the trip, the parents were naturally worried about their welfare. Many of them had called the Big Bend National Park headquarters to find if they had any news of our crew.

The people at the headquarters would assure them that we were doing fine —no problems. They told my wife the rangers had talked to us, while we were camped on the Mexican side. I suppose this information calmed the fears of the parents, but it was a snow job. The only times we even saw a Park Ranger on our seven day trip, was when the fellow came down to tell us we had camped in the wrong place at Castolon, and when the ranger met us at Rio Grande Village to collect a dollar a head for camping in the area.

This was Raft Trip Number 1.

P.S. We learned several valuable lessons on our first raft trip. The most important was this: anything which is to be kept dry must not be packed in one of those weather-making plastic and canvas bag combinations.

Raft Trip Number 2 was a lot more ambitious than our first raft trip. We planned to start where we ended our first trip at Rio Grande Village. This was near the east edge of Big Bend National Park. Our proposed trip was to take us to Langtry, Texas, a distance of between 160 and 200 miles on the river. A short distance from Rio Grande Village, you run out of the Park and are more or less on your own.

There are no towns on the Texas side between our starting point and Langtry, and the few ranch houses are from thirty to sixty miles from the river. This is about the same situation you find on the Mexican side. In other words, you had better carry everything you need, and be prepared to take care of any emergency with the equipment on hand. After you leave the Park, the lower canyons are so remote that if you had to summon help, it would take at least four days to get aid to you. We carried a very complete first aid kit and felt that we could handle anything short of an operation in the wilderness.

There were thirty-six members in our bunch of rafters, and we divided these into three crews. This time, all of our food, sleeping bags and personal gear were packed in waterproof plastic buckets, which held from three to five gallons. We allowed each crew member two of these containers. All of our food was packed, by meals for each crew, and we were certain that we would not have to contend with drinkable bread and penicillin-covered jerky.

We started out with 200 plastic gallon jugs of water. We knew that on this longer trip we would probably have to boil water at least three times. There were some springs along the river, but they were bunched pretty close together, and we couldn't depend on them for water.

Each raft had 100 feet of half-inch nylon rope, and with that in the supply rafts we had about 1,600 feet of rope. We carried plenty of extra paddles, and several rolls of duct tape to patch the rafts. We were going to use eight, six-man rafts on this trip, and the crews had come up with some very descriptive names for their crafts. We had—Old Yeller—Sea Cow—Trident—Speedy —Jet—Bud Man—Pegasus—and one raft marked with a large question mark. The names had been painted on the rafts, using red and black markers.

After spending the night at Rio Grande Village, we got up, cooked, ate breakfast and packed the rafts. The river was on a seven and a half foot rise, and the current was really moving along. We pushed out into the river and started our long journey.

We hadn't been gone very long before we started through Boquillas Canyon. This is a beautiful canyon, but the walls are not as high as those in Santa Elena and Mariscal Canyons. Another feature of this canyon is that the walls are further back from the river's edge, and one does not have the feeling of being completely overshadowed by the towering walls. This canyon has something which I have never found in any of the other canyons. There are sand dunes in the floor along the river. A short distance into the canyon we stopped and took some pictures of a large sand dune with a big cave at the top of the dune.

Of course, our boys had to climb up to the cave, but they found that this wasn't as easy as it seemed. The climb was very steep and you took two steps and slid back one. While we were at the foot of the large dune, a man and his wife and three children, came walking into the canyon. The entire family decided to climb up to the cave. The man and the three kids made it to the top in fine fashion, but when we started down the river, the poor woman was still struggling to reach the top.

The river was up and the current was very strong, and we went barreling along with a minimum of paddling. We would paddle to keep our rafts headed in the right direction and would have to paddle a little to keep from bouncing off a rock as we went through the rapids.

We came around a shallow bend in the river and noticed three of our lead rafts had pulled in to the shore. We stopped to investigate and found a very large calf had gotten into the same predicament I got in when I found myself in the quicksand. Evidently, the calf, a very large one of the Black Angus variety, had gone down to the river bank to get a drink. He became mired in the mud and sand and couldn't get out. You could see where he had struggled to get out, but all to no avail. The calf had just about quit struggling and seemed resigned to his fate.

We decided to get him out, but this was easier said than done. The animal weighed several hundred pounds, and it was difficult to get enough manpower around him to lift him out of the mud. When you stooped down to raise the calf, you found yourself sinking into the gooey mess. At first you would be in over your ankles, then over your knees, and end up buried all the way to your hips.

The crew came to the conclusion that the only way to save the calf was to use some of our nylon ropes. We tied several around the calf, using good ol' bowlines, and had several crew members stand on top of the river bank holding the ropes. Some of the larger boys and the leaders got around the calf, ready to heave him out of the mud.

At the signal, with our heaving and the boys pulling on the ropes, we were finally able to get the animal up the river bank. We removed the ropes, and he lay there on the ground for a few minutes. The calf finally struggled to his feet, took a few shaky steps and trotted off into the brush. We got back in our rafts and started down the river again, with that warm feeling of having done our "daily good turn."

The first day out of Rio Grande Village we made twenty-seven miles on the river. I had told the other leaders we needed to make as many miles as possible each day because we had planned our trip to take nine days on the river. Because of the portages, there might be several days where we would be limited to the number of miles traveled.

About 5 o'clock in the afternoon we pulled into the shore to camp. There was a high cliff on the Texas side, so we camped in old Mexico. As we were making camp, I caught a flash of light on top of a hill about a mile down the river. I had a powerful telescope in my bucket and got it out to see what was the source of the flash of light. I focused it on the hill and could see a couple of men looking at us through binoculars. I hoped that they would decide that we were harmless and had no plans for invading old Mexico. I think the thing which helped them to decide that we had no plans for annexation were those crazy kids of ours.

The river had been up and the place where we got out of the rafts was covered with about four inches of water. There was a clear space, about fifty yards square, where the sand and mud had washed in from the river. There was no brush or weeds in this area, and the kids discovered this cleared space. They immediately set about converting this clear spot into a "lob-lolly." If you are not familiar with a "lob-lolly," this is a term used in some parts of Texas to describe a large mudhole where the mud is about the consistency of apple butter. To create this mudhole, all of the boys got in this area and started jumping up and down. Sure enough, in a very short time we had a "lob-lolly."

I wondered why they were going to all of the trouble to make this super mudhole—but I soon found out. The kids would take a running start and literally dive into this ooshy, gooey mess. They would go completely out of sight and would come up laughing, gasping, with mud in their eyes, nose, hair and mouth, looking like some "creature from the Black Lagoon." I was afraid that there might be a rock or two lurking in their mudhole, but they assured me, that they had checked it out and thought the mud went all the way to China.

After about an hour of this, we called a halt and told them to get cleaned up. They went down to the river and washed off several tons of mud. I was certain that, if any engineer at the huge Amistad Dam several hundred miles downstream had just happened to be checking that day, he might have wondered about the increase in sediment flowing into the reservoir.

I called the entire crew together the next morning and told them we were going to have to paddle a little more because the river was beginning to drop. We had excellent topographical maps which were large enough and contained enough detail to give us a good idea of the terrain on both sides of the Rio Grande. One of my ex-Scouts had made this same trip a couple of times, and we were using his maps. Each map, which covered an area of about ten miles along the river, was sealed in waterproof plastic and was marked with compass headings and notes to suggest that you might want to leave the river at a certain point to check on the rapids up ahead.

The area through which we were traveling, was a favorite place for "wetbacks" or illegal aliens to cross the river in to Texas. This part of Texas is so remote and covers such a large area that it is impossible for the Border Patrol to cover it. We had camped one evening on the Mexican side, and it was very obvious that this was a spot where the "wetbacks" crossed into Texas. Where we were camped, there was a shallow cave with some rusty sardine cans and some pieces of sandals which the aliens make from old automobile tires. On the Texas side there was a hill about 400 feet high with a tree limb sticking in the rocks at the top. A white piece of rag was tied to this pole and was waving in the breeze.

As we were eating breakfast the next morning, we were talking about how some "would-be wetbacks" planning to cross the river, would feel if he topped the hill behind our camp and saw the rafts and all of the kids strung out for about fifty yards along the river. As we were talking, here came a couple of Mexican nationals. One man was riding a horse and the other fellow was walking. The man who was walking was carrying a small flour sack with something in it and a small plastic jug in the other hand. One of our Scouts, Hector, could speak excellent Spanish, so I told him to ask them where they were going. The man who was walking said that he was going to Texas by himself. When asked where he was going, he told us that he was going to Levelland, Texas. This was about 500 miles from where we were. I instructed Hector to ask him how he was going to get across the river, as it was still very muddy and the current was swift. He told Hector, that he couldn't swim, but that his friend would swim his horse across, and he would hold on to the horse's tail.

We offered to take him across in the raft, and he accepted. The only food the man had was one can of sardines. It was about fifty miles to the nearest ranchhouse from the river. The kids were appalled to find how little food the man had. They gave him some hard candy, some non-green jerky and a few cans of food. As we were going across the river, he leaned over the side of the raft and filled his plastic jug with that muddy river water. Immediately, the kids started giving me a hard time about not drinking that untreated stuff. I had warned them that they would end up with a good case of "Montezuma's Revenge" if they drank the river water. They said, "Look at this guy— he's drinking it!" I reminded them that his stomach was used to drinking the untreated stuff and he could get by with it.

As we let the man out on the Texas bank, the kids yelled at him, "If you ever come to San Angelo, be sure to come by 523 South Monroe," which is my address. I wouldn't have been too surprised to have found him knocking on my door, one day. Take note, all of my friends in the Border Patrol. To my many other sins, you may now add "wetback smuggling."

All of our Scouts were very impressed to find that a man would put his life on the line because he wanted to work so badly. He could have fallen and broken a leg or been bitten by a rattlesnake, and it might have been weeks before anyone came along and found him.

There is a place in the lower canyons called "The Canoe Eating Cliff." This spot, very appropriately named, has demolished several canoes and has caused the demise of a number of rafts. On the Texas side of the river a sheer cliff rises straight up from the water to the height of several hundred feet. The bottom edge of the cliff comes to within a foot or two of the surface of the river, and the wall is undercut for fifty to seventy-five feet back from the face of the cliff.

The place doesn't look particularly dangerous as the river flows in a broad, sweeping curve, straight into the face of the cliff. The day we arrived at this spot there was a very large whirlpool out about fifteen feet from the face of the cliff. The river was flowing so smoothly that you are lulled into feeling there isn't much danger from the place. Our topo maps showed this place very plainly, but the day we arrived there our lead raft was not the one containing the maps. On the map for this area was a notation to get out of the river and look over the situation before you tried to get by the cliff.

Our first raft, containing a man and three Scouts, was on the curve heading toward the cliff, at a very fast pace. They decided to go between the whirlpool and the cliff and this turned out to be the wrong decision. As the raft went by the whirlpool, the hydraulics was so strong the craft was dashed against the face of the cliff, and remained wedged under the rock with about one third of the raft sticking out. When the raft hit the cliff, one of the Scouts, Kevin, was thrown out and disappeared, as the current pushed him up under the undercut portion of the cliff. The second raft was so close behind the leader, it hit part of the raft sticking out from under the cliff and it overturned, throwing its three passengers, David, Chuck and Jackie, into the river, and they disappeared from my sight. The third raft saw what was happening and decided to go on the other side of the whirlpool, away from the cliff. This raft made it all right and went on down the river a short distance, where they pulled in to the shore.

I was in the fourth raft and stopped the rest of the crews. The bunch under the cliff was making a valiant effort to get their raft out from under the wall of rock but were not having much success. There was not any room between the bottom of the cliff and the top of the raft. We could see Eddie, the leader in the raft, but could not tell whether or not the other two kids were in the raft.

One of our leaders, Bill, and my son-in-law were tying some ropes together to see if Bill could wade out far enough to toss a rope to the raft under the cliff. He just couldn't get out far enough before the current started pulling him into the whirlpool, so he had to give up on this idea.

While we were trying to figure out something to do, three young Mexican men came running up to where Bill and Ted were standing. The Mexicans were trying to tell Bill something, but he couldn't understand what they were trying to say. Hector, the Scout who could speak Spanish fluently, was in the raft hung under the cliff.

Finally, one of the young men made my son-in-law understand what he was trying to say. He would take several of the ropes, tie them together, with one end around his waist, and let the current pull him down the river to where the raft was wedged under the "Canoe Eating Cliff."

As I stood there holding back the other rafts, I was absolutely sick with worry. I knew Kevin had been knocked out of the raft and swept up under the cliff. The other three boys in the overturned raft had disappeared and I was afraid that they had drowned.

When one thinks of tragedy, you naturally think of a dark, gloomy day, with possibly some rain to add to the gloom. On this day, the sun was shining brightly with nary a cloud in the sky. I felt that we had lost four boys in about three minutes, and the worst part was my feeling of helplessness. There just wasn't anything I could do about the situation until we could free the raft under the cliff.

The young Mexican man started taking off his clothes and Bill and Ted started tying the ropes together. He was about ready to step into the river, when we heard a yell. Eddie, the leader in the wedged raft, had finally managed to get a paddle against the cliff, and pushed enough to free the craft. When they floated free, I could see that the only one missing was Kevin, who had been washed up under the cliff.

We all went rushing down to check on the four missing boys and found that they were all safe. Kevin said he went up under the cliff for about fifty feet and then was washed back out into the river. He said the rocks under the cliff were as slick as glass. I had been afraid that there might be a lot of debris in the undercut, but he said there was absolutely nothing but the slick rocks. He had been washed down the river for quite a distance before he could get to the shore, and he had just now been able to get back to let us know that he was OK.

The three boys in the overturned raft had quite a story to tell. When their craft flipped, two of the Scouts were thrown clear. The other boy was caught under the raft with one foot caught in the rope which went around the outside of the raft. One of the kids grabbed his knife and cut the rope, releasing the trapped boy.

The only casualties of our mishap were two big aluminum stockpots, used to boil water and a few of our tools such as a shovel or two and some hatchets. The kids were worried about losing the gear, but I reminded them how grateful we should be. We could replace the equipment—but it is very difficult to replace our boys. When we went back to thank the young Mexican man for his help—he was gone. He had left his hat lying on the bank of the river. We weighted it down with rocks so it wouldn't blow away.

In our day you hear constantly about people not wanting to get involved. They use it as an excuse for not helping people in trouble, and this helps to hide their indifference. I pointed out to the Scouts that here was a good example of getting involved. This young Mexican man had never seen us before, and it was unlikely that our paths would ever cross again, yet he saw we were in trouble and needed help. He offered to become involved with total strangers, and there was the chance that he might be injured or even lose his life—and he didn't even wait around to accept our thanks.

One final word of caution—if you are ever rafting or canoeing in the lower canyons of the Rio Grande, and you approach the "Canoe Eating Cliff," get out on the bank to look it over. You just might decide to portage around this dangerous spot.

One source of interest on this long trip were the many buzzards. They seemed to float effortlessly along the canyon walls as they caught the thermals and soared and circled with hardly any movement of their wings. One day we were watching the buzzards flying high overhead, and one kid remarked that, if there was anything to this reincarnation bit, he would like to come back as a buzzard. They seemed so carefree and happy that he thought that this would be the ideal life. Another kid pointed out that flying around all day in the canyons of the Rio Grande would be great fun—but he wasn't too excited about the food they ate.

For several days we thought that the same buzzard was following us. He had two gaps in the feathers of his left wing, and we were sure that it was our friend. When we would leave in the morning, the kids would look for him and then yell when they spotted him. The boys wondered why this particular buzzard was following us, until I mentioned that the boys had been a little lax in their bathing and the smell probably made the buzzard think that we were fast approaching the ripeness of buzzard bait.

San Francisco Canyon is a very large, deep canyon which runs into the Rio Grande. When there has been a rain in this area, the volume of the water flowing from the canyon into the river is almost as large as the Rio Grande. When this happens, at the junction of the canyon and the river, you are liable to have some humongous rapids or haystacks, the name pinned on the waves of the rapids. The day we approached this dangerous spot we heeded the admonition on the topo maps: "Get out at this point to look over the rapids."

There wasn't a lot of water flowing from San Francisco Canyon, and the turbulence was not as bad as we had imagined. After looking the rapids over carefully we decided that we would run the haystacks by sticking close to the bank on the Texas side. One of our leaders, Mr. Wiedenfeld, thought that this would be an opportune time to get some good pictures of our crews running rapids.

On these raft trips, we were always disappointed because we were unable to get good pictures as we were shooting the rapids. Usually, everyone in the raft was too busy trying to avoid the rocks and whirlpools to have time to take any pictures. Another bad thing about trying to take pictures in the turbulent water was the fact that you stood a good chance of ruining your camera from the water. On our first raft trip I tried to take some pictures of our crews making like white water river rats and had ended up ruining a good camera.

Mr. Wiedenfeld climbed out on top of a flat rock which was about fifteen feet high and stuck out over the river. As the various rafts would come into focus, he would catch the rafts climbing up the waves, which were about eight feet high, and then snap the crews as the water would pour over the raft and the craft would go down into the trough between the waves.

He got some excellent pictures of my raft as we climbed one of the enormous haystacks. I was sitting on the front of my raft and there were four boys with me. The raft was climbing at such a steep angle, I was visible on the front and you can see the shoulders of the two boys in the rear of the raft. In the next picture, he caught our raft as it started down the trough between the waves. The water is coming completely over the raft and you can just spot our heads sticking out of the waves.

It was during this picture taking session that we came to the conclusion that Mr. Wiedenfeld had nerves of steel. As he stood on top of the bank, snapping the shutter, the raft containing his son, David, came around under the rock. Just before the raft passed under the spot where Mr. Wiedenfeld stood, the waves caused David to be thrown from the raft. Not only was David tossed overboard, but several of our waterproof buckets containing food, joined him in the fierce waters of the Rio Grande.

His dad continued his picture taking, calmly aiming his camera and shooting, while his son floundered around in the big waves. The pictures came out very well showing David floating along behind the raft, surrounded by plastic buckets and other gear thrown from the raft.

The last raft picked up our photographer and we retrieved our wet river rat a short distance down the river after we had cleared the last rapids. David said that he was a little scared when he first fell overboard, but he was a little irked that his dad hadn't thrown himself from the top of the rock to at least join him in the rapids.

A couple of days later, we ran some rapids, which were sort of rough, but nothing like those at San Francisco Canyon. As we cleared the turbulence, the water was very smooth but the current was moving right along. I was in the front of the raft and my little grandson sat right behind me on my left. All of a sudden I saw this big rock, just a few inches below the surface right in front of the raft. I yelled at the kids to pull to the right to avoid ripping the bottom out of the raft. I thought that it would be better to remove my weight from the front of the raft to give it a little more clearance.

I went over the side into the river and the sudden shifting of my weight from the front of the raft caused it to rear up. The surface was wet from the recent rapids and the lurching of our craft caused my grandson to follow me into the water.

We took a lot of kidding about the episode, but it helped to keep the rock from ripping out the bottom of the raft. The kids in the other rafts would not let us forget this little scene. For days after this happened, the boys in any raft 300 yards ahead of us on the river would start yelling, "Rock! J.T., Rock!"

When compared to those kids remembering embarrassing moments, an elephant would almost be considered absent-minded.

We proceeded on to Langtry where we got out of the river and ended our long float trip. Mr. Jack Skiles, the Director of the Tourist Information Center, had told me to call on him if we needed any assistance. While the rest of the crews were setting up camp, I decided to go into town to see about the possibility of getting some much-needed hot showers. As I crossed the main street, some Mexican workers were patching the street. I had on a big straw hat, khaki shirt and pants and nine days' growth of beard. The workers laughed and pointed to me, and I am sure they thought I was one of the older "wetbacks" who had crossed into Texas illegally.

I was a little embarrassed to go into the tourist center because there were about three bus loads of tourists inside. Mr. Skiles welcomed me like a long-lost brother and offered his services to make our stay in Langtry more pleasant. I told him we could certainly use some baths to wash off the many layers of dirt. Bathing in the Rio Grande leaves a lot to be desired as you are dirtier when you get out than when you went in.

He arranged for us to take showers and even offered to take us to his ranch for a barbecue. I told him that we appreciated his offer, but felt that the boys should stay down at the river where we had set up camp and had all of our equipment. Several of the leaders did go to his ranch and really had a good time.

After we finished bathing, I called a meeting of all our crews. I told them we could eat in camp or go to a fast food place and have hamburgers and shakes. You know, I didn't have a single taker to stay in camp to eat the "freeze-dried" food.

Mr. Skiles later told me that our crew of thirty-six persons made only 250 people to ever make this long trip from Rio Grande Village, in the Big Bend Park, to Langtry.

We returned home to where our parents and families were amazed to find that we had conquered the lower canyons of the Rio Grande. This had been accomplished with a minimum of cuts, a few bruises, some minor cases of sunburn, a few chapped lips and one stubbed toe.

And this was Raft Trip Number 2.

Raft Trip Number 3 was to be a repeat performance of our first raft trip. We would put in the river at Lajitas, Texas, about eleven miles about the Park and float the full length of Big Bend National Park, coming out of the river at Rio Grande Village.

This was to be the largest bunch from our unit to make a raft trip as we planned on a crew of forty. We were much better prepared for this trip because of the information and experience we had gained from the two earlier trips. On our first float trip we had eight little boys who were only eleven years old. On this last trip, five of the eight were going on this expedition, so I guess that they must have liked the fun and adventure of a Rio Grande Float Trip.

We carried our food in the waterproof buckets, and also our personal gear such as clothes and sleeping bags. On this excursion we even carried two extra rafts just in case some lurking rock or stump ripped the bottoms out of our crafts.

We had sub-divided our crew of forty into three crews: two with thirteen members each and one crew of fourteen. For the most part we were using "freeze-dried" food, which required a minimum of preparation and also very few cooking utensils.

Our crews boarded our chartered bus and we proceeded to the Park where we had to check in at headquarters to get our "float permit" and to fill out some information forms showing our projected trip and where we hoped to be on each of the seven days covering our trip.

We were a little shocked to learn that a new regulation had been put into effect since our first trip through the Park. This regulation required the use of gasoline or kerosene stoves if you were camping in the park area. We felt that we would have to have at least six stoves to take care of our three crews, and we just didn't have the extra money or the time to obtain the stoves. We decided just to camp on the Mexican side of the river as we floated along the Park.

We went to Lajitas and camped on the same island by the Rio Grande. We made camp, ate supper and inflated our rafts. Several of the leaders and boys in our crews had been on that first trip when the rain almost washed us away. We went to bed pretty early since we needed to get an early start. We planned to get to Santa Elena Canyon and portage the "rock slide." Our boys thought it would be fun to camp in the canyon at the lower end of the portage, so we knew that we had a long way to go.

The next morning our rafts were floating down the river making good time when we came upon two rafts of people just playing around in the river. There were three men and about six teenagers, sixteen or seventeen years old. They had some big inner tubes tied to the rafts with pieces of rope about twenty to thirty feet long, and some of the kids were floating in these. As we went by, one of the older men asked me where we were going. I told him our plans were to go through Santa Elena Canyon and camp below the portage. He asked me if we were going to portage the "rock slide" or run the rapids. I told him that we planned to portage around the rapids because we had so many kids in our crew and thought running the rapids was dangerous. This joker told me that his bunch was going to run the rapids because he was an expert on white water. I didn't argue with him and we soon left them behind as we were trying to reach Santa Elena as soon as possible.

We entered the canyon and soon reached the rock slide. We started deflating our rafts and got our gear ready to start and were coming back to get another load. We saw the "experts" two rafts coming so we stopped to see how the experts ran the rapids.

The first raft, containing two men, a girl and two boys was about seventy-five yards ahead of the other raft. It crashed into a large rock sticking out of the water. The craft was sucked under the rock so that only about two feet of the front part was visible. When the raft crashed into the rock, the two men and a boy were thrown out into the water on the Texas side. The other boy and the girl were caught in the middle of the rapids, where they were frantically holding on to an inner tube tied to the sunken raft. The two kids didn't have any life jackets on, and we were afraid that they would lose their hold on the inner tube and be washed into the main part of the rapids by the "rock slide." The two men and boy on the Texas side had no ropes and couldn't get to the two in the middle of the river.

We had competed in a Council Camporee a few weeks before our raft trip and one of the events was the "Rope Throw Rescue." A victim sat on a heavy piece of cardboard, and the rest of the patrol tied their ropes together, using sheet bend knots. The end was tossed to the victim, who tied a loop in the end of the rope using a bowline knot. The patrol then pulled the victim across the finish line. Our patrols had done very well in this event, so we decided that this was an opportune time to test our "rope throw rescue."

Paul, one of the original eleven year olds on our first trip, was to be the rescuer. The boys tied several of the half-inch nylon ropes together and had Paul tie one end around his chest, using a bowline. He was to take another rope with him to throw to the two teenagers. He tied a loop in the end of the rope, and started working his way out from rock to rock in the rapids. The kids on the shore held the rope tied around his chest, so that if he got caught in the swirling waters, they could pull him out.

Paul finally got near enough to the two in the water to try to get the rope to them. He threw the rope to the boy first, who grabbed hold of it. Paul yelled at him to slide down the rope and put the loop over his chest. The boy kept screaming that he was going to drown, and he was just frozen to the rope. Paul talked to him for about ten minutes before he finally coaxed him to slide down the rope and place the loop over his shoulders. He pulled him out on to the rocks and the kid just lay there, like he was in shock. Our rescuer threw the rope to the girl and had no trouble at all getting her to pull the loop over her shoulders. She was pulled out on the rocks and seemed to be in much better shape than the boy.

While this was taking place, some of our other boys had managed to get a rope to the people stranded across the river, and helped them to get to our side of the river. The "experts" were not wearing any life jackets, had lost part of their paddles and didn't have a single foot of rope except the short pieces tied to the inner tubes. The other raft had come up by now and the men seemed to think that they could get the raft out from under the rock.

We left them and started across the portage with our second load of equipment and rafts. As we were making the last trip across the portage, we met the great rafters coming across the portage. The girl, who was caught out in the rapids, was the only one of the bunch who thanked Paul, and I had to bite my tongue to keep from saying, "Some Experts!"

The next day we floated on through Santa Elena Canyon and camped at the Cottonwood Camp Grounds. This was a very nice place to camp with plenty of water, and small cook stoves which were fired with wood. This was to be the last place on our trip where we could camp on the Texas side of the river because of the cooking regulation.

As we were cooking supper, a Park Ranger came by to ask us about a report the headquarters had received concerning some people who had some trouble in Santa Elena Canyon at the "rock slide." We told him about the little episode and said our crew fished them out. I asked the Ranger about the questions you were required to answer before the headquarters would issue a float permit. These questions were asked about life jackets, rope, extra paddles and patching gear for your rafts. The Ranger said they asked the questions but never checked to see if you were telling the truth about the necessary equipment.

The Ranger said it was a good thing we were there because they would not have even been aware of their danger for several hours. He said that the only way they could get to the people on the rocks was to come up the canyon in air boats.

I told him that I guessed that it was quite a chore taking care of the foolish people who took such grave chances on the river. He said that they were constantly having to bail out the so called "experts."

He said, "You know, we have picked up several people out of Santa Elena

Canyon after they have drowned, and the d%$#~! fools still refuse to listen to us when we tell them about the dangers of a float trip on the river."

After spending the night at the Cottonwood Camp Ground, we started the long haul to Mariscal Canyon. This part of the river has no canyons and the river banks are not very high. The river was low, the current sluggish and the wind was blowing directly into our faces most of the time. We really had to lean into the paddles to make any headway, which prompted Lance, who was in my raft, and one of the smallest kids on the trip, to grumble, "I thought this was supposed the be a float trip, not a paddle trip."

I reminded him and the other boys in my raft, that, if they didn't put a little more effort into their paddling, we might not make it to Mariscal Canyon by Christmas.

The first night out from Cottonwood Campground, we stayed on the river longer trying to make up some lost time for our poor progress against the wind. It finally reached the point where we had to find a camp in order to get in, set up camp and eat supper before it got dark.

At last, our lead raft swung in to the shore, and the leader in the raft said that he thought this might be a good spot to camp. The river came around a big bend and the shore sloped away from the river into a sandy flat covered with a few patches of brush. Down next to the river the bank looked as if it had been paved with cobblestones, each rock about the size of a volleyball. We pulled our rafts far enough away from the river to prevent their floating away in case of a sudden rise.

All of the boys and the other leaders had unrolled their sleeping gear in the open patches of sand away from the river. I had put my sleeping bag nearest the river in a small open area. There was a small bush at the foot of my bag, but the rest of the open space was clear of even any weeds.

I had made one mistake in choosing my sleeping spot, though. My bag seemed to be located in the path of anyone going down to the area where all of our gear was stored next to the rafts. Every time someone needed something from our supplies, they came through my area and stepped on or over my sleeping bag.

I finally announced in a loud voice that anyone walking on my bed would be chastised, severely. I am certain that my doomsday pronouncement did not make much of an impression on the kids, as they continued their tromping through my bedroom.

It was completely dark by now and we were making ready to retire for the night. I had gone down to make sure our rafts were anchored to the trees, and had returned to my sleeping area. Here came one of the boys walking up from the river, and he was headed straight for my sleeping bag.

I told him, "Mike, if you step on my sleeping bag, I'm going to lean on you."

He disclaimed any plans for walking on my bed and stepped over my bag down near the foot where the small bush was growing. Just as he put his foot down by the bush, we heard the rattle of a rattlesnake.

I turned on my big lantern and spotted the reptile in the bush. I made the mistake of telling everyone to stay where they were as we had found a rattler. As soon as I got the words out of my mouth, here came thirty-nine people galloping through the brush.

We got rid of the varmint and were sort of carefully searching around the brush to be sure there were no more pets lurking in the area, when we were amazed to see one of our leaders, Marcus, with his sleeping bag over his shoulder going down to the river area.

I asked him where he was going and he told me that he was going to sleep down by the river. I reminded him that the river bank was covered with those large round rocks, and that he couldn't sleep there.

He answered, "I can sleep a lot better there than up here where there are rattlesnakes."

This was the first time we realized that the man was very afraid of snakes. After things had settled down a little, some of the kids thought it might be fun to take the dead snake down and put it near the leader's bag. I vetoed the idea and suggested that they just throw the snake in the river and provide a tasty meal for the alligator gars in the water.

We went on to Mariscal Canyon and traveled through until we came to the big rocks blocking the river. We got out to decide our route in portaging around the rocks and started getting our gear ready to carry overland. After we completed the portage, which is a piece of cake, some of the kids who had been with us on our first trip, started looking for the "hermit," who had been living here, and who came up to ask me if we had brought his mail.

We climbed up to the two caves, which had been his home, and found them in very good condition. It was evident that there had been no one living here for some time, but the crude furniture and his hot shower arrangement were still in the caves. Outside the main cave was a small statue of St. Francis of Assisi. Some of the boys decided that the "hermit" had changed his religion from Buddhist to Catholic.

We went through Mariscal and decided to camp on a very large sandbar, where the river made a big "S" curve. Late that afternoon, after we had eaten supper, one of our leaders needed some first aid attention. Jack Moore, our council executive, was one of the leaders on our expedition, and he complained about his urgent need for some medical assistance. It seems that our noble leader had developed a very large blister on the bottom of his foot. We were quick to point out that, if he had really been putting his shoulders into the paddling, the blister would have developed on his hands, or on his posterior from shifting his weight back and forth as he stroked.

Jack, with the proper sling around his sore foot,
does a repair job on a pesky blister.

He could offer no explanation as to the location of the blister, but he did get the idea across to us that he was suffering extreme pain and could go into "shock" at any moment. We sat him down on a convenient log and prepared to perform this very delicate operation. We discussed the feasibility of having one of our leaders standing by to administer the last rites, just in case Jack's constitution could not stand the terrible pain accompanying such a traumatic experience. However, we could not decide who was best qualified for such a delicate task, so we thought it best to just forget the whole matter.

We opened our three first aid kits and laid out everything needed to work on a blister. Two of our leaders removed Jack's shoe, which was about the size of a small kayak. The blister had broken and there was about a pound of river silt around the edges of the wound. We felt that while we were working on the blister we needed to immobilize his foot. In our equipment we found an athletic supporter, which made a perfect sling. We draped the supporter around his neck and put the other end around his leg.

We cleaned out the silt, trimmed the dead skin from around the edges of the broken blister, dabbed his foot with antiseptic, placed a bandage on the wound and promptly presented him with a bill for our services. He thanked us for our expertise in taking care of his blister, but suggested that if we planned on being paid, we would have to contact his insurance company.

After we went to bed that night, the wind started to blow. It was blowing about forty miles an hour with gusts up to sixty. Being camped out in the open on that huge sandbar, we really caught the full force of the sandstorm. The only way we could breathe was to cover our head or to get down in your sleeping bag to keep out the wind and sand. It blew like this for several hours before it finally quieted down. The next morning when I got up to check out our situation, you couldn't see the sleeping bags of the members of our crew. There were only small mounds of sand to indicate the location of each very dry, very sandy river rat. When we finally went around and aroused everyone, we were a sorry looking lot. Most of us had sand in our hair, our eyebrows and eye lashes, our ears, and I found that I had small amounts of sand gritting on my teeth.

After bathing in the muddy, chocolate-colored Rio Grande, we found that we hadn't really got rid of the pesky sand—just moved it around to where we could see and breathe a little better.

Breakfast was cooked and eaten, we put a little air into our rafts, and packed for our journey on down the river.

There was a little incident which happened that day to make us realize that rafts were not the most maneuverable craft for moving on the river, and that water can exert a terrific force. The river made a sharp bend to the right, and thick cane was growing on the left side of the bank and sticking out over the water. The cane had drooped down so that there was very little clearance between the cane and the surface of the river. The river, in making the bend, caused the current to flow directly into the cane, and to make matters worse, there was water flowing from a higher level of the river bank down into the main current.

This caused a terrific force throwing your raft into the cane along the bank. The first raft tried to avoid going under the growth, but the current pulled them right into the cane. The second raft saw what was happening, and got over as far as they could toward the opposite shore. The river was narrow here and the water from the higher level forced them to crash into the cane and disappear as their raft was pulled by the force of the water.

I told my crew that we should profit by the mistakes of the first two rafts, and that we could avoid trashing out under the cane. We moved over to the opposite shore away from the cane and started really paddling to offset the pull of the current. We did very well until we got within about thirty feet of the cane, and then the hydraulics of the water took effect. We were paddling as hard as possible but were losing the battle. Our raft was being pulled relentlessly into the cane. I yelled at the kids in our raft to lie down and cover their faces to prevent being cut by the sharp leaves of the cane or being swept overboard by the hard stems of the growth.

With no one guiding our craft we hit the shore and the raft turned completely around. The current swept us along at a fast clip, and we finally came out from under the cane. We took inventory and everyone was OK except one kid who had lost his big straw hat. We pulled over to the shore and waited, and sure enough, in a few moments his hat came floating down the river.

Our council executive, Jack Moore, and his crew had seen what had happened to our first three rafts. Jack told his boys that they were not going to be caught in the current and forced in under the cane. Famous last words — his group made the same mistake my raft did and they went crashing through the cane as the current pulled them down the river.

When we finally came out in the open, they found that their crew hadn't been quite as lucky as the other three rafts. It seems that our noble council executive, after making those rash statements, as to what they were not going to do, had found that frail man could not fight with the river and win, and that he had lost his wrist watch in the process.

Even now, a long time after the raft trip, we are inclined to remind him of the time he was feuding with the mighty Rio Grande, and he lost not only the gauntlet he cast down, but his watch as well.

The rest of the rafts saw what had happened to us and they used the proper technique to get past the cane. They got out and pulled the rafts past the cane. We were happy that no one had been cut by the cane because sometimes the sharp leaves can slice you like the blade of a knife.

We continued on down the river to make camp for our last night before reaching our destination at Rio Grande Village. After we had eaten our evening meal, I called everyone together for a meeting. I reminded them that we still had a long ways to travel, and we needed to get an early start the next morning. In my little speech, I told all of the boys and leaders that when I yelled at them to get up the next morning, I expected everyone to come out of their sleeping bags, running. Of course, after all of my fiery rhetoric, I wasn't real sure that they would pay much attention to what I said.

After we had gone to bed, about 2:30 in the morning something happened to make me believe that, just maybe for once, my words of great wisdom had soaked into their brains and made an impression there. A couple of wild donkeys had wandered into camp and started braying. As the animals continued their braying, all over camp you could hear the kids yelling, "OK, J.T. We are getting up. Just don't yell at us anymore."

At first this tickled me until I thought about it a little more. I had never thought my yelling sounded like the braying of a wild jackass, but who was a better judge than the kids I had been yelling at for years? After my donkey friends left camp, we went back to sleep for some well-deserved rest. We continued on to our destination the next afternoon, and came out of the river in great shape. We spent a night at the campgrounds and then our chartered bus carried us back to our families in San Angelo.

And this was our last raft trip on the mighty Rio Grande.

After rafting down the Rio Grande, we were amazed at the remoteness of this vast area of the United States. Another fact which made quite an impression on us was the lack of medical attention in case of a major injury.

Before we made our first float trip, I checked with an old, grizzled river guide who had spent a lot of time guiding parties on raft and canoe trips. He shared many bits of useful information with us and had an admonition which became quite clear after our first trip when we became aware of the necessity of trying to prevent any accidents in this remote area.

His words of advice were very short and to the point, "Don't break no legs!"

If you go rafting or canoeing on the Rio Grande, take a good, complete first aid kit. Take everything you need because you cannot depend on someone else to help you out in case of an emergency, and "Don't break no legs!"

Chapter 25
Summary

As I reflect on fifty-seven years of Scouting, I realize just how much Scouting has meant to me. I have received several awards from Scouting and from my community, but my greatest award came from a totally unexpected source.

In our troop there was a little boy who was having a very difficult time adjusting after his father had been killed in an accident. I suppose I gave him a little more of my time to try to help him fill the void left by his father.

We were on a weekend campout, and he and I were sharing a cooking fire. He looked across the fire, grinned shyly and said, "You know, I wish you were my dad." I had to turn away to pretend I was getting some more wood for the fire in order to hide my tears. I always felt that this was the greatest award I ever received because it came straight from the heart of a little boy.

I have a great many wonderful memories of the Scouting part of my life:

As a boy on my first overnight camp, when I suddenly realized that my dream had come true—at long last I had finally become a Boy Scout.

The many hikes I went on as a Scout, on which I suffered blistered feet, sunburned noses, running out of water, and picking about a jillion cactus thorns out of my anatomy. But we always went back—we were tough— we were Boy Scouts!

The fun and adventure in attending our council's first summer camps.

The feeling of great accomplishment in being a member of the council Exhibition Troop, which helped to get Scouting started in the smaller communities in our council.

The thrill of receiving my Eagle award at a Court of Honor.

As a Scoutmaster, my thirty-nine years of overnight camps, in which I ruined my stomach from tasting the horrible messes (food) prepared by the kids working on their Second and First Class cooking.

Hiking over the trails of Philmont and feeling that we were rubbing elbows with the Mountain Men.

Attending a great many summer camps and enjoying them all—especially the council fires where I watched the Scouts present the same old moth-eaten skits, which were ancient even when I was a Scout.

Paddling over the clear, cool waters of Northern Minnesota and Canada and feeling almost like Lewis and Clark.

Attending four National Jamborees and seeing Scouts from all the states and many foreign countries, and finding that Scouting was a mighty big movement throughout the whole world.

The faces of the many boys I had in my units during my thirty-nine years as a Scoutmaster. Many of the faces I can remember—but some are only a name.

The great satisfaction which comes from seeing a fumbling, bumbling Tenderfoot changed into a poised young man, as he completes his requirements for the Eagle award.

And last, the feeling of warm contentment and maybe just a little mystery as I gazed into the flickering flames of "a thousand campfires."

Boy Scouts of America
P.O. Box 152079
Irving, Texas 75015
214/580-2000

Charles L. Sommers Canoe Base
Northern Tier Adventure Programs
Box 509
Ely, Minnesota 55731
218/365-4811

Concho Valley Council
Boy Scouts of America
P.O. Box 1584
San Angelo, Texas 76902
915/655-7107

Philmont Scout Ranch
Cimmaron, New Mexico
505/376-2281

Rio Grande Ranger Station
Big Bend National Park
Panther Junction, Texas
915/477-2251

MORGAN PRINTING
BOOKS AND PUBLISHING SERVICES

900 Old Koenig Lane, Suite 135
Austin, Texas 78756
Tel (512) 459-5194   Fax (512) 451-0755

Alligator Gar - Nick-name for a freshwater ganoid fish with an elongated body and many sharp teeth. Can grow to large size similar to small alligators

Cat Claw Bushes - A bush with sharp thorns that are curved like a cat's claw.

Coral snake - a small, poisonous snake with coral-red, yellow and black bands around its body, found in the southern U.S.

Council - As pertaining to Scouting; an administrative assembly representing an area usually more than one city or one county.

Durkle - Your guess is as good as ours. *Pub.*

Garter snake - Any of various small, harmless, stripped snakes common in N. America. Some varieties are very similar to coral snakes.

Gully Washer - A torrential downpour of rain.

Haystacks - Nick name for a certain type of fierce river rapids.

Jamboree - a boisterous party or revel. (b) a gathering with planned entertainment. 2. A national or international assembly of Boy Scouts.

Jillion - Ten or twenty times a Zillion.

Lister Bag - A large canvas bag with a waterproof lining to store liquids. Usually has several spigots and a wood tripod to suspend it. Has a capacity of approx. 25 gallons.

Natural Patrols - Sub group within a standard Boy Scout troop.

Portage - The act of carrying boats and supplies overland between navigable rivers, lakes, etc. (b) any route over which this is done.

Shooting the breeze - Slang term for casual conversation.

Sky hooks - A tool used to anchor a tent in case of a strong wind.

Snollygosters - A cute (we think) small animal that lives along the banks of the Concho River and eats old Montgomery Ward catalogues

Strap oil - A liquid used to waterproof canvas tents and shelters.

Tent Stretcher - A legendary tool used to pull the canvas of your tent back into shape.

Widow maker - A large limb on a tree that may fall and injure people sleeping under it. Any hazard likely to cause injury or worse.

Slicker - Long rain coat

Monkey Bridge - A suspension type personnel bridge made of rope or cable with three primary spans arranged in a 'V' with the top two spans as hand holds and the bottom span as a walk way.

FIG. 1—FIRST AID IS ONE OF THE REQUIREMENTS OF A BOY SCOUT TRAINING

SAFETY FIRST

West Texas Utilities Co.

EVERYTHING ELECTRICAL

FIG. 5—DON'T DROWN A FAINTING PERSON—SPRINKLE HIM (SEE INSET)

IT IS BEST TO BE PREPARED FOR EMERGENCIES

FIRST AID

A RELIABLE REFERENCE FOR GENERAL USE

Written and Illustrated by George W. French, Former Scout Executive and Physical Director and Co-Author of The Scout Master's Guide

Approved by Joseph E. Pollard, M. D.

How to Render First Aid

First aid embraces exactly what the term indicates—aid which, in the absence of a doctor, or while one is coming, will prevent more serious developments. Always, when in doubt, get a doctor.

Fortunately, the majority of everyday accidents are such that the cause is readily understood and therefore can be treated promptly without the necessity of studying symptoms. Cases that require a study of symptoms or signs will be discussed first, and although doctors have many signs or symptoms for which they look, there are five *common signs* that you can easily remember to look for that will help you to decide what the trouble is in cases where it is not readily recognized. See Fig. 1.

Now then, First Aid, in cases where the trouble is not readily evident, embraces, in order, three steps, viz: *Observance of five general rules; diagnosis or study of the five common signs, and first aid treatment.*

Five General Rules

1. Send for a doctor.
2. Move the patient to a safe, cool, well-ventilated spot and place in a comfortable position.
3. Loosen tight clothing, and remove only enough, if necessary, to expose the wound. Keep the head on a level with the shoulder.
4. If stimulants need be given, give aromatic spirits of ammonia, hot tea or coffee, or even hot water, in preference to alcohol.
5. Do not attempt to clean a wound if a doctor is coming—stop the bleeding and apply proper dressings. A good rule to follow is—leave all that is expedient to the doctor. DON'T DO TOO MUCH!

The Five Common Signs

1. *Consciousness* (Is it present, or is the patient unconscious?)
2. *Color* (Is it normal, or pale, or flushed?)
3. *Breathing* (Is it normal—18 to 24 times a minute—or is it faster or slower?)
4. *Pulse* (Is it normal—70 to 80 a minute—or is it faster or slower?) See Fig. 7 for method of "taking the pulse."
5. *Temperature* (Is it normal—98.6° Fahrenheit—or is it higher or lower?)

Diagnosis or Study of the Five Common Signs, and First Aid Treatment

The cases diagnosed here are those in which the trouble is not readily evident. There are two groups, viz.—Depressed Conditions, and Head Injuries.

DEPRESSED CONDITIONS

Fainting, Hemorrhage, Heat Exhaustion, and Shock. In this group, with the exception of fainting, the subject is conscious, but pale. The respiration is inclined to be rapid, the pulse also rapid (90 to 120 a minute) but weak, and the temperature is low (below 98.6°) as a result of which the skin is cool and covered with a clammy sweat. If, on examination of a patient, you find these conditions present, then you may be pretty sure that the case is one of the four following:

Fainting, Heat Exhaustion, Hemorrhage (external hemorrhage is readily self-evident, but internal hemorrhage is not) or *Shock*.

Fainting

Place the patient with the head lower than the body; loosen clothing; sprinkle water on the face; apply smelling salts; when the person is conscious give aromatic spirits of ammonia (one-half teaspoonful in one-third glass of water.)

Heat Exhaustion

Symptoms—Patient is depressed and weak, but not unconscious; pale, cold sweat; breathing shallow; pulse weak and rapid; temperature below normal.

Treatment—Send for a doctor; remove to cooler place; loosen clothing; give stimulants such as hot coffee, or tea.

Hemorrhage (Bleeding)

If an artery is ruptured, the blood spurts and is bright red; if a vein, the blood flows steadily and is dark red or purple.

Treatment—For a ruptured vein, place a piece of sterile compress over the bleeding point and bind on tightly with a bandage.

For a ruptured artery use a regulation tourniquet or devise one with a handkerchief and stick. Twist the handkerchief with the stick thrust through it, until the pressure stops the bleeding. If the tourniquet must be left on a long time before the doctor comes, loosen it once an hour till the color in the limb returns, even if the wound bleeds freely while doing it. This will prevent gangrene setting in. While it is loose, press your thumb just above the wound; it will check a lot of the bleeding, and the blood will reach the rest of the limb through many little bypaths.

When the wound is below the knee or elbow, place a pad in the bend of the joint and double the limb back over it, holding the pad tightly. Tie the limb in this position.

Remember that a tourniquet must always be placed between the wound and the heart, and at points where the arteries come near the surface. A small stone or other pad in the tourniquet over the artery will increase the effectiveness of the tourniquet. See Fig. 6 for demonstration of tourniquet on thigh, and for chart of "pressure points."

Internal Hemorrhage

Symptoms—Increasing pallor (the person is probably in shock, anyway); a steadily increasing pulse rate, determined by taking the pulse every 15 minutes and keeping a record of it; increasing thirst, and difficulty in breathing.

Treatment—A doctor at once is imperative, for an operation may be necessary.

Shock

Symptoms—Patient is dull or semi-conscious, and often shivers even on a hot day; he is pale and frequently has a cold sweat; pulse and respiration are weak and rapid.

Treatment—Remove to a warm place and stimulate in every way possible—hot blankets, rub limbs vigorously toward body and give hot black coffee.

Common Stimulants

For External Use:

1. Aromatic Spirits of Ammonia.
2. Smelling Salts.
3. Household Ammonia.
4. Cold water—on chest and face.
5. Chafing of hands and feet.
6. Warm blankets.

For Internal Use:

1. Aromatic Spirits of Ammonia. Dose: ½ teaspoonful (30 drops) in ½ glass of water.
2. Strong tea or coffee.
3. Alcohol (if (1) and (2) are not available), either brandy or whiskey—one to three teaspoonfuls.

These internal stimulants are to be used only on return of the patient to consciousness.

HEAD INJURIES

Alcoholic Intoxication, Apoplexy, Concussion, Skull Fracture, Epilepsy, Sunstroke.

In each of these cases consciousness is very much dulled, or entirely absent for hours; the color is flushed, the respiration deep, noisy and possibly slow, the pulse full but slow (50 to 70 per minute), the temperature high, (maybe as high as 113°), and the skin hot, but either sweaty or dry.

Alcoholic Intoxication

Treatment—Pour aromatic spirits of ammonia on a handkerchief and hold it very close over the nose and mouth; keep it away from the eyes; this may restore consciousness; or you may rouse the patient by pressing hard with your thumb in the middle of his eyebrow; if he rouses from one of these treatments, make him vomit, if possible, by tickling his throat with a feather or straw, and give him one to two teaspoonfuls of aromatic spirits of ammonia with an ounce of epsom salts in a glass of water.

CAUTION—Before treatment, be certain that the case is not one of apoplexy, or skull fracture. If uncertain, get a doctor at once.

Apoplexy

Cause—Bursting a blood vessel in the brain.

Symptoms—Unconsciousness (usually paralysis on one side); flushed face; pupils large and unequal in size; can touch eyeballs without the patient's winking; pulse slow but full; breathing deep and snoring; temperature above normal.

Treatment—Send for doctor; rest the patient in a dark room, lying down, with his head and shoulders propped up on pillows; apply ice and cold cloths to his head; rub limbs, and apply hot bottles to his feet. Give no stimulants!

Concussion

Treatment—Proceed as for fainting; lay the person in a cool place; loosen tight clothing at neck and belt; sprinkle cold water on face and chest and let him smell of a cloth wet with aromatic spirits of ammonia.

Epilepsy

Cause—Something wrong in the brain.

Symptoms—The person suddenly cries out in a hoarse way, falls and becomes perfectly rigid; his breathing stops and he quickly turns purple in the face; after a short while, gasping, and then foaming at the mouth occurs, followed by a limp and still unconscious condition. When consciousness does return he probably will be dazed for a while, or he may drop into a heavy, long sleep.

Treatment—Keep the patient from hurting himself, by placing something soft under his head, and slipping something between his back teeth to keep his mouth partly open—for instance, a piece of wood, the small handle of an umbrella, etc. Don't try to hold him still.

Loosen tight clothing and call a doctor. When the fit is ended remove to a warm, quiet place.

(*Continued on following sheet*)

FIG. 2 — RESUSCITATION. YOU MAY HAVE OCCASION TO KNOW HOW TO SAVE A LIFE. DO YOU KNOW HOW?

Resuscitation—Schaeffer Method

For Drowning Accidents

1. Clean out the mouth and pull the tongue forward.
2. Lift the patient by the hips, allowing his head to hang downward so that water can run from throat and lungs.
3. Lay him face downward, arms extended above the head, with face a little to one side and a folded coat under his chest.
4. Kneel astride the body in such a position that when your weight is relaxed you will be sitting back against the patient's calves, and place your hands on the short ribs with thumbs nearly touching near the spine. Again see that the tongue is pulled forward. Tie a string or handkerchief to it and keep it out, if necessary. Loosen tight clothing about neck and chest.
5. Let your weight fall on your hands by leaning forward, then relax the pressure, and repeat this process about fifteen times a minute. An hour or two may be necessary to produce breathing, but don't give up.
6. When breathing starts, promote circulation by rubbing the legs and body towards the heart, and apply blankets.
7. When the patient can swallow, give aromatic spirits of ammonia, one teaspoonful in half a glass of water; if glass and drinking water are not available, a small quantity may be placed on the back part of the tongue.
8. Don't allow patient to rise until breathing is regular.
9. The patient should be put to bed as soon as possible after resuscitated. Remember that fresh air and a doctor are needed.

If someone is present to help you, while you are giving artificial respiration have him loosen tight clothing about the patient's neck, chest, and waist; also remove any foreign body such as tobacco, false teeth, etc. from the mouth and keep the patient warm with coverings, warm water, bottles, etc. The same procedure, almost in detail, applies to resuscitation after electric shock and asphyxiation.

FIG. 4 — THE CHAIR CARRY (INSET) AND THE FIREMAN'S LIFT

The Fireman's Lift

This is the most common method of carrying an unconscious person, single handed. Proceed as follows:

Turn the patient on his face. Straddle him, facing toward his head. With hands under his armpits, lift him to his knees; then clasp your hands under his abdomen, and lift him to his feet. Grasp his left wrist with your left hand and draw his left arm around your neck, moving meanwhile to his left side, and supporting him with your right arm around his waist. Now, grasp his right wrist with your left hand and draw his right arm around your neck, releasing his left arm, and stooping in front of him, thus bringing his head and chest across your shoulders. Reach between his legs with your right arm and pass it around his right thigh. Lift so that he rests easily on your shoulders. Then, shift his right wrist to your right hand, and grasp his left wrist with your left hand to steady him as you straighten up. See Fig. 4.

When about to lower the patient pass your left hand between his legs and grasp his left leg just back of the knee.

The Four-Hand Carry

This requires two carriers and is used for carrying conscious patients for short distances. Each carrier grasps his own left wrist with his right hand and his partner's right wrist with his left hand, thus forming a seat. The patient when seated puts his arms around the carriers for balance. See the inset in Fig. 4.

The Two-Hand Carry

Two carriers required; they clasp opposite hands, one right and one left only, and each places his other hand on his fellow's shoulder, thus forming a back against which the carried leans while sitting across the carriers' clasped hands.

FIG. 3—DON'T MISTAKE POISON IVY FOR VIRGINIA CREEPER

LINE DRAWINGS TAKEN FROM THE BOOK "FIRST AID FOR BOYS" BY COLE AND ERNST COURTESY D. APPLETON AND CO., NEW YORK

FIG. 6—IN CASE OF BLEEDING THE FIRST THING TO DO IS STOP IT! THE INSET SHOWS POINTS AT WHICH TO APPLY PRESSURE. SEE HEMORRHAGE

SAFETY FIRST

Everlasting watchfulness is the price of safety. Think of your loved ones and you won't "take a chance."

One thoughtless act of a moment often causes untold suffering and loss that cannot be repaired in a lifetime.

Do all things the Safety Way.

Practice Safety yourself and others will follow you.

Life is sweet—keep it by boosting for Safety.

Preach Safety and practice what you preach.

Look before you act—at home, in the street and at work.

It's fine to know what to do in case of accident and this First Aid Poster tells you, BUT it's better yet to follow the Safety Way—keep well and avoid accidents.

Think Safety First always.

Guard your health—keep fit—a good body means a clear mind and clear minds protect themselves and others from accidents and disease.

Safety saves sickness, suffering, sadness.

It's cheaper and easier to keep well than to get well.

A pay check is always bigger and better than a relief check.

It is better to be safe than sorry—don't take chances.

Think of your loved ones and you won't "take a chance."

Never depend on the other fellow doing exactly what he should—do the safe, sensible thing yourself. It's the only way.

The gun that "wasn't loaded" and the match that "was out" destroy countless lives. Be careful.

SEE SECOND PAGE FOR ADDITIONAL FIRST AID AND SAFETY FIRST INFORMATION.

Front side (Back not shown) of a reproduction of a 1926 "Safety First" poster, written by Scouter George W. French and featuring Scouts. The original was found in the attic of a house near the site of the "Scout Village" as mentioned in Chapter 6 of *A Thousand Campfires.*

10" X 15" B & W Reproduction — $2.00

Note: Dated First Aid Information

A Thousand Campfires

ORDER FORM

Did you enjoy *A Thousand Campfires?* Would you like another copy or a Hardcover Edition? Would you like to have one sent to a friend, library or a Scout Troop in your name? If so, please photocopy or copy information on a separate sheet.

YES, I want to order J. T. Henderson's book *A Thousand Campfires*.

Qty.			Extension
_____	*Softcover editions* (ISBN #0-9631648-0-5)	*@$10.95*	_____
_____	*Hardcover Editions* (ISBN #0-9631648-1-3)	*@$17.95*	_____
_____	*10' X 15" B & W "Safety First" Poster*	*@$2.00*	_____

Sub Total _____

(Texas Residents Please Add 7.75% Sales Tax) ———

Shipping = $3.00 for the first book.
$1.50 for each additional book per destination. _____

Total _____
(Canadian Residents Send Postal Money Order in U.S. Funds.)

❑ *My check is enclosed.*
❑ *Please bill my (circle one):*   DISCOVER   VISA   MasterCard   American Express Cards

Card # _____ Exp. Date _____

Purchased by:

_____
(Your Name)   (please print)   (Street Address)

( )
_____
(City)   (State)   (Zip)   (Phone)

Signature: _____

Ship to:

_____
(Name)   (Street Address)

( )
_____
(City)   (State)   (Zip)   (Phone)

Send Orders To: **Ambush Publishing**
419 West Avenue C
San Angelo, TX 76903
(Allow up to 30 days)

Coming Soon from Ambush ...
Four and Twenty Girls Scouts by J. T. Henderson (Dec. 1992)
The Brownsea Trail: A Brave, Clean and Reverent Path (Summer 1993)

Write for more information about books on Scouting from Ambush.